M & E Handbooks are recommended reading for examination syllabuses all over the world. Because each Handbook covers its subject clearly and concisely books in the series form a vital part of many college, university, school and home study courses.

Handbooks contain detailed information stripped of unnecessary padding, making each title a comprehensive self-tuition course. They are amplified with numerous self-testing questions in the form of Progress Tests at the end of each chapter, each text-referenced for easy checking. Every Handbook closes with an appendix which advises on examination technique. For all these reasons, Handbooks are ideal for pre-examination revision.

The handy pocket-book size and competitive price make Handbooks the perfect choice for anyone who wants to grasp the essentials of a subject quickly and easily.

Other M & E books of interest:

THE M & E HANDBOOK SERIES

Company Secretarial Practice

L. Hall
ACIS, AMBIM

*Formerly Senior Lecturer in Secretarial Practice at the
City of London Polytechnic*
Revised by G. M. Thom, LLB (Hons)

*Senior Lecturer in Law, Department of
Business Studies, Bristol Polytechnic*

SIXTH EDITION

MACDONALD AND EVANS

Macdonald & Evans Ltd
Estover, Plymouth PL6 7PZ

First published 1965
Reprinted (with amendments) 1967
Second Edition 1969
Reprinted 1970, 1972
Third Edition 1974
Reprinted 1975, 1976
Fourth Edition 1977
Fifth Edition 1981
Sixth Edition 1984

British Library Cataloguing in Publication Data

Hall, L.
  Company secretarial practice.—6th ed.—(M&E
  handbook series)
  1. Corporation secretaries—Great Britain
  2. Office practice—Great Britain
  I. Title   II. Thom, G.M.
  344.106′664   HD2741

ISBN 0–7121–0478–X

Photoset in Times by
Northern Phototypesetting Co., Bolton
and printed in Great Britain by
Hollen Street Press Ltd, Slough

Preface to the First Edition

In preparing these study notes it has been the author's intention to reduce the subject of company secretarial practice to its bare essentials and, so it is hoped, meet the requirements of students preparing for the final examinations of the *Institute of Chartered Secretaries and Administrators*.

It is not suggested that these notes will completely replace the textbooks recommended for the use of students taking college or correspondence courses; indeed, textbooks are an essential part of their course. Nevertheless, for many years it has been the author's experience as lecturer in the subject that students are always appreciative of "hand-outs", and this HANDBOOK will supply that need—particularly for the purpose of revision.

In order to derive maximum benefit from this HANDBOOK the text ought to be used in conjunction with the classified examination questions appearing at the end of each chapter. Most of the questions are taken from past examination papers of the former *Chartered Institute of Secretaries* and the *Corporation of Secretaries* (now combined to form the *Institute of Chartered Secretaries and Administrators*), to whom the author tenders grateful acknowledgment. It will be noted that many of the questions are cross-referenced to the relevant paragraph(s). Those which have not been cross-referenced are principally questions the answers to which rely upon the students' own practical experience, powers of observation, initiative, tact and diplomacy in letter-writing, and skill in report-writing. Practice in answering questions of this type is an essential part of a student's training for the professional secretarial examinations.

In order to keep this edition to HANDBOOK size, it has not been possible to include a separate chapter on company meetings; nevertheless, a good deal of attention has been given to meetings in the course of the many detailed procedures included in the text.

A separate HANDBOOK on the Law of Meetings is now available to meet the requirements of students preparing for the final professional examinations.

1967   L.H.

Preface to the Sixth Edition

It has become necessary to update this HANDBOOK in view of the provisions of the Companies Act 1981, and it has therefore been revised on the basis that this Act is fully operative.

As in previous editions all sectional references are to the principal Act (Companies Act 1948) unless otherwise stated.

1983   G.M.T.

Contents

Table of Cases

CHAPTER I

Formation of a Company

TYPES OF COMPANY

1. Basic types. There are three basic types of company:
(*a*) statutory companies,
(*b*) chartered companies,
(*c*) registered companies.

2. Statutory companies.

(*a*) These are, or were, formed under special Acts of Parliament which carefully define their powers.

(*b*) As they were principally public utility companies, such as gas, water, electricity, railway, dock and harbour undertakings, most of them have been brought under State control.

3. Chartered companies.

(*a*) These are companies granted a charter by the Crown, the charter usually conferring special statutory powers.

(*b*) They are rarely formed nowadays as trading companies but the granting of charters to charitable or public bodies is not uncommon.

4. Registered companies.

(*a*) These are formed under the Companies Acts 1948 to 1981. It is this type of company with which we are principally concerned.

(*b*) As the name implies, the essential feature is public registration, that is, the registration of certain documents with the Registrar of Companies, an official of the Department of Trade and Industry.

(*c*) Registered companies are often known as *limited* companies or *joint stock* companies although, as will be explained later, all registered companies are not necessarily limited companies.

5. Types of registered company.

(*a*) In forming a company, the promoters must first decide which type of registered company they wish to form.

(*b*) They must choose between *limited* and *unlimited* liability. If the company is to be engaged in trade or industry they are unlikely to choose the latter.

(*c*) If they decide upon a limited company, there is still a choice between a company with liability *limited by shares* and one with liability *limited by guarantee*.

(*d*) Another point they may consider is whether or not the company is to have share capital, bearing in mind that if they decide on a guarantee company it cannot have a share capital now that the Companies Act 1980, s.1(2) has come into operation. (This does not affect guarantee companies registered with share capital before the 1980 Act came into operation.)

(*e*) Finally, is the company to be a public company or a private company?

NOTE: In practice, companies limited by shares are by far the most numerous. Unlimited companies are rare, and the comparatively small number of companies limited by guarantee that have been formed are principally non-trading companies such as professional bodies.

6. Classification of companies.

(*a*) *A public company* is defined in the Companies Act 1980, s.1 as a company that is limited by shares or limited by guarantee, has a share capital, has stated in its memorandum of association that it is a public company, and has registered or re-registered as a public company in accordance with the requirements of the 1980 Act, s.3.

(*b*) *A private company*, unless the context otherwise requires, means a company that is not a public company: Companies Act 1980, s.1.

NOTE: Part II of Table A (Regulations for the Management of a Private Company Limited by Shares) is repealed by the Companies Act 1980, and Part I of Table A applies to *both* public and private companies limited by shares registered after the 1980 Act came into operation. This repeal does not, however, affect companies of the kinds mentioned which were registered before that date.

REGISTRATION

7. Preliminary considerations. Prior to registering a company there will be preliminary discussion by the promoters, particularly concerning the following important matters.

(*a*) *Type of company* to be formed, taking into consideration the points raised in 5 above.

(*b*) *Objects.* What are to be the company's main objects, ancillary objects and borrowing powers (if any)?

(*c*) *Capital requirements.* This is a vitally important matter and ought to be considered with a view to assessing the required authorised capital with which the company proposes to be registered and the division thereof into shares of a fixed amount—unless, of course, the company is to be limited by guarantee. It must be borne in mind, however, that the "authorised minimum capital" for a public company is £50,000 (nominal value), or such other sum as may in future be specified by statutory instrument: Companies Act 1980, ss.3 and 85. In assessing the capital requirements, the following matters should be taken into account:

(*i*) *purchase price* of any business to be acquired if, for example, a partnership is being converted into a limited company;

(*ii*) *preliminary expenses* covering the legal and other expenses to be incurred in the formation of the company;

(*iii*) *working capital*: after meeting the above items, there must be sufficient capital remaining to enable the company to meet its everyday commitments;

(*iv*) *future requirements*: not only immediate requirements but also long-term requirements should be taken into account. The promoters ought to be sufficiently optimistic to anticipate that the company will develop, and development should not be hindered for lack of capital.

(*d*) *Name.* Consideration might be given at this stage to the choice of a suitable name for the company, but it must be borne in mind that the name chosen must not be contrary to the provisions of the Acts (*see* **22** *below*).

(*e*) *Registered office.* As the company must have a registered office it might be as well to consider where it is to be situated, bearing in mind that its situation must be stated in the registration documents and that the domicile of the registered office determines the nationality of the company, i.e. English, Welsh or Scottish.

(*f*) *Directors.* Although the first directors cannot be officially appointed at this stage, the constitution of the board may be fixed and the first director(s) named. In the case of a private company one director only would suffice, but two directors constitute the minimum requirement for every public company registered on or after 1st November 1929: s.176.

(*g*) *Secretary.* Every company must have a secretary: s.177; therefore, a person may be named as such at this stage, although his appointment will have to be ratified later. It should be noted, however, that a sole director cannot also act as secretary of the company. (*See also* **XIV, 32** as to qualifications required in the case of a secretary of a public company.)

(*h*) *Solicitors.* The promoters may now decide to instruct a solicitor to prepare the necessary documents, and it is usually advisable to choose one who specialises in company formation.

8. Underwriting. If a public company is to be formed, consideration will almost certainly be given to the question of underwriting the issue of any shares to be offered to the public—if that is the immediate intention—but the contacts with firms of underwriters and the drafting of an underwriting agreement are best left to the solicitors.

9. Documents. The solicitors will be instructed to prepare the necessary documents. These will vary according to the decisions already taken, but some or all of the following will be required.

(*a*) *Documents to be filed* with the Registrar of Companies, including the Memorandum of Association and the Articles of Association. These and the other necessary documents are explained later in this chapter.

(*b*) *Business purchase agreement* where the company is being formed to acquire an existing business, e.g. where the business of a sole trader or of a partnership is being converted into a company.

(*c*) *Prospectus* (or equivalent document) where the company is to be a public company and intends to offer its shares (or debentures) to the public.

(*d*) *Underwriting contract.* This will be required if it is decided to ensure the success of a public issue of shares (or debentures), the underwriters agreeing in the contract to take up any shares which are not subscribed by the public on payment of underwriting commission.

10. Signing of documents. When the registration and other documents are prepared:

(*a*) *attend the solicitors' office*: where convenient, those responsible for signing the various documents will attend the solicitors' office to examine the documents;

(b) *after approval* they will sign the various documents, the only exception being the statutory declaration in prescribed form which the solicitor who has prepared the documents usually signs, although it may be signed by a person named as a director or secretary of the company: Companies Act 1980, s.3(5). This also declares that all requirements of the Companies Acts in respect of registration have been complied with;

(c) *payment of capital duty and registration fees:* a cheque to cover capital duty and registration fee may be signed at the same time. Alternatively, payment may be arranged by banker's draft and, if there is any urgency, this method can save a certain amount of delay, as the Registrar will not usually issue a Certificate of Incorporation until the cheque for capital duty etc. has been cleared.

11. Documents to be filed with the Registrar. The following are the documents to be lodged with the Registrar of Companies before incorporation of a company with share capital.

(a) *Memorandum of Association*, bearing the appropriate registration fee stamp.

(b) *Articles of Association* (if any). If Articles are *not* filed, the company will be deemed automatically to have adopted Table A, Part I, whether public or private company, Table A, Part II having been repealed by the Companies Act 1980 (*see* **38** *below*).

(c) *A statement on Form PUC 1*, stamped for capital duty at the current rate calculated on the greater of the nominal value of the shares issued or allotted and the actual value of assets of any kind contributed, less any liabilities which have been assumed or discharged by the company in consideration of the contribution: Finance Act 1973.

(d) *The statutory declaration* referred to in **10**(b) above.

(e) *A statement in the prescribed form:*

(i) signed by the subscribers to the memorandum, giving particulars of the first directors and secretary (or joint secretaries) and containing a consent signed by each person named in it to act in the relevant capacity; and

(ii) specifying the intended situation of the company's registered office.

12. Procedure on filing documents.

(a) *Examination of documents.* The person presenting the

documents at the Registrar's office (probably the solicitor who prepared the documents, or his clerk) is generally asked to leave them for examination and return at a stated time on the next or a subsequent day.

(b) *After examination.* Any defects will be pointed out to the solicitor (or other person presenting the documents) on his return to the Registry. Defects of a trivial character may be corrected on the spot, but it may be necessary to take away any documents requiring material alterations. Such documents ought to be referred back to their respective signatories and any alterations made should be initialled by them.

(c) *After approval.* When the documents are approved, the fees and stamp duties will be paid, usually by cheque or banker's draft.

13. Certificate of Incorporation.

(a) *Issue of certificate.* All registration documents having been approved and all fees and stamp duties paid, the Registrar will issue the Certificate of Incorporation, usually within two weeks.

(b) *Effect of the certificate.*

(*i*) The certificate provides conclusive evidence that all requirements of the Companies Acts in respect of registration have been complied with, and that the company is duly registered under the 1948 Act as (say) a public company. The certificate also bears the company's registered number and this must be quoted in all formal returns made to the Registrar of Companies. It must also be quoted on all business letters and order forms.

(*ii*) The company comes into existence as a body corporate.

(*iii*) In the case of a *private* company, it is entitled to commence business and exercise its borrowing powers; in the case of a *public* company, it cannot do business or exercise borrowing powers until it has received from the Registrar a certificate to that effect: Companies Act 1980, s.4 (*see* **14** *below*).

14. Section 4 certificate.

As stated above, a public company cannot commence business or exercise any borrowing powers unless the Registrar has issued it with a certificate under s.4 of the 1980 Act.

The certificate will be issued when the Registrar is satisfied that the nominal value of the company's allotted share capital is not less than the authorised minimum (£50,000), and not less than one-quarter of the nominal value of each issued share in the company plus the whole of any premium on such shares have been paid up, though employees' shares may be excluded from this calculation.

In order to obtain such a certificate a statutory declaration in the prescribed form signed by a director or secretary of the company must be filed with the Registrar; it must state:

(*a*) that the nominal value of the company's allotted share capital is not less than the authorised minimum;

(*b*) the amount paid up, at the time of the application, on the allotted share capital of the company;

(*c*) the amount, or estimated amount, of the preliminary expenses and the persons by whom any of those expenses have been paid or are payable; and

(*d*) any amount or benefit paid or given or intended to be paid or given to any promoter of the company, and the consideration for the payment or benefit.

If a company does business or exercises borrowing powers in contravention of s.4, the company and any officer of the company who is in default shall be liable on conviction on indictment to a fine and on summary conviction to a fine not exceeding the statutory maximum.

RE-REGISTRATION

15. Re-registration of companies. The procedure outlined in **7–14** above refers to a company on its *original* incorporation.

The Companies Act 1980 sets out in some detail the requirements for re-registration in the following cases:

(*a*) re-registration of a private company as a public company;

(*b*) re-registration of an unlimited company as a public company;

(*c*) re-registration of a public company as a private company.

The requirements in each case are outlined below. The 1980 Act also made provisions for the re-registration of old public companies (i.e those which on 22nd December 1980 were public companies as defined under the former law) in accordance with the new classification of public and private companies introduced by that Act. Failure on the part of such a company to re-register under the new classification by 22nd March 1982 exposed the company and its officers to criminal sanctions, and where the default continued after 22nd June 1982 entitles the Secretary of State to petition the court to wind up the company.

16. Re-registration of a private company as a public company. A private company with share capital wishing to re-register as a public limited company must comply with the requirements of the Companies Act 1980, s.5:

(*a*) A special resolution must be passed:

(*i*) that the company be re-registered as a public company;

(*ii*) altering the company's Memorandum of Association so that it states the company is to be a public company;

(*iii*) making such other alterations in the Memorandum of Association as are necessary to conform with requirements of the Companies Act 1980 with respect to the requirements of a public company;

(*iv*) altering the Articles of Association as required in the circumstances.

NOTE: A private company cannot be re-registered as a public company unless, at the time the resolution is passed, the nominal value of the company's allotted share capital is not less than the authorised minimum. (*See* Companies Act 1980, s.6(1) for further requirements in this connection.)

(*b*) An application for re-registration in the prescribed form, signed by a director or secretary of the company, must be delivered to the Registrar, together with:

(*i*) a printed copy of the Memorandum of Association and Articles of Association as altered in accordance with the special resolution;

(*ii*) a copy of a written statement by the auditors of the company that, in their opinion, the relevant balance sheet shows that, at the balance sheet date, the amount of the company's net assets was not less than the aggregate of its called-up capital and undistributable reserves;

(*iii*) a copy of the relevant balance sheet, together with a copy of an unqualified report by the company's auditors in relation to that balance sheet;

(*iv*) a copy of any report with respect to the value of the allotment, where shares are allotted by the company between the balance sheet date and the passing of the special resolution;

(*v*) a statutory declaration in the prescribed form by a director or secretary of the company that the special resolution (mentioned above) has been passed and that between the balance sheet date and the application of the company for re-registration there has been no change in the financial position of the company that has resulted in the amount of the company's net assets becoming less than the aggregate of its called-up share capital and undistributable reserves.

If the Registrar is satisfied that the application and documents comply with the requirements for re-registration, he will retain the application and other documents and issue to the company a Certificate of Incorporation, stating that the company is a public company.

17. Re-registration of an unlimited company as a public company. The procedure laid down in the Companies Act 1980, s.7 for re-registration of an unlimited company as a public company is the same as that described in **16** above, except that the special resolution must, in addition:

(*a*) state that the liability of the members is to be limited by shares and what the share capital of the company is to be; and

(*b*) make such alterations in the company's Memorandum of Association as are necessary to bring it in substance and in form into conformity with the requirements of the Companies Acts with respect to the Memorandum of a company limited by shares.

If the Registrar is satisfied that application and documents comply with the requirements for re-registration, he will issue to the company a Certificate of Incorporation, stating that the company has been incorporated as a company limited by shares, and that:

(*a*) the company shall by virtue of the issue of that certificate become a public company so limited; and

(*b*) the certificate shall be conclusive evidence of the fact that it is such a public company.

18. Re-registration of a public company as a private company. The requirements in this case, as laid down in the Companies Act 1980, s.10 are as follows.

(*a*) A special resolution must be passed:

(*i*) that the company be re-registered as a private company;

(*ii*) altering the company's Memorandum of Association so that it no longer states that the company is to be a public company, and making such other alterations in the company's Memorandum and Articles as are requisite in the circumstances.

NOTE: The Court has power to cancel this resolution on the application of a specified number (or proportion) of members who had not consented to or voted in favour of the resolution, made within 28 days after passing the resolution.

(*b*) An application for re-registration in the prescribed form, signed by a director or secretary of the company must be delivered to the Registrar, together with a printed copy of the Memorandum and Articles of the company as altered by the resolution.

After the period during which an application for the cancellation of the special resolution in accordance with the Companies Act 1980, s.11, has expired without any such application having been made, or, if an application has been made, it has been withdrawn, or the Court has made an order confirming the resolution, and a copy of that order has been delivered to the Registrar, then:

(a) if satisfied that the company has complied with re-registration requirements, the Registrar will retain the application and other documents delivered to him; and

(b) issue to the company a Certificate of Incorporation appropriate to a company that is not a public company.

The effects of the issue of the Certificate of Incorporation to the company are:

(a) the company, by virtue of that certificate becomes a private company;

(b) the alterations in the Memorandum and Articles set out in the special resolution take effect accordingly; and

(c) the company has conclusive evidence that the requirements in respect of re-registration and of matters precedent and incidental thereto have been complied with, and that the company is a private company.

OVERSEA COMPANIES

19. Oversea companies. An oversea company is a company incorporated outside Great Britain which establishes a place of business within Great Britain.

Within one month of establishing such a place of business an oversea company must deliver the following documents to the appropriate Registrar: s.406:

(a) a certified copy of the charter, statutes or memorandum and articles of the company or other instrument defining the constitution of the company, and, if the instrument is not written in the English language, a certified translation of it;

(b) a list of the directors and secretary, with similar particulars to those required by s.200 in the case of an English or Scottish company;

(c) the name and address of a person resident in Great Britain authorised to accept, on behalf of the company, service of process and notices;

(*d*) a list of the above documents.

The Registrar must be notified of any alterations in the above documents.

MEMORANDUM OF ASSOCIATION

20. Main purpose. The Memorandum of Association is often described as a company's charter, since it defines and limits its powers, particularly as regards the company's dealings with the outside world.

Internally, the Memorandum and Articles bind the company and its members to the same extent as if they respectively had been signed and sealed by each member (s.20).

21. Contents. The Memorandum of Association of a public company limited by shares must be in the form set out in Part I of Schedule I to the Companies Act 1980. Briefly, its contents are:

(*a*) name of the company,

(*b*) a statement that the company is to be a public company,

(*c*) domicile of the company's registered office, i.e. in which country it will be situated,

NOTE: If the Memorandum states that the registered office is to be situated in Wales, both Memorandum and Articles may be in Welsh; if they are, they must be accompanied by a certified translation in English: Companies Act 1976, s.30(6).

(*d*) the objects for which the company is established,

(*e*) a statement that the liability of the members is limited,

(*f*) the amount of the company's share capital, and the number and denomination of shares into which it is divided,

(*g*) a subscription clause.

The Memorandum of Association of a *private* company limited by shares, set out in Schedule 1, Table B, of the Companies Act 1948, omits (*b*) above but is identical in other respects.

The Memorandum of Association of a *public* company limited by guarantee and having a share capital contains an *additional* clause, stating that every member of the company guarantees to contribute to the assets of the company in the event of its being wound up, subject to certain conditions: Companies Act 1980, Schedule I, Part II.

22. Name of the company; Companies Act 1981, ss.22–23 and 31.
By s.22 of the 1981 Act a company shall not be registered under the
1948 Act by a name:

(a) which includes otherwise than at the end of the name any of
the following words and expressions, that is to say, "limited",
"unlimited" or "public limited company" or their Welsh equivalents;

(b) which includes otherwise than at the end of the name abbrevia-
tions of any of those words or expressions;

(c) which is the same as a name appearing in the index which the
Registrar is required to keep under s.23 of the Act (*see below*);

(d) the use of which by the company would in the opinion of the
Secretary of State constitute a criminal offence; or

(e) which in the opinion of the Secretary of State is offensive.

Further, except with the approval of the Secretary of State, a company may not be registered under the 1948 Act by a name which:

(a) in the opinion of the Secretary of State would be likely to give
the impression that the company is connected in any way with Her
Majesty's Government or with any local authority; or

(b) includes any word or expression for the time being specified
under regulations made under s.31 of the 1981 Act (*see below*).

The index of names required to be kept by the Registrar under s.23
of the 1981 Act contains the names of all existing companies, incorporated and unincorporated bodies and limited partnerships and
it is against this index that the promoters of a company check to
ensure that the proposed name of the company they intend to form is
not the same as that of an existing company. Assuming that such is
not the case, that the proposed name ends with the appropriate designation and is not in the opinion of the Secretary of State offensive or
one the use of which would be a criminal offence, the proposed name
will be accepted by the Registrar. The Registrar's prior approval to a
choice of name is only required where the name includes any word
specified under s.31 of the 1981 Act or gives the impression that the
company is connected with Her Majesty's Government or with any
local authority. Among the words specified under s.31 of the 1981
Act are the words British, Queen's, International, European,
Council, Society, Group and Trust.

23. Companies exempt from requirement to use word "limited" etc.
A company is permitted under s.25 of the 1981 Act to omit the word
"limited" from its name if it fulfils the following conditions (and submits a statutory declaration to that effect):

(*a*) it is or is about to be registered as a private company limited by guarantee; or

(*b*) it is immediately before the day on which s.25 of the 1981 Act comes into force a private company limited by shares the name of which does not, by virtue of a licence granted under s.19 of the 1948 Act, include the word limited, and which satisfies the following requirements:

(*i*) its objects are or in the case of a company about to be registered are to be the promotion of commerce, art, science, education, religion, charity or any profession and anything incidental or conducive to any of those objects; and

(*ii*) it is a company the memorandum or articles of which:

(1) require its profits, if any, or other income to be applied in promoting its objects;

(2) prohibit the payment of dividends to its members; and

(3) require all the assets which would otherwise be available to its members generally to be transferred on its winding up either to another body with objects similar to its own or to another body the objects of which are the promotion of charity and anything incidental or conducive thereto (whether or not the body is a member of the company).

A company so exempted from the requirements of the 1948 Act relating to the use of the word "limited" as any part of its name is also exempted from the requirements of the 1948 Act relating to the publishing of its name and the sending of lists of members to the Registrar of Companies.

24. Trading under a misleading name.

(*a*) It is an offence for a "person" who is *not* a public company to carry on any trade, profession or business under a name which includes the words "Public Limited Company", or their Welsh equivalent.

(*b*) A public company will be guilty of an offence if, where it is likely to be material, it uses a name which may give the impression that it is a private company: Companies Act 1980, s.76.

(*c*) A company or any officer of the company in default in either of the above cases is liable to a fine.

25. Domicile of the registered office.

(*a*) The Memorandum must state whether the registered office is to be situated in England or in Scotland (s.2(1)(b)), but the

Companies Act 1976, s.30 provides that a company may instead make a statement that its registered office is to be situated in Wales. This, in effect, indicates the company's nationality.

(*b*) As already stated earlier in this chapter (*see* 11), the intended situation of the registered office must be given in a statement in the prescribed form and delivered to the Registrar when the Memorandum is presented for registration.

(*c*) Subject to the exception stated in (*d*) below, a company cannot change its domicile, but it may change its address at will within the country of domicile, so long as the requisite 14 days' notice is given to the Registrar: Companies Act 1976, s.23.

(*d*) A company with its registered office in Wales may alter its Memorandum by *special* resolution so that it provides that its registered office is to be situated in Wales.

26. Objects of the company.

(*a*) The "objects" clause in the Memorandum sets out the purpose(s) for which the company is formed. It may be brief, like those shown in the specimen forms of Memorandum in Schedule I, Parts I and II to the Companies Act 1980, but in many cases it may be quite extensive and contain:

(*i*) one or more main objects, which might be described as the "substratum" of the company;

(*ii*) several subsidiary clauses, including, for example, the company's borrowing powers (if any) and any limits imposed thereon; and

(*iii*) a final clause, giving the company power to do things "incidental to" the main object(s).

(*b*) This definition of the company's objects gives some degree of protection to shareholders and to persons dealing with the company; thus, such parties are protected in the following ways:

(*i*) if the "substratum" (i.e. the main purpose) of the company fails, a shareholder may petition for a winding up: *Re German Date Coffee Co.* (1882);

(*ii*) any act of the company which is outside the scope of its objects is *ultra vires* the company and void; moreover, the act cannot be ratified even if all the shareholders agree: *Ashbury Railway Carriage Co.* v. *Riche* (1875).

27. "Limitation of liability" clause.

(*a*) This is merely a statement that the liability of members is limited, i.e. limited to the amount (if any) unpaid on their respective shares.

(*b*) Obviously, the Memorandum of an *unlimited* company does not include this clause, nor does it require a capital clause. (*See* specimen Memorandum of an unlimited company in Schedule I, Table E, Companies Act 1948.)

(*c*) In the case of a company limited by guarantee, it can no longer be formed as or become a company limited by guarantee with a share capital: Companies Act 1980, s.1(2).

An *additional* clause is, however, required, stating that every member of the company guarantees to contribute to the assets of the company in the event of its being wound up—subject to various conditions—but not exceeding the sum guaranteed.

NOTE: A member's right to limitation may be lost if a company carries on business without having at least two members and does so for more than six months. In such circumstances a person who, for the whole or any part of the period that it carries on business after those six months, is a member of the company and knows that it is carrying on business with only one member, becomes liable (jointly and severally with the company) for payment of the debts of the company contracted during (i.e. after) the period or part of it: Companies Act 1948, s.31, as amended by the Companies Act 1980, Schedule 3.

28. Capital clause.

(*a*) This sets out the authorised capital of the company, and states the number and denomination of its shares. Types of shares are not usually stated in the Memorandum; they are generally named and described (where necessary) in the company's Articles of Association.

(*b*) Formerly, the authorised capital determined the amount of capital duty payable on registration but, since the Finance Act 1973 came into force, it is calculated on the *greater* of the nominal value of the shares issued or allotted and the actual value of assets of any kind contributed less any liabilities which have been assumed or discharged by the company in consideration of the contribution.

29. Association (or subscription) clause.

(*a*) This is a statement by the subscribers to the Memorandum that they desire to be formed into a company, and agree to take up one or more shares in the company.

(*b*) It must be subscribed by at least *two* persons, irrespective of whether it is a public or a private company.

(*c*) Their signature must be attested (one witness is sufficient to all signatures) and the document dated.

(*d*) Subsequently, it will bear the registration fee stamp at the current rate.

MATTERS AFFECTING THE MEMORANDUM

30. Alteration of the Memorandum.

(*a*) *When permissible.* Subject to certain exceptions (*see below*), any condition in the Memorandum which could lawfully have been contained in the Articles of Association instead of in the Memorandum may be altered by *special* resolution: s.23. If, however, the specified proportion of shareholders object to the alteration, it will have no effect unless it is confirmed by the Court (s.23(1),(3)).

(*b*) *Exceptions.* The right to alter a condition in the Memorandum does *not* apply:

(*i*) where the Memorandum itself provides for, or prohibits, the alteration of its conditions;

(*ii*) where alteration of the Memorandum would vary or abrogate the special rights of any class of members;

(*iii*) where alteration of the Memorandum would compel a member to take up more shares, or increase liability, unless the member agrees in writing, either before or after the alteration, to be bound by it: s.22;

(*iv*) where an order under s.75 of the 1980 Act requires a company not to make any, or any specified alteration in the Memorandum, unless the court gives leave to make an alteration in breach of such a requirement (s.75 of the 1980 Act).

31. Alteration of the "objects" clause.

(*a*) *When permissible.* The Companies Act 1948, s.5, permits alteration of the objects clause of the Memorandum by *special* resolution to enable a company:

(*i*) to carry on some other business that may conveniently be combined with its own;

(*ii*) to enlarge or change the local area of its operation;

(*iii*) to attain its main purpose by new or improved means;

(*iv*) to carry on its business more economically or more efficiently;

(*v*) to restrict or abandon any of the objects specified in its Memorandum;

(*vi*) to sell or dispose of the whole or part of the undertaking of the company; or

(*vii*) to amalgamate with any other company or body of persons.

A company to which s.25 of the 1981 Act applies (*see* **23** *above*) and the name of which does not include "limited" cannot alter its memorandum or articles of association so that it ceases to be a company to which s.25 of the 1981 Act applies.

(*b*) *Procedure.*

(*i*) *Check the purpose.* Ensure that the reason for altering the objects is one of those permitted by s.5.

(*ii*) *Notify the stock exchange.* If the company's shares are listed on the stock exchange, notify its Share and Loan Department without delay, giving particulars of the proposed alteration.

(*iii*) *Convene a general meeting.* A general meeting of the company must be convened, giving at least 21 days' notice. The notice must state that it is proposed to pass a *special* resolution, and should be sent to:

1. all members of the company; and

2. all debenture holders (if any) who are entitled to object to the alteration.

(*iv*) *Special resolution.* At the general meeting a *special* resolution is passed, i.e. by a majority of not less than three-fourths of the members voting in person or (where proxies are allowed) by proxy: s.141.

(*v*) *File a copy* of the special resolution with the Registrar within 15 days of its being passed: s.143.

(*vi*) *Forward to the stock exchange* (Quotations Department) *four* copies of the special resolution, if the company's shares are listed.

(*c*) *Objections to the alteration.*

(*i*) Any applications for cancellation of the special resolution must be made to the court within 21 days after the resolution was passed, by those entitled to object, namely:

(1) the holders of not less in the aggregate than 15 per cent in nominal value of the company's issued share capital, or any class thereof; or

(2) not less than 15 per cent of the company's members, if

the company is not limited by shares; or

(3) the holders of not less than 15 per cent of the company's debentures secured by a floating charge created prior to 1st December 1947.

NOTE: An application cannot be made for cancellation of the alteration by any person (in any of the above cases) who has consented to, or voted in favour of, the alteration.

(*ii*) If application is made by objectors (who are entitled to do so) within 21 days after the passing of the resolution:

(1) notify the Registrar forthwith that such an application has been made;

(2) the court has power to confirm the alteration wholly or in part, to cancel the alteration, to postpone the matter, or require alteration of the company's name so as to indicate the changed objects;

(3) file an office copy of the court order within 15 days of the date of the order; and

(4) if the order confirms the alteration, deliver to the Registrar, at the same time, a printed copy of the Memorandum in its altered form.

(*iii*) If no application is made by objectors within 21 days after passing the resolution:

(1) the alteration cannot be questioned;

(2) the company must, within a further 15 days (after expiration of the 21 day period) deliver to the Registrar a printed copy of the Memorandum in its altered form.

(*d*) *Subsequent issues of the Memorandum.* Every copy of the Memorandum issued after the date of the alteration must embody the alteration. The company and every officer of the company in default are liable to fines (s.25).

32. Change of name.

(*a*) *Conditions.* A company is permitted by s.24 of the 1981 Act to change its name by special resolution.

(*b*) *Procedure.*

(*i*) Ensure that the proposed new name complies with the requirements of s.22 of the 1980 Act.

(*ii*) *Notify the stock exchange* concerned. If the company's shares are listed, notify the appropriate department of the proposed change of name as soon as possible.

(*iii*) *Convene a general meeting* of the company giving not less than 21 days' notice.

(*iv*) *Pass a special resolution* at the meeting, sanctioning the change of name. A three-fourths majority of those actually voting in person (or, where permitted, by proxy) is required for this purpose.

(*v*) *File copies* of the special resolution, as follows:

(1) one copy with the Registrar, within 15 days after the passing of the resolution together with a copy of the Memorandum as altered and the appropriate fee;

(2) four copies with the stock exchange, if the company's shares are listed.

(*vi*) The Registrar shall, subject to s.22 of the 1981 Act, enter the new name on the register in place of the company's former name, and shall issue a certificate of incorporation altered to meet the circumstances of the case.

(*vii*) *Subsequent procedure.* The change of name having become official:

(1) ensure that every copy of the Memorandum issued after the date of the alteration embodies the alteration, otherwise the company and every officer of the company in default are liable to fines (s.25);

(2) arrange for the alteration of the company's name on the common seal, nameplates, stationery, etc.;

(3) if the company's shares are listed, have new share certificates (and debenture certificates, if applicable) printed, using the company's new name, and submit a specimen (or two advance proofs) to the stock exchange for approval;

(4) as it is unlikely that the company will call in share and debenture certificates, alterations or replacements are usually made as and when the documents are submitted for registration in connection with transfers;

(5) advertise the change of name in the *London Gazette* and, where appropriate, in one or more provincial papers.

(*c*) The Secretary of State has power under s.24 of the 1981 Act to direct a company to change its name within twelve months of registration in the index of company names if the name is the same as one already on the index: s.24(2) of the 1980 Act.

(*d*) Where it appears to the Secretary of State that a company has provided misleading information for the purposes of its registration by a particular name or has given undertakings or assurances for that purpose which have not been fulfilled, the Secretary of State may within five years of the date of its registration by that name in writing direct the company to change its name within such period as he may specify.

(*e*) *Power of Department of Trade and Industry* to require a company to abandon a misleading name.

(*i*) The Companies Act 1967, s.46, gives the Department of Trade and Industry power to direct a company to change its name where it has been registered with a name which is so misleading as to be likely to cause harm to the public.

(*ii*) The company is, however, permitted to apply to the court to set the direction aside.

(*f*) *Trading under a misleading name.*

(*i*) The Companies Act 1980, s.76, makes it an offence to trade under a name that is misleading as to a person's status or, in the case of a company, its classification; where, for example, a person or company that is *not* a public company trades under a name that includes the words "Public Limited Company" or an abbreviation, or their Welsh equivalent or its abbreviation.

(*ii*) Any person or, if the "person" is a company, any officer of the company in default will be liable to a fine.

33. Publication of a company's name (s.108).

(*a*) The Act requires every company:

(*i*) to have its name painted or affixed on the outside of every office or place of business, in a conspicuous position and in letters easily legible;

(*ii*) to have its name engraven in legible characters on its seal;

(*iii*) to have its name mentioned in legible characters in all business letters, on notices and other official publications, on bills of exchange, promissory notes, endorsements, cheques and orders for money or goods, and in all bills of parcels, invoices, receipts and letters of credit of the company.

(*b*) Failure to comply with the above requirements renders the company and every officer in default liable to fines. Moreover, any officer of the company may be held *personally* liable on documents such as cheques, bills of exchange etc. from which the company's name has been omitted.

(*c*) Where a limited company with a registered office in Wales has adopted "Cyfyngedig" as the last word of its name, the fact that the company is a limited company must be stated in English in all prospectuses, bill heads, letter paper, notices and other official publications of the company; and in a notice conspicuously displayed in every place in which the company's business is carried on. The company and every officer in default are liable to fines: Companies Act 1976, s.30. The Companies Act 1980, s.77, makes a similar provision where the name of a *public* limited company includes, as its last part, the equivalent in Welsh of the words "Public Limited Company". Failure to comply renders the company and every officer in default liable to fines.

34. Business names. Section 28 of the Companies Act 1981 provides that any company which has a place of business in Great Britain and which carries on business in Great Britain under a name which in the case of a company, being a company which is capable of being wound up under the 1948 Act, does not consist of its corporate name without any addition shall not, without the written approval of the Secretary of State, carry on business in Great Britain under a name which:

(*a*) would be likely to give the impression that the business is connected with Her Majesty's Government or with any local authority; or

(*b*) includes any word or expression for the time being specified under regulations made under s.31 of the 1981 Act (*see* **22** *above*).

Where a company falls within the scope of s.28 of the 1981 Act, s.29 of the 1981 Act requires that company to state in legible characters on all business letters, invoices and receipts issued in the course of business and written demands for payment of debts arising in the course of the business its corporate name and an address within Great Britain at which service of any document relating in any way to the business will be effective; and, in any premises where the business is carried on and to which the customers of the business or suppliers of any goods or services to the business have access, to display in a prominent position, so that it may easily be read by such customers or suppliers, a notice containing such name and address.

Further, a company falling within the scope of s.28 of the 1981 Act must provide the name and address specified by that section immediately, in writing, to any person with whom any thing is done or discussed in the course of the business and who asks for such name and address.

ARTICLES OF ASSOCIATION

35. Articles of Association. A company limited by shares *may*, and a company limited by guarantee or unlimited *must*, register Articles of Association along with its Memorandum of Association (s.6).

36. Purpose. The Articles contain regulations for management of the internal affairs of the company, e.g.:

(*a*) rights of the various classes of shareholder;
(*b*) rules governing meetings;
(*c*) appointment and powers of directors;
(*d*) common seal, its custody and use;
(*e*) alteration of share capital;
(*f*) procedure for making calls;
(*g*) forfeiture of shares etc.

37. Legal effects.

(*a*) The Memorandum and the Articles, when registered, bind the company and its members to the same extent as if they respectively had been signed and sealed by each member, and contained covenants on the part of each member to observe all the provisions (s.20).

(*b*) All money payable by any member to the company under the Memorandum or Articles is in the nature of a speciality debt (s.20).

(*c*) In *Eley* v. *Positive Government Security Life Assurance* (1876), the courts decided that the Memorandum and Articles can only have a contractual effect as between the company and its members as such; that is, neither the company nor its members are bound to "outsiders" by virtue of those documents.

(*d*) In *Royal British Bank* v. *Turquand* (1856), the court ruled that persons dealing with the company are deemed to know the contents of the Articles, but are not bound to see to it that the provisions of the Articles are carried out.

(*e*) Articles are inoperative if they conflict with statutory requirements, e.g. the right of shareholders to present a winding-up petition cannot be abolished by the articles. Likewise, if the provisions of the articles conflict with those of the memorandum the provision of the latter prevail.

38. Table A.

(*a*) This is a model set of Articles of Association, setting out regulations for the management of a company limited by shares. It is set out in Schedule 1 to the Companies Act 1948 and now applies to *both* public and private companies limited by shares, as Part II of Table A was repealed by the Companies Act 1980.

(*b*) A company may elect to follow any one of the following methods in relation to its Articles of Association.

(*i*) A company limited by shares may register its own special set of Articles, in which case Table A provisions will apply only on any matters omitted from the special Articles.

(*ii*) Alternatively, a company may adopt Table A in its entirety or in a modified form.

(*iii*) If, however, Articles are not registered, then the regulations of Table A will automatically become the regulations of the company.

39. Form of Articles. If a company registers its own Articles, they must be:

(*a*) in printed form;
(*b*) divided into paragraphs, consecutively numbered;
(*c*) signed, witnessed and dated.

40. Stock exchange requirements of the Articles. Before the stock exchange will give "permission to deal" the Articles of the company applying for such permission must comply with the requirements of the stock exchange concerned. In particular:

(*a*) fully-paid shares must be freely transferable and free of lien;
(*b*) share certificates must be under seal, and the seal affixed under authority of the directors;
(*c*) directors are not entitled to vote (except as provided in Table A, Article 84) on contracts in which they have a personal interest.

41. Alteration of Articles of Association.

(*a*) The Companies Act 1948, s.10, permits alteration of the Articles:

(*i*) subject to the provisions of the Companies Acts 1948 to 1981 and the conditions contained in its Memorandum of Association;

(*ii*) by *special* resolution of the company.

(*b*) Other restrictions of the power to alter the Articles have arisen out of various cases decided in the courts, namely:

(*i*) any alteration in the Articles must be legal; thus an alteration which gives a company power to purchase its own shares is invalid: *Trevor* v. *Whitworth* (1887);

(*ii*) a company cannot justify a breach of contract by altering its Articles: *Baily* v. *British Equitable Assurance Co.* (1906);

(*iii*) any alteration of the Articles must be made for the benefit of the company as a whole; it will not be invalid merely because it inflicts hardship upon any individual shareholder: *Allen* v. *Gold Reefs Ltd.* (1900).

CAPITAL STRUCTURE

42. Authorised, nominal or registered capital.

(*a*) *Various considerations.* As already indicated (*see* 7) capital requirements are determined by taking into account:

(*i*) the *purchase price* of any business to be acquired, or assets to be taken over;

(*ii*) *preliminary expenses;*

(*iii*) *working capital;*

(*iv*) *future requirements* arising out of anticipated development of the business.

(*b*) *Classes of shares.* Although shares need not be classified it is usually advantageous to do so in order to give the investors a wider choice of investment. Basically shares may be divided into three classes:

(*i*) preference shares;

(*ii*) ordinary shares;

(*iii*) deferred shares.

43. Preference shares.

(*a*) These entitle the holder to a fixed rate of dividend out of the profits of the company, to be paid in priority to other classes of shareholder.

(*b*) Other rights are sometimes given in the company's Articles and conditions of issue, the following in particular.

(*i*) *Cumulative preference shares.* All preference shares are presumed to be cumulative unless otherwise described; that is, arrears of dividend are to be made up in subsequent years, when profits are available. No dividend will be paid to other classes of shareholder until preference dividends (including arrears) are paid to date.

(*ii*) *Non-cumulative preference shares.* The holders of such shares are entitled to a specified rate of dividend, but only out of profits of the current year. If the profits do not warrant payment of a dividend, the arrears are *not* carried forward to subsequent years.

(*iii*) *Participating preference shares.* Such shares entitle the holder to preferential dividend at a fixed rate and to participate further in any profit remaining after the ordinary shareholders have received, say, 10 per cent dividend. In the absence of express provisions, preference shares are deemed to be non-participating: *Will* v. *United Lankat Plantation Co.* (1914).

(*iv*) *Preference as to repayment of capital.* This is a right which may be given in addition to, or instead of, some of those already mentioned. It gives the preference shareholders the right to repayment of their capital in full in priority to the ordinary shareholders in the event of a winding up. Unless this right is expressly given in the Articles or conditions of issue, preference shareholders rank equally with other shareholders as to return of capital.

(*v*) *Participation in surplus assets.* The preference shareholders may be entitled to participate with the ordinary shareholders in any surplus assets, but this is a right that must be expressly conferred by the company's Articles, Memorandum or conditions of issue: *Scottish Insurance Corporation* v. *Wilson's & Clyde Coal Co.* (1949).

(*vi*) *Entitlement to arrears of dividend on winding up.* The right to arrears of preference dividend may be provided for in the company's Articles; even so, however, it does not necessarily entitle the holders to payment of their arrears before the repayment of capital to other classes of shareholder. If, for example, the Articles provide for payment of arrears of preference dividend "due" at the date of the winding up, no arrears will be payable unless a dividend has been declared, because a dividend is not due *until* it has been declared: *Re Roberts & Cooper Ltd.* (1929).

44. Ordinary shares.

(*a*) The holders of these shares are the main risk-bearers of a company, since ordinary shares confer no special dividend rights apart from an implied right to participate in the profits, if any.

(*b*) In most companies the ordinary shares constitute the equity share capital, i.e. the holders are entitled to the "equity" or residue of profits after payment of dividends on prior ranking shares and of any surplus assets in a winding up.

(*c*) In recent years some companies have issued *non-voting* ordinary shares, sometimes described as "A" shares. Such shares apart, however, the ordinary shareholders carry the bulk of the voting power in most companies. Preference shareholders, on the other hand, are often without any voting power, or are entitled to voting power only when their dividends are in arrears.

45. Deferred shares.

(a) These are sometimes issued to the vendors in full or partial settlement of the purchase price of the business acquired by the company. If, for example, A. Brown Ltd. is formed to acquire the business of A. Brown, he may be allotted deferred (or founder's) shares in consideration of the purchase price.

(b) They are usually valuable shares, as they may have the right to all profits remaining after payment of prior dividends and to all surplus assets on winding up the company. In that event the deferred shares, and not the ordinary shares, will form the "equity" of the company.

(c) Deferred shares, although they are sometimes of small denomination, usually give the holder heavy voting power, e.g. on a poll vote, where each share is worth one vote, £5000 worth of 5p deferred shares might well out-vote the ordinary shares. Thus the deferred shareholders can retain control of the business, and it is for this reason that deferred shares are sometimes referred to as management shares.

46. Redeemable shares.

(a) Section 45 of the Companies Act 1981 enables a company limited by shares or limited by guarantee and having a share capital, if authorised by its articles, to issue shares which are, or at the option of the company or a shareholder are liable, to be redeemed.

(b) However, no such shares may be issued at any time when there are no issued shares of the company which are not redeemable; redeemable shares may not be redeemed unless they are fully paid; and the terms of redemption must provide for payment on redemption.

(c) In general redemption may only take place by utilising distributable profits or the proceeds of a fresh issue; and any premium payable on redemption must be paid out of the company's distributable profits.

(d) On redemption out of the profits of the company, the company is required to establish a capital redemption reserve equivalent to the amount by which the company's issued share capital is thereby reduced. Such a fund is a capital fund, though it may be used to pay up unissued shares for the purpose of a bonus issue: s.53 of the 1981 Act.

(e) Shares so redeemed are treated as cancelled on redemption, but although the company's issued share capital is reduced thereby a redemption of shares under the provision is not treated as reducing the amount of the company's authorised share capital. A company which has issued shares up to its maximum nominal capital is permitted to issue fresh shares for the purpose of redeeming an existing issue of redeemable shares.

(*f*) Section 54 of the 1981 Act extends the power provided by s.45 of that Act in that it enables a private company limited by shares or limited by guarantee and having a share capital, if authorised to do so by its articles, to redeem its own shares out of capital. The procedure to be followed on redemption of such shares out of capital is the same as that entailed when a private company purchases its shares out of capital (*see* 57 *below*).

47. Stock.

(*a*) A company cannot make an original issue of stock, i.e. stock can only be created out of fully paid shares:

(*i*) if authorised by the Articles; and

(*ii*) by resolution of the company in general meeting. An ordinary resolution is adequate unless the Articles require some other form of resolution (s.61) (*see* XI, 7).

(*b*) There is only one real advantage in converting shares into stock; the requirement of the Act that shares shall bear distinctive numbers does not apply to stock. Thus the conversion will be expected to lead to some simplification of work in the company's registration department.

NOTE: Even this advantage has been nullified to some extent, as s.74 permits a company to dispense with the numbering of all its issued shares (or all the issued shares of a particular class) so long as they are fully paid up and rank *pari passu* for all purposes.

(*c*) Theoretically, there is a further advantage, in that the stock created is transferable in fractional amounts. In fact, however, this would create more work for the registration department, and the Articles invariably provide for the transfer of stock in units or multiples of fixed amount.

NOTE: Table A permits conversion of paid-up shares into stock by ordinary resolution but gives the directors power to fix the minimum amount of stock transferable, the minimum not to exceed the nominal amount of the shares from which the stock arose.

48. Debentures.

(*a*) Strictly, debentures do not form part of a company's true capital; they may, however, be described as "borrowed" or "loan" capital and are included in this section for that reason. They are dealt with in greater detail in XV.

(b) The term "debenture" is usually applied to any form of long-term borrowing, but it is also used to describe any document which acknowledges the indebtedness. In most cases, such a document is under seal and sets out the conditions for securing repayment of the loan, date of repayment, and payment of interest.

49. Deter[ ] capital structure.

(a) Va[ ] lerations. If capital is to be raised in various forms, so[ ] he following points ought to be considered.

(i) [ ] y. Share capital is essentially *permanent*, i.e. it cannot b[ ] cept with the sanction of the Court under s.66 or redeen[ ] ased in accordance with the provisions of the Compani[ ] . Debentures are a *redeemable* security and might, th[ ] preferred to satisfy a long term (but not permanent) [ ] ncial assistance.

(ii) [ ] tures are usually more economical than preference sh[ ] ed adequate security is offered to the debenture holders, t[ ] lly prepared to accept a comparatively low rate of interes[ ] compared with the dividend that would have to be offered to make preference shares attractive.

(iii) *Capital gearing*, i.e. the ratio of fixed interest capital to "equity" capital, ought to be considered very carefully. If, for example, a large issue of debentures (or preference shares) is contemplated, it might be well to consider the effect upon the capital gearing. If the capital gearing is high (where the proportion of fixed interest bearing capital is high in relation to "equity" capital), the company's ordinary shares might appear less attractive to prospective investors, who realise that both debenture holders and preference shareholders must be satisfied before they would earn any dividend on their ordinary shares.

(b) *Under-capitalisation.* In calculating capital requirements, the aim must be neither too much nor too little. Under-capitalisation is almost certain to result in all kinds of difficulties, in particular:

(i) lack of working capital;

(ii) inability to meet present commitments;

(iii) inability to obtain credit;

(iv) failure to work to optimum capacity.

(c) *Over-capitalisation* must also be avoided, for the following reasons.

(*i*) The excess capital must be invested outside the business, probably at a low rate of interest.

(*ii*) As a result, dividends paid on the company's capital may be reduced or, in the case of preference shares, fall into arrears.

(*iii*) Failure to maintain dividends will soon have an adverse effect upon the market value of the company's shares.

(d) *Taxation.* Debenture interest is charged against profits, whereas dividend on shares is regarded as a distribution of profits—a very important consideration as regards taxation.

MAINTENANCE OF CAPITAL

50. Maintenance of capital. The Companies Act 1980 contains various provisions which are designed to ensure that a company maintains its capital, i.e. by compelling the directors to warn the shareholders when a serious situation affecting the capital has developed, and by preventing a company from acquiring an interest in its own shares directly or indirectly. However, these provisions must now be viewed in the light of certain provisions to be found in Part III of the Companies Act 1981. The relevant provisions of both Acts are examined in **51–58** following.

51. Serious loss of capital: 1980 Act, s.34

(*a*) If a serious loss of capital occurs, i.e. if the assets of a *public* company fall to half or less of the amount of the company's called-up capital, the directors of the company must convene an extraordinary general meeting of the company to consider whether any, and if so what, measures should be taken to deal with the situation. (The object is, of course, to give the shareholders an opportunity to consider the position of the company before it becomes insolvent and is compelled to cease trading.)

(*b*) The meeting must be convened not later than 28 days after the earliest date on which the situation became known to a director of the company, for a date not later than 56 days from that date.

(*c*) The notice of the meeting must comply with the requirements of the 1948 Act, s.133, for convening an extraordinary general meeting, i.e. not less than 14 days' notice in writing—unless it is intended to pass a special resolution at the meeting for any reason, in which case not less than 21 days' notice in writing is required.

(*d*) Failure on the part of any director of the company who knowingly and wilfully authorises or permits the failure to convene an extraordinary general meeting—or permits the failure to continue after expiry of the 28-day period—will be liable to a fine.

52. Acquisition of a company of its own shares: 1980 Act, s.35.
Except as permitted by the Companies Acts, the courts have consistently refused to allow a company to reduce its capital, however attempted, a principle established in *Trevor* v. *Whitworth* (1887) which held that a company could not purchase its own shares, even though there was express power to do so in its Memorandum of Association.

This important basic principle is reinforced in the following terms.

(*a*) No company limited by shares or limited by guarantee and having a share capital shall acquire its own shares, whether by purchase, subscription or otherwise (s.35(1)).

(*b*) If a company acts in contravention, it becomes liable to a fine, and any officers of the company in default are liable to a fine or imprisonment or both, and the purported acquisition will be *void* (s.35(3)).

However, s.35(4) provides that the basic prohibition in s.35(1) does not apply in relation to:

(*a*) the redemption or purchase of any shares in accordance with Part III of the Companies Act 1981;

(*b*) the acquisition of any shares in a reduction of capital, duly made;

(*c*) the purchase of any shares under an order of the court under ss.11 or 75 of the 1980 Act or s.5 of the 1948 Act;

(*d*) the forfeiture of any shares or the acceptance of any shares, surrendered in lieu of forfeiture, in accordance with its Articles of Association, for non-payment of any sum due in respect of those shares.

Under s.35(2) a company limited by shares may also acquire its own fully-paid shares "otherwise than for valuable consideration" (e.g. by way of gift). This means that shares so acquired need no longer be put into the name of a nominee.

53. Acquisition of shares in a company by company's nominees.
(*a*) The 1980 Act (s.36) provides that a limited company (whether public or private) is regarded as having no beneficial interest in any shares it has issued to a nominee of the company, nor in any partly paid shares acquired by a nominee of such company for a third

person; that is, for all purposes, the shares will be treated as being held by the nominee on his own account.

(*b*) If, in the case of partly paid shares, a nominee fails to pay the amount of any call in respect of the nominal value or premium on such shares within 21 days of his being called upon to do so, then

(*i*) if the shares were issued to him as a subscriber to the Memorandum of Assocation, the *other* subscribers to the *Memorandum*; or

(*ii*) if the shares were otherwise issued to him, or acquired by him, the directors of the company at the time of the issue or acquisition

will be jointly and severally liable with him to pay that amount.

(*c*) A subscriber or director who believes that a claim will, or might, be made against him in (*b*) above may apply to the court for relief. The court has power to grant such relief either before or in the course of any proceedings for recovery of any amount due, if it appears that the person or persons concerned acted honestly and reasonably and, in the circumstances of the case, he ought to be excused from liability, either wholly or partly.

(*d*) The above provisions do *not* apply

(*i*) to shares issued or transferred in consequence of an application or agreement made before the appointed day; or

(*ii*) to shares acquired by a nominee of a company when the company has no beneficial interest in the shares (other than any rights the company may have as trustee, whether as personal representative or otherwise); or

(*iii*) to shares acquired otherwise than by subscription by a nominee of a public company with the financial assistance of the company, and where the company has a beneficial interest in those shares—*see* **54**(*a*)(*iv*).

54. Treatment of shares held by or on behalf of a public company: 1980 Act, s.37.

(*a*) *Cases affected.* Section 37 provides for the treatment of forfeited and surrendered shares, and shares held by a nominee of a public company in the following cases:

(*i*) where shares in the company are forfeited or are surrendered to the company in lieu of forfeiture, in accordance with the Articles of Association, for failure to pay any sum due on the shares;

(*ii*) where the nominee of a public company acquires shares of the company from a third person without financial assistance by the company for the purpose, and the company has a beneficial interest in the shares;

(*iii*) where shares in the company are acquired by the company otherwise than by any of the methods mentioned in s.35(4) (*see* **54**), and the company has a beneficial interest;

(*iv*) where any person acquires shares in the company without financial assistance being provided by the company for the purpose, and the company has a beneficial interest in those shares.

NOTE: In determining whether a company has a beneficial interest in any shares, any rights the company has as trustee or personal representative to recover expenses, or to be remunerated out of the trust property, must be disregarded.

(*b*) *Treatment* of shares held in the above cases.

(*i*) Unless the shares (or any interest of the company in them) are previously disposed of, the company must not later than the end of the "relevant period" (*see* (*c*) *below*) from the date of their forfeiture, surrender or acquisition, as the case may be,

(1) cancel them and diminish the amount of the share capital by the nominal value of the shares; and

(2) if the effect of the cancellation is to reduce the nominal value of the company's allotted share capital below the authorised minimum, the company must apply for re-registration as a private company, stating the effect of the cancellation.

NOTE: The directors of the company may take such steps as are necessary to comply with the above requirements, and the usual procedures for reduction of capital under ss.66 and 67 of the 1948 Act can be dispensed with for this purpose.

(*ii*) The company, the company's nominee, or, as the case may be, the other shareholder, must not exercise any voting rights in respect of the shares involved, and any purported exercise of such rights is *void*.

(*c*) The *"relevant period"* referred to in (*b*)(*i*) above means:

(*i*) *three years*, in the case of shares forfeited or surrendered to the company (case (*a*)(*i*)) or acquired, as in cases (*a*)(*ii*) and (*a*)(*iii*) above.

(*ii*) *one year*, in the case of shares acquired, as in case (*a*)(*iv*) above.

(*d*) *Penalties.* Failure to cancel shares or to apply for re-registration, as required in (*b*)(*i*) above renders the company, and every officer of the company, in default liable to fines.

55. Charges taken by a public company on its own shares. A lien or other charge that a public company holds on its own shares is generally *void*, but s.38 of the 1980 Act permits the following exceptions:

(*a*) in a company of every description, a charge on its own partly-paid shares for any amount remaining unpaid on them;

(*b*) in the case of a company whose ordinary business includes the lending of money or providing hire-purchase (or both), a charge of the company on its own shares (whether fully or partly-paid) in connection with any transaction which the company enters into in the ordinary courses of its business;

(*c*) in the case of a company (other than a company referred to in (*d*) below) which is re-registered or registered as a public company, a charge on its own shares held immediately before it applies for re-registration or, as the case may be, registration;

(*d*) in the case of any company which after the end of the re-registration period remains or remained an old public company and did not apply to be re-registered before the end of that period as a public company, any charge on its own shares which was in existence immediately before the end of that period.

NOTE: A lien or charge taken by a company which is a trustee and where the trust property includes its own shares, is not specifically excepted.

56. Financial assistance for acquisition of shares: ss.42–44, 1981 Act.

(*a*) Section 42 of the 1981 Act provides that:

(*i*) where a person is acquiring or is proposing to acquire any shares in a company it shall not be lawful for the company or any of its subsidiaries to give financial assistance directly or indirectly for the purpose of that acquisition before or at the same time as the acquisition takes place; and

(*ii*) where a person has acquired any shares in a company and any liability has been incurred (by that or any other person) for the purpose of that acquisition it shall not be lawful for the company or any of its subsidiaries to give any financial assistance directly or indirectly for the purpose of reducing or discharging the liability so incurred.

(*b*) Neither of the prohibitions stated in (*a*) however, prohibit a company from giving any financial assistance for the purpose of any acquisition of shares in the company or its holding company or from giving financial assistance to reduce or discharge any liability incurred by a person for the purpose of the acquisition of any shares in the company or its holding company if:

(*i*) such is not the principal purpose of the assistance, but is an incidental part of some larger purpose of the company; and

(*ii*) the assistance is given in good faith in the interests of the company.

Nor do they prevent:

(*i*) any distribution of a company's assets by way of dividend lawfully made or any distribution made in the course of the winding up of the company;

(*ii*) the allotment of any bonus shares;

(*iii*) anything done in pursuance of an order of the court made under s.206;

(*iv*) anything done under an arrangement made between a company and its creditors which is binding on the creditors by virtue of s.306;

(*v*) anything done under an arrangement made in pursuance of s.287;

(*vi*) any reduction of capital confirmed by order of the court under s.68;

(*vii*) a redemption or purchase of any shares made in accordance with ss.45 to 62 of the Companies Act 1981.

(*c*) Further, neither of the general prohibitions is declared to prohibit:

(*i*) where the lending of money is part of the ordinary business of the company, the lending of money by the company in the ordinary course of its business;

(*ii*) the provision by a company in accordance with an employees' share scheme of money for the acquisition of fully paid shares in the company or its holding company;

(*iii*) the making by a company of loans to persons, other than directors, employed in good faith by the company with a view to enabling those persons to acquire fully paid shares in the company to be held by themselves by way of beneficial ownership.

Though in the case of a public company these three exceptions only operate if the company has net assets which are not thereby reduced or, to the extent that those assets are thereby reduced, if the financial assistance is provided out of distributable profits.

(*d*) If a company acts in contravention of s.42 of the 1981 Act the company and any officer who is in default commits a criminal offence.

(*e*) Section of the 1981 Act provides a further exception to the general prohibitions established in s.42 of that Act in that it provides that they do not prohibit a private company from giving financial assistance in any case where the acquisition of the shares in question is or was an acquisition of shares in the company or if it is a subsidiary of another private company, in that other company, provided that the following conditions are satisfied:

(*i*) The company must have net assets which are not thereby reduced or, to the extent that they are reduced, the financial assistance must be provided out of distributable profits.

(*ii*) The assistance must be approved by a special resolution.

(*iii*) The directors are required to make a statutory declaration giving details of the assistance and certifying that in their opinion the company can pay its debts and will continue to be able to do so during the ensuing twelve months. This must be supported by a report made by the auditors confirming that the directors' conclusions are reasonable.

(*iv*) The holders of 10 per cent of the company's issued share capital or any class thereof may apply to the court to cancel the resolution authorising the assistance.

57. Purchase by a company of its own shares: ss.46–52, 1981 Act.

(*a*) Section 48 of the 1981 Companies Act provides that a company limited by shares or limited by guarantee and having a share capital may, if authorised by its articles, purchase its own shares (including any redeemable shares). However, a company may not purchase any of its shares if as a result of such purchase there would no longer be any member of the company holding shares; and any such purchase must be in accordance with the procedures set out in the Act.

(*b*) The procedure prescribed for the purchase of shares varies according to whether or not the purchase takes place through a recognised stock exchange.

(*i*) *Off market purchase.* Such must be in pursuance of an interim contract of purchase, approved in advance by a special resolution of the company. The contract, or a memorandum thereof, must have been available for inspection by members for fifteen days before the meeting and at the meeting at which it is approved.

(*ii*) *Market purchase.* Such a purchase must have been authorised by an ordinary resolution of the company, specifying the maximum number of shares that may be purchased, the maximum and minimum prices to be paid and the date the authority expires.

In either case, within twenty-eight days of the transfer to the company of the shares concerned the company must deliver to the Registrar a return stating with respect to shares of each class purchased the number and nominal value of the shares and the date on which they were transferred to the company. Further, in the case of a public company this return must also state the aggregate amount paid by the company for the shares and the maximum and minimum price paid in respect of each class purchased.

Details of the purchase must be disclosed in the directors' report.

(c) The provisions of s.53 of the 1981 Act (*see* **46**(*c*) *above*) apply to the exercise of the power to purchase own shares, in the same way as they apply to the exercise by the company of the power to issue redeemable shares.

58. Redemption or purchase of own shares out of capital: ss.54–58, 1981 Act. Section 54 of the Companies Act 1981 extends the powers provided by ss. 45 and 46 of that Act (**46** and **56** above respectively) in that it enables a private company limited by shares or limited by guarantee and having a share capital, if authorised to do so by its articles, to redeem or purchase its own shares out of capital.

A payment out of capital to redeem or purchase the company's own shares will not be lawful, however, unless:

(*a*) The directors of the company make a statutory declaration specifying the amount of capital required and stating that having made full inquiry into the affairs and prospects of the company it will not thereby become insolvent, and will still be able to continue to carry on business as a going concern. Such declaration must be supported by, and have annexed to it, an auditors' report.

(*b*) A special resolution approving the payment out of capital is passed within the week immediately following the date on which the directors make the statutory declaration.

(*c*) Within the week immediately following the date of the resolution for payment out of capital, and having delivered a copy of the statutory declaration and the auditors' report to the Registrar, the company must cause to be published in the *London Gazette* and in an appropriate newspaper (or give notice in writing to that effect to each of its creditors) a notice detailing its intention and actions and bringing to the attention of creditors the statutory rights of objection.

(*d*) The payment out of capital must be made not earlier than five or more than seven weeks after the date of the resolution.

The right of objection referred to in (*c*) above is exercisable within five weeks of the date on which the resolution was passed and is exercised by:

(a) any member of the company other than one who consented to or voted in favour of the resolution; or

(b) any creditor of the company who may apply to the court for the cancellation of the resolution.

On the hearing of such an application the court may make such order as it thinks fit.

PROGRESS TEST 1

1. The company of which you are secretary has recently been changed from private to public. The directors are contemplating further expansion and you are asked to prepare a memorandum for consideration by the Board setting out the advantages and disadvantages, from the point of view of the company, in having an official quotation. (6)

2. Tabulate the documents to be lodged with the Registrar before incorporation of a private company with a share capital can be effected. What additional documents are required in the case of a public company? Where applicable, state against each document the stamp duty and registration fees payable. (11)

3. (a) Set out the procedure for forming a private company, and (b) specify the matters which you would expect to be dealt with at the first board meeting. ICSA (9–12; II, 3)

4. What is a Certificate of Incorporation? What is its effect in regard to (a) the existence of a company; (b) the legal rights to trade? Write fully. CCS (13)

5. As a practising secretary, you are approached by Messrs Smith and Robinson to convert their firm into a private limited company. Report to them, outlining the procedure and indicating the principal advantages and disadvantages of such a conversion. (9–13)

6. You are asked by your directors to arrange for the formation of a wholly owned subsidiary company, which is to be a private company with a nominal capital of £100. The suggested name for the company is Exe Limited. In numbered paragraphs, explain the action you would take up to the time of delivery to the Registrar of Companies of the documents necessary to obtain a Certificate of Incorporation. (NOTE: It should be assumed that you are expected to undertake all the work involved.) (7, 9–13)

7. You are asked to apply for the registration of a private company limited by shares. List the items of information about the proposed company which you would require to enable you to draft the memorandum and articles of association. *ICSA*   (**11, 21, 22, 26**)

8. For what purposes are companies limited by guarantee usually formed? What are the advantages of using this type of company, rather than other possible methods of organisation, for such purposes? What is the nature of the "guarantee"? *ICSA*   (**5, 6, 27**)

9. What are the statutory requirements for publishing a company's name and the names of its directors? *ICSA*   (**27, 28**)

10. Set out in numbered paragraphs the procedure to be followed by a company which desires to alter the objects clause of its memorandum of association. Who, apart from members, may object to such an alteration, and what steps may objectors take?   (**31**)

11. Your directors wish to change the objects of the company. In a memorandum advise them how this may be achieved. *ICSA*   (**31**)

12. Your company wishes to change its name, and also to trade under a different name from its registered name. Set out in detail the steps that are required for these purposes. *ICSA*   (**32**)

13. Where would you expect to find the rights attaching to different classes of your company's shares, and how may these be varied? *ICSA*   (**36, 41**)

14. Your directors would like to issue preference shares. In the form of a memorandum to them, summarise the rights attaching to such shares, and explain how they may be repaid. *ICSA*   (**43**)

15. Your company is considering raising further capital. Consider the relative advantages and disadvantages to the company and the investor of raising capital by means of shares and convertible loan stock. *ICSA*   (**42–49**; XV, **6**)

16. Comment briefly on the usual rights of holders of preference shares as to dividends, return of capital and participation in the distribution of surplus assets.   (**43**)

17. The directors of a company seek your advice as to the relative merits of preference and ordinary shares as a means of raising capital What are the general considerations involved?   (**43–44**)

18. The issued shares of your company are now fully paid up and the board considers it desirable to de-number them. The articles require that the shares be numbered. What is the appropriate procedure?   (**47**)

19. Write a letter to the directors of your company, explaining the significance of redeemable shares. Indicate briefly in your letter a comparison with an issue of debentures as a means of raising money.

ICSA **(46, 48–49)**

20. Examine the power of a company to purchase its own shares. **(57–58)**

CHAPTER II

Procedure after Incorporation

FIRST BOARD MEETING

1. Appointment of first directors.

(*a*) Before the Companies Act 1976 came into force, the first directors were named as such in the company's articles or, failing that, they were appointed by the subscribers to the Memorandum of Association.

(*b*) But, the Companies Act 1976, s.21, provides that a Memorandum delivered for registration must be accompanied by a statement in prescribed form, signed by the subscribers to the Memorandum, giving particulars of the first directors (and secretary or joint secretaries) and containing a consent signed by each person. On incorporation, the persons named shall be deemed to have been appointed as first directors (and secretary or secretaries).

2. The first board meeting. This should be held as soon as possible, i.e. after the first directors have been appointed and following receipt of the Certificate of Incorporation. Some or all of the following items are likely to be included in the agenda, but it should be borne in mind that certain items might not be relevant in the case of a private company.

(*a*) Record receipt of the *Certificate of Incorporation.* This will be produced by the Secretary.

(*b*) Record appointment of the *first directors.* The first directors having already been appointed, this is merely a question of producing formal evidence of their appointment so that it can be recorded in the minutes.

(*c*) Appoint the *Chairman of the Board.* The person appointed will usually also take the chair at general meetings of the company.

(*d*) Record the appointment of the first secretary. As stated above, the person named as secretary is deemed to be appointed on incorporation of the company in a Memorandum delivered for registration, accompanied by a statement signed by the subscribers to the Memorandum, and containing the signed consent of the person appointed first secretary.

(e) Appoint the company's *solicitors*.

(f) Appoint the company's *brokers*. This item would not normally appear on the agenda of a private company. In the case of a public company, the appointment would be necessary in order to obtain permission to deal in the company's shares on the stock exchange.

(g) Appoint the company's *bankers*. The resolution passed for this purpose will usually be in the form required by the bank concerned; in fact the London clearing bankers have adopted a standard form which requires the signatures of all persons authorised to sign cheques, bills of exchange, etc. on behalf of the company.

(h) Appoint the company's *auditors*. Although it is not essential to make such an appointment at this stage, a public company intending to offer shares in a Prospectus would, no doubt, consider it advisable to include the name of a well-established and reliable firm of auditors. The company's accounting reference date would be established.

(i) Submit and adopt a design for the common seal. At the same time it will be necessary to lay down rules for the use and custody of the seal, unless these have been included in the company's Articles. An impression of the company's seal would be made in the minute book.

(j) Determine the method (or methods) to be adopted for obtaining capital. In the case of a public company intending to offer shares and/or debentures to the public, the principal methods available are by Prospectus, offer for sale and stock exchange placing.

(k) Arising out of the previous item:

(i) prepare and/or consider draft Prospectus, or equivalent document, submitted by the Secretary;

(ii) consider the terms of draft underwriting contract, submitted by the Secretary.

(l) Execute any purchase agreement, e.g. for purchase of the business from the vendor.

NOTE: Even after a Certificate of Incorporation has been received, a *public* company is still not entitled to do business until it has received a certificate to commence business from the Registrar. If such a company does business or exercises its borrowing powers in contravention of these requirements, the company and any officer of the company in default will be liable to a fine; moreover, the validity of any purported transaction is not affected and, if the company fails to comply with its obligations in connection with the transaction within 21 days of being called upon to do so, the directors become jointly and severally liable to indemnify the other party to the transaction for any resultant loss or damage (*see* I, **14**).

(*m*) Instruct the Secretary to:

(*i*) submit an application to the stock exchange for permission to deal;

(*ii*) deal with the appointment of bankers;

(*iii*) purchase the necessary books and stationery;

(*iv*) arrange for the engagement of staff;

(*v*) register the company with HM Customs and Excise for the purpose of VAT and supply particulars to the Inland Revenue for tax purposes.

3. After the first board meeting, apart from drafting minutes of the meeting the Secretary will have the following business to attend to.

(*a*) Forward to the bank appointed under a covering letter:

(*i*) one copy of the resolution of appointment, signed by the chairman and all authorised signatories;

(*ii*) a copy of the company's Memorandum of Association, and of the Articles of Association, if required;

(*iii*) the company's Certificate of Incorporation, for inspection only.

NOTE: Later, in the case of a *public* company, the bank will also wish to inspect the certificate to commence business when it is obtained.

(*b*) Notify the brokers of their formal appointment and, in due course, submit formal application for permission to deal to the stock exchange.

NOTE: The application must be signed by the brokers and supported by at least two dealers (or jobbers) in the market concerned. Various documents must be lodged at the same time, together with a cheque for the appropriate stock exchange charges.

(*c*) Purchase the necessary books and stationery, if this has not already been dealt with. In particular, the Secretary must ensure that all books required by the Act (usually referred to as statutory books) are provided, namely:

(*i*) Register of Members; s.110;

(*ii*) register of Directors and Secretaries; s.200;

(*iii*) register of Directors' Interests: s.29, 1967 Act (*see* **XIV, 18**);

(*iv*) register of Mortgages and Charges: s.104;

(*v*) Minute Book: s.145;

(*vi*) books of account;

(*vii*) register of Interests in Shares: s.73, 1981 Act (*see* **XII, 23**).

(*d*) Also various *non-statutory* books may be purchased, such as:

(*i*) Register of Debenture Holders.

NOTE: If the company issues debentures, the conditions of issue may require the keeping of such a register; in that event, the Act provides for its location, inspection, etc.: s.86.

(*ii*) Minute Book for board meetings.

NOTE: Although the Act provides for the keeping of minutes of both general directors' and managers' meetings, only the minutes of general meetings are required to be kept open for inspection by shareholders; therefore, it is usually considered advisable to have separate minute books.

(*iii*) Register of Documents Sealed (or Seal Book). Most companies find this useful for recording particulars of documents issued under the company's seal.

(*iv*) Register of Transfers (or Transfer Register). Although this is no longer a statutory requirement, many companies still find it a useful medium for the posting of transfer particulars from transfer forms to the Register of Members.

(*v*) Register of Important Documents. To record receipt of various documents lodged with the company for purpose of registration, a comprehensive register of this kind may suffice, but large public companies usually prefer to have separate registers, such as Register of Power of Attorney, Register of Probates and Letters of Administration, etc.

RAISING CAPITAL

4. Principal methods. If the founders themselves are unable to raise the necessary capital, then the balance may be raised by one or more of the following methods:

(*a*) by *private issue* of shares to relatives and friends;

(*b*) by *direct public issue* of shares and/or debentures, requiring a full Prospectus;

(*c*) by *allotting shares and/or debentures to an "issuing house"*, which subsequently offers the shares to the public in an offer for sale, or places large blocks of the securities with its clients;

(*d*) by *stock exchange "placing"*, the shares and/or debentures being "placed" through the agency of an issuing house or stockbrokers on the stock exchange, where a market is created for the securities. As they will subsequently become available to the public, a Prospectus (usually in modified form) is required.

NOTE: It will be appreciated that *all* the above methods are available to a public company, whereas a private company (other than a company limited by guarantee and not having share capital) is prohibited from offering its shares or debentures to the public: Companies Act 1980, s.15(1).

5. The Prospectus.

(*a*) *Definitions.* Section 455 defines a Prospectus as "any prospectus, notice, circular, advertisement or other invitation, offering to the public for subscription or purchase any shares or debentures of a company".

(*b*) A Prospectus is required in all cases where the public are invited to subscribe for a company's shares or debentures, but it is not always clear what constitutes an invitation "to the public". In an attempt to remove this uncertainty there are the following provisions.

(*i*) Section 55 provides that an offer of shares or debentures to any section of the public, including the company's members or debenture holders, is deemed to be an offer to the public, subject to any provision to the contrary contained in the offer.

(*ii*) Section 55(2) provides that any offer which in all the circumstances might be regarded as a "domestic concern" of the persons making and receiving it, shall not be treated as an offer to the public.

(*iii*) Section 55(3), added by the Companies Act 1980, provides that, unless the contrary is proved, an offer of shares in or debentures of a private company, or an invitation to subscribe for such shares or debentures, will be regarded as a domestic concern and not an offer to the public in the case of an offer or invitation made to any member of the relevant class, or in the case of an offer or invitation to subscribe for shares or debentures to be held under an employees' share scheme.

(*c*) *Unlawful issue.* Section 38 provides that it shall be unlawful to issue any form of application for shares or debentures of a company unless the form is issued with a Prospectus which complies with the requirements of the section.

NOTE: This does *not* apply to a form of application issued to a person who is being invited to enter in to an underwriting agreement, nor in relation to shares or debentures which are not being offered to the public: s.38(3)(*a*).

(*d*) *Main purpose of the Prospectus*. The general aim is to protect the investing public by compelling the disclosure of information or relevant facts from which the risks of investment can be assessed.

6. Contents of the Prospectus. Section 38(1) requires that a prospectus state the matters specified in Part I of the Fourth Schedule to the Act (as amended by s.33 of the Companies Act 1976), set out the reports specified in Part II of that Schedule and comply with s.16 of the Companies Act 1980.

Essentially, the specified matters and reports seek to ensure disclosure of the following:

(*a*) the name of the company's directors and the benefit they will obtain from their directorship;

(*b*) the profit being made by the promoters;

(*c*) the amount of capital required by the company to be subscribed, the amount actually to be received in cash, and the precise nature of the consideration given for the remaining part. Section 16 of the 1980 Act requires the prospectus to state whether or not the shares will be alloted even if the issue is not fully subscribed;

(*d*) details of the company's financial history;

(*e*) the company's contractual obligations and in particular those with regard to commissions and preliminary expenses;

(*f*) the voting and dividend rights of each class of shares.

7. Filing the Prospectus. The Act provides that before any Prospectus can be issued the following requirements must be carried out.

(*a*) *Filing*. A copy of the Prospectus, together with any relevant reports, must be delivered to the Registrar of Companies on or before the date of publication: s.41.

(*b*) *Date*. The Prospectus must be dated and that date shall, unless the contrary is proved, be taken as the date of publication: s.37.

(*c*) *Signatures*. It must be signed by every person named in it as director or proposed director, or by his agent authorised in writing: s.41.

(*d*) *Statements by experts*. It must contain, where applicable, a statement by any expert whose report appears in the Prospectus that he has consented to the issue of the Prospectus and has not withdrawn his consent: ss.40 and 41.

(*e*) *A copy of every material contract* must be endorsed on the Prospectus or attached to it. If the contract is not reduced to writing, a memorandum giving full particulars must be endorsed or attached: s.41.

(*f*) A statement of the adjustments made in preparing figures extracted from previous year's accounts: s.41.

(*g*) *Every Prospectus* issued must, on the face of it, state that a copy has been filed with the Registrar and refer to, or specify, any documents attached to, or statements endorsed on, the filed copy: s.41.

8. Stock exchange listing. A public company of any significance will undoubtedly wish to obtain a stock exchange listing and the consequential advantages which follow from such. To obtain a listing the company concerned must, *inter alia*, comply with the requirements of the stock exchange as set out in the exchange's publication *Admission of Securities to Listing*. This not only details the procedure to be followed on making an application for permission to deal (*see* **9** *below*), but also requires that the company enters into what is termed the "listing agreement"—a resolution passed by the board of directors of the company to observe rules and procedures appropriate to its status as a listed company and detailed in *Admission of Securities to Listing*.

The implications of this undertaking have been, and will be, referred to throughout this text as and when appropriate.

9. Application for permission to deal on the stock exchange.

(*a*) *When to apply.* If a Prospectus contains a statement that "application has been, or will be made, for permission to deal" in the shares or debentures offered, then application ought to be made before the third day after first issue of the Prospectus. The reason is explained in **10** below.

(*b*) *Application procedure.* Application is made through the company's brokers to the Quotations Department of the stock exchange concerned.

(*c*) *Documents required.* A formal application, signed by the company's brokers and supported by at least two dealers on the stock exchange market concerned, together with a remittance for the appropriate charges, must be lodged at least two days before the hearing of the application by the Committee on Quotations.

In addition, some or all of the following documents will be required at the same time, depending upon whether the application relates to an original issue or a subsequent issue:

(*i*) copy of the Prospectus, offer for sale or equivalent document;

(*ii*) certified copy of the board's resolution, authorising the issue;

(*iii*) certified copy of every report, balance sheet, etc., referred to in the Prospectus;

(*iv*) certified copy of the written consent of any expert to the inclusion of his report or statement in the Prospectus;

(*v*) specimen (or two advance proofs) of the allotment letter, or letter of acceptance;

(*vi*) specimen (or two advance proofs) of share certificate, or other definitive certificate, such as debenture stock certificate;

(*vii*) statement setting out particulars of shares to be listed and, where applicable, indicating when the shares or other definitive certificates will be ready;

(*viii*) an undertaking to submit, as soon as possible after grant of the listing, a statutory declaration as to compliance with the stock exchange requirements.

(*d*) *Additional documents.* The following documents may also be required:

(*i*) Certificate of Incorporation;

(*ii*) certificate entitling the company to commence business;

(*iii*) two copies of the Memorandum and Articles of Association;

(*iv*) two copies of any trust deed, or debenture if the debentures are not secured by a trust deed;

(*v*) general undertaking, in the form of the Listing Agreement, to comply with various stock exchange requirements.

NOTE: The above is not a complete list of documents which the stock exchange concerned may require; it is merely an indication of what are considered to be the most important documents included in the stock exchange regulations.

(*e*) *Final checking.* Before giving permission to deal, the stock exchange will carefully examine the documents lodged and make a thorough investigation of the company's promotion and of any matters arising out of documents submitted which might appear suspicious. Assuming everything is in order, permission will be granted, but only after publication of the Prospectus or equivalent document.

10. Failure to obtain permission to deal: s.51. Applicants for shares offered in a Prospectus regard marketability of the shares they apply for as an important factor, so there is almost invariably a statement in the Prospectus that "application has been or will be made for permission to deal".

If a Prospectus (or offer for sale) contains such a statement and permission to deal is *not* obtained for either of the following reasons:

(*a*) *because permission was not applied for* before the third day after the first issue of the prospectus; or

(*b*) *because permission was refused* before the expiration of three weeks from the date of closing the subscription lists, or longer period not exceeding six weeks where the stock exchange gives notice to that effect within the three-week period,

then protection is given to applicants relying on the statement under s.51.

Thus, if for either of the above reasons, permission to deal is not obtained:

(*i*) any allotment of shares (or debentures) to applicants relying on the statement is void;

(*ii*) application money must be refunded "forthwith", without interest;

(*iii*) if the money is not repaid within eight days (after the company became liable to repay), the directors of the company become jointly and severally liable to repay the money, with interest at 5 per cent per annum, calculated after expiration of the eighth day—except where a director can prove there was neither misconduct nor negligence on his part;

(*iv*) all money received on application and liable for repayment, for either of the above reasons, must be kept in a separate bank account and remain there so long as the company remains liable to repay it.

11. Stock exchange certificate of exemption: s.39.

(*a*) Section 39 permits certain prescribed stock exchanges to give a "certificate of exemption", which permits some relaxation of the Fourth Schedule's requirements affecting Prospectuses, in the following circumstances:

(*i*) where it is proposed to offer shares or debentures in a prospectus issued *generally*, i.e. to persons who are *not* existing members of debenture holders of the company; and

(*ii*) application is made to a prescribed stock exchange for permission to deal in the shares or debentures; and

(*iii*) where the prescribed stock exchange is of the opinion that compliance with the Fourth Schedule to the Act would be unduly burdensome having regard to:

(1) the size of the issue;

(2) any limitations on the number and class of persons to whom the offer is made; and

(3) other circumstances connected with the issue, e.g. the expense and difficulty of obtaining certain information may be out of all proportion to its value to the public.

(*b*) The certificate of exemption has the following effects.

(*i*) It permits the company to publish an advertisement which complies with the stock exchange requirements, and this will be deemed to be a Prospectus complying with the Fourth Schedule to the Act.

(*ii*) It may save time and expense for the company, e.g. in obtaining and collating information for the Prospectus which, in all the circumstances, the stock exchange considers would serve little useful purpose.

(*c*) The prescribed stock exchanges usually grant exemption under s.39 in suitable cases where an issue of shares or debentures is effected through an issuing house or through stockbrokers, who place the shares with their clients.

(*d*) In such cases the company allots the shares or debentures to the issuing house (or stockbroker) which, in turn, offers them by circular or advertisement in the modified form permitted by the stock exchange, to their clients.

NOTE: This method of "placing" is now deemed to be an "issue to the public" under s.55.

12. Offers for sale.

(*a*) *When preferable.* Another way of raising capital is by means of an offer for sale. This is more popular than the more direct Prospectus method, particularly in the case of large original issues.

(*b*) *Method.* By this method the company allots the whole, or a large part, of the shares or debentures to an issuing house, and the issuing house offers the security to the public in an offer for sale.

(*c*) *When the offer for sale is a Prospectus.* Prior to the 1929 Act, this method was frequently used to avoid the use of a Prospectus and the detailed disclosure which that necessitated. However, the 1929 Act made provisions intended to close the statutory gap and the 1948 Act (s.45) provides that an offer for sale is deemed to be a Prospectus if:

(*i*) the offer of the shares or debentures is made to the public within six months after the allotment, or agreement to allot, to the issuing house; or

(*ii*) at the date of the offer for sale, the company has not received the whole consideration for the shares or debentures.

NOTE: Although this is deemed to be sufficient evidence that the allotment to the issuing house was with a view to a subsequent offer to the public, proof to the contrary may be given.

(*d*) *Contents.* An offer for sale must, therefore, contain all the information required for a Prospectus issued generally, and the following additional information (s.45(3)):

(*i*) the net amount of the consideration received (or to be received) by the company in respect of the shares or debentures to which the offer for sale relates; and

(*ii*) the place and time at which the contract of allotment can be inspected.

(*e*) *Registration.* The provisions of s.41 as to registration of a Prospectus apply equally to an offer for sale, but s.45 makes the following variations.

(*i*) The copy filed with the Registrar, in the case of the issuing house being a limited company, must be signed by *two* directors, i.e. it is not necessary for all directors to sign, as in the case of a Prospectus.

(*ii*) If the issuing house is a partnership, the copy filed must be signed by no fewer than half the partners.

(*f*) *Liability.* Where an offer for sale is deemed to be a Prospectus in the circumstances laid down in s.45, those responsible for its issue are liable, as though the document were a Prospectus and they were named in it as directors, for non-disclosure, mis-statements or failure to register the document under s.41.

(*g*) *Advantages of the offer-for-sale method.* The principal advantages for the issuing company are that:

(*i*) it is relieved of a great deal of the paper work which a large share or debenture issue usually entails;

(*ii*) the success of the issue is assured, as the issuing house has, in effect, underwritten "firm" the whole issue. The significance of "firm" underwriting is explained in **16.**

13. Placings.

(a) *Two methods.* Currently, the "placing" of shares is a more popular method than either direct Prospectus or offer for sale issues. It must be explained, however, that a "placing" may refer to either of two quite separate methods, as follows.

(*i*) An arrangement whereby the company allots the securities with an issuing house, and the latter agrees to purchase the securities and "place" them with its clients; or, alternatively, the issuing house is merely paid a commission for "placing" the securities and does not purchase them.

(*ii*) A "stock exchange placing" refers to the method whereby an issuing house (or the company's brokers) "place" the whole or part of the company's shares with stock jobbers, to be "made available" to brokers at a certain price. Investors wanting to take up such shares must either wait until they become available on the open market—when the supply is likely to be very limited and the price higher than the opening price—or ask their brokers to put in an order for the shares on their behalf.

(b) *"Placing" and "introduction" of shares.*

(*i*) There is often some confusion between a "placing" and an "introduction" of shares; to make matters even more confusing, one occasionally reads of a "placing coupled with an introduction".

(*ii*) If, in connection with a stock exchange placing, the brokers are given the opportunity to place advance orders with the jobbers, the operation is known on the stock exchange as a "placing".

(*iii*) If, on the other hand, brokers are not permitted to deal in the shares until the first advertised dealing day, the operation is known as an "introduction".

(*iv*) The "placing" method is undoubtedly more orderly than the "introduction" method with its "first come, first served" principle, so it is not surprising that the stock exchange virtually abolished the latter a few years ago.

(*v*) Both these stock exchange "placing" methods have their critics, as it is contended that the average investor is put at a disadvantage: by the time the "placed' shares become available to him, professional investors have already snapped up all the shares available on starting day and at the starting price.

(*vi*) Nevertheless, the method is cheaper than any other in most cases and, moreover, this is one of the occasions, referred to earlier in this chapter (*see* 11) when the stock exchange will usually permit the use of a modified form of Prospectus. This accounts for the frequent appearance in the financial papers of an advertisement headed (say)

FOR INFORMATION ONLY which, although it gives information similar to that required in a Prospectus, does not invite applications from the public.

14. Underwriting.

(a) *Underwriting* is merely a form of insurance against the risk of a poor public response to an issue of shares or debentures.

(b) *An underwriting contract* is, therefore, one between the company offering the shares to the public and the underwriter who relieves the company of the risk. Such a contract has been aptly defined as:

> "An agreement entered into before the shares are brought before the public that in the event of the public not taking up the whole of them, or the number mentioned in the agreement, the underwriter will, for an agreed commission, take an allotment of such part of the shares as the public has not applied for": *Re Licensed Victuallers' Association* (1889).

(c) *Advantages of underwriting.* Apart from the obvious advantage, that is, of relieving the issuing company of all or a large part of the risk, there are at least two further advantages, namely:

(i) any risk of not reaching the minimum subscription is removed as is the unpleasant necessity of returning application money under s.47;

(ii) there is good advertising value in the fact that a firm of underwriters has been prepared to accept the risk—particularly if it has done so at a comparatively low rate of commission.

(d) *Statutory provisions affecting underwriting commission.* Section 53 permits both public and private companies to pay underwriting commission, subject to the following provisions.

(i) The company's Articles must permit such payment.

NOTE: At common law, authority in the Memorandum alone is apparently not sufficient: *Re Bolivia Republic Exploration Syndicate Ltd.* (1914).

(ii) The commission must not exceed 10 per cent of the issue price of the shares, or the amount or rate authorised by the Articles, whichever is less.

(iii) The amount or rate of commission paid or agreed to be paid on shares offered to the public must be disclosed in the Prospectus.

(iv) The amount or rate per cent of commission paid, or agreed to be paid, on shares which are *not* offered to the public must be disclosed in a statement in the prescribed form signed by every director of the company, or by his agent authorised in writing, and delivered, before the payment of the commission, to the Registrar of Companies for registration.

(v) The number of shares which persons have agreed to subscribe absolutely for commission must also be disclosed in the manner described above.

NOTE: It is also provided (in the eighth Schedule to the Act) that the amount of commission must be disclosed in every balance sheet, so far as it has not been written off.

(e) *Underwriting of debentures.* Section 53 does not apply to debentures; therefore, they may be underwritten at *any* rate of commission, unless the company's Articles impose a limit (where debentures are concerned, there is no restriction on their issue at what amounts, in effect, to a discount, as debentures (unlike shares) do not, of course, form part of a company's capital).

EXAMPLES: (1) Exe Ltd. agree to underwrite an entire issue of 100,000 shares of £1 each, offered to the public by Zed Plc. If the *whole* issue is subscribed, Exe Ltd. are under no obligation to take up any of the shares. If, however, the public subscription is for only (say) 80,000 shares, Exe Ltd. will be liable to take up the whole of the 20,000 balance.

(2) If, in the above example, Exe Ltd. had underwritten only 75,000 of the 100,000 offered, they would then be liable *rateably* for the balance, i.e.

$$\frac{75,000}{100,000} \times 20,000 = 15,000.$$

15. Sub-underwriting.

(a) *Method.* In most cases (and particularly when the whole of a large issue is underwritten by one underwriter), underwriters "spread" their risk by sub-underwriting, i.e. the main underwriter makes separate contracts with various sub-underwriters, each of them agreeing to take a specified share of the risk.

(b) *Over-riding commission.* If the main underwriter agrees to procure sub-underwriters, the commission he receives for that service is known as "over-riding commission" (that commission is, of course, additional to the one paid to the sub-underwriters). It must be emphasised that, where the main contract takes the form just described, the primary underwriters' service to the company is to ensure that the issue is fully and reliably underwritten.

NOTE: The term "over-riding commission" is also sometimes used in a different context, i.e. it may be applied to the *difference* between the underwriting commission paid to the principal underwriter and the slightly lower commission he pays to the sub-underwriters.

(c) *Statutory provisions.* The provisions of s.53 apply equally to both underwriting and over-riding commission, i.e. in any form of underwriting contract to which the issuing company is a party.

EXAMPLE: Wye Ltd. agreed to underwrite 80,000 shares out of an issue of 100,000 shares of £1 each and subsequently procured sub-underwriting contracts with Jay and Ess for 30,000 and 10,000 respectively.

The public response was poor, as only 60,000 of the shares were subscribed—an under-subscription of 40,000, of which the *total liability of underwriters* is 80,000/100,000×40,000 = 32,000 shares.

Wye Ltd........ $\dfrac{40,000}{80,000} \times 32,000 = 16,000$ shares

Jay Ltd. .... $\dfrac{30,000}{80,000} \times 32,000 = 12,000$ shares

Ess Ltd. .... $\dfrac{10,000}{80,000} \times 32,000 = 4,000$ shares

Total liability of underwriters $\quad \overline{32,000}$ shares

NOTE: In such a contract, the principal underwriters, Wye Ltd., are *primarily* liable to take up the whole of the 32,000 shares; if either Jay or Ess fail to take up any of the shares they have underwritten, then Wye Ltd. must make up their deficiency.

16. "Firm" underwriting.

(a) An underwriter may agree to *take firm* all or part of the shares he agrees to underwrite.

(b) He will then be allotted whatever number of shares he has agreed to take "firm", no matter whether the issue is under-subscribed or over-subscribed, but any other shares underwritten will be dealt with by the usual method, i.e. in the case of an under-subscription, the total liability of the underwriters is apportioned amongst them rateably.

(c) The effect of the "firm" underwriting upon all the underwriters will depend upon the terms of the contract; that is, whether the "firm" subscriptions are to be applied:

(i) exclusively in relieving the liability of those who have underwritten "firm"; or

(ii) to reduce the respective liabilities of *all* underwriters proportionately.

EXAMPLE: A public company issues 250,000 shares. The issue is underwritten as follows: X, 100,000 shares (including 25,000 firm); Y, 50,000 shares (including 25,000 firm); and Z, 100,000 shares. The public subscription totalled only 150,000 shares. The following table shows the alternative methods of dealing with the "firm" underwriting.

		X, 4/10	Y, 2/10	Z, 4/10
Shares offered to public	250,000			
Public subscription	150,000			
Gross liability of underwriters	100,000	40,000	20,000	40,000
Less relief for "firm" subscriptions		50,000	25,000	25,000	—
		50,000	15,000	5,000	40,000
Allocation of Y's excess (X, 4/8; Z, 4/8)			*2,500*	5,000	*2,500*
(i) *Final liability* of underwriters where "firm" subscriptions are used to reduce liability of those underwriting "firm"		50,000	12,500	—	37,500
(ii) *Final liability* of underwriters where "firm" subscriptions are used to reduce respective liabilities of all underwriters proportionately		50,000	20,000	10,000	20,000

SUMMARY

	Method (i)		Method (ii)	
X: Final liability	12,500		20,000	
Add "firm" subscription	25,000	37,500	25,000	45,000
Y: Final liability	—		10,000	
Add "firm" subscription	25,000	25,000	25,000	35,000
Z: Final liability	37,500		20,000	
Add "firm" subscription	—	37,500	—	20,000
		100,000		100,000
Public subscription		150,000		150,000
Total issue		250,000		250,000

17. Brokerage.

(*a*) Brokerage might be defined as a payment to a person, who in some way carries on the business of a broker, for "placing" shares.

(*b*) It must not be confused with underwriting commission. The placing of shares does not involve the broker in any risk of having to take up the shares, whereas risk-taking is the main feature of an underwriting contract.

(*c*) Brokerage can, in fact, be paid in addition to underwriting commission and s.53(3) clearly indicates that a company has the right to pay such brokerage as was previously lawful. In *Metropolitan Coal Consumers' Association* v. *Scrimgeour* (1885) it had previously been held that the payment of brokerage was legal, so long as it was "reasonable" and payable in the ordinary course of business.

18. Prohibition on issue of shares at a discount.

(*a*) The Companies Act 1980, s.21(1) specifically prohibits the allotment of shares at a discount and thus repeals s.57 of the 1948 Act.

(*b*) Shares allotted in breach of s.21 shall be treated as paid up by the payment to the company of the amount of the nominal value of the shares less the amount of the discount, but the allottee shall be liable to pay the company the latter amount and shall be liable to pay interest thereon at the appropriate rate: s.21(2), 1980 Act.

(*c*) The prohibition in s.21(1) of the 1980 Act does not apply to debentures. These can be issued at a discount, as they do not form part of a company's capital.

19. Issue of shares at a premium: s.56.

(*a*) There are no restrictions imposed upon the issue of shares or debentures at a premium, i.e. at more than the nominal value of the security; for example, a £1 share may be issued for 125p, giving the company a capital profit of 25p per share.

(*b*) However, there are restrictions as to the use which the company can make of a share premium, as s.56 provides that a sum equal to the aggregate amount or value of the premiums must be transferred to a "share premium account", which is to be treated as though it were paid-up shares capital of the company and subject to provisions of the Act relating to reduction of capital.

(*c*) Although the company cannot use the premium as it thinks fit—as, for example, to pay a dividend—it is permitted by s.56 to apply the balance in the following ways:

(*i*) to allot fully-paid bonus shares to its members:

(*ii*) to write off preliminary expenses of the company;

(*iii*) to write off expenses of, or commission paid or discount allowed on, any issue of shares or debentures;

(*iv*) to provide for any premium payable on redemption of debentures.

In addition, by virtue of s.54 of the Companies Act 1981 the share premium account may be used by private companies to pay off any premium on a redemption or purchase by such companies of their own shares.

(*d*) The balance (if any) of a company's share premium account must be shown in any balance sheet subsequently issued, until such time as it may be written off by reason of its having been used in any of the ways permitted under s.56.

(*e*) The provisions of s.56 do *not* apply to debentures. If, therefore, a company issues debentures at a premium, the company is not legally bound to transfer the amount of the premium to a debenture premium account (although it is common practice to do so). Nor are there any restrictions placed upon the use to which the company can put the debenture premium.

(*f*) Further, ss.36–41 of the Companies Act 1981 in order to facilitate the concept of merger and acquisition accounting seek to provide relief from s.56 of the 1948 Act in certain defined situations.

20. Arrangements for a Prospectus issue. If the issue is to be a large one, a great deal of the office work entailed can be passed on to firms specialising in new issue work. It has been assumed, therefore, that the work of underwriting and publishing the Prospectus is being dealt with by such a firm, leaving further arrangements to be handled as follows.

(*a*) *Arrangements with the company's Bankers.* Most banks, and certainly all the large banks, have specialist departments for handling share issue work. The following arrangements will be made with one of these banks:

(*i*) to receive application forms and application moneys;

(*ii*) to credit all application moneys received to a separate "Application Account", or "Application and Allotment Account", if that method is preferred;

(*iii*) to number serially all applications received;

(iv) to keep a progressive total of the number of shares applied for;

(*v*) to return direct to applicants any applications (and accompanying remittances) received after the closing of the subscription lists.

(*b*) *Office staff and stationery.* Finally, even before the actual issue of the Prospectus, the following matters ought to be arranged, to ensure that the application and allotment procedure is handled with speed, accuracy and efficiency.

(*i*) Available office staff must be well organised to handle the work, so that each section is responsible for a particular aspect of the work, and the whole of the work to be under the supervision of either the Secretary himself, or his registrar.

(*ii*) If necessary (and it might well be necessary if the issue is a large one), engage temporary office staff preferably with experience of share issue work. Practising secretaries may be able to help in this direction by hiring out temporary staff.

(*iii*) Ensure that all necessary documents, such as allotment sheets, allotment letters, letters of regret, share certificates, etc., will be available when required.

(*iv*) Stock exchange requirements must be borne in mind, if "permission to deal" has been applied for, e.g. as regards the form of certificate, which must have stock exchange approval, and allotment letters, which must be accompanied by a "letter of renunciation".

(*v*) If more than one class of share is being offered to the public (or where both shares and debentures are being offered simultaneously) the task of sorting and filing can be eased considerably by the use of application forms in different colours or (in the case of newspaper application forms) by coding. Similar methods can also be adopted to simplify identification of existing shareholders, if it is intended to give preference to their applications.

PROGRESS TEST 2

1. (*a*) What formal business should be considered at the first meeting of the directors of the company?

(*b*) Describe the procedure for opening a bank account for a company which has just received its certificate of incorporation. *ICSA* (**2, 3**)

2. You are secretary of A Plc., which has recently been changed from a private to a public company. Business continues to expand, and your directors decide to consider the advisability of seeking a stock exchange official listing for the company's shares. They ask you to prepare a memorandum setting out the advantages and disadvantages, from the point of view of the company, in having an official listing. *ICSA* (**8, 9, 11**)

3. A company sometimes issues capital by means of a "placing". In certain circumstances, a company's shares are said to be "placed" or "introduced" on a stock exchange. Explain fully what is meant by the terms "placing" and "introduction". (**13**)

4. Draft a memorandum for the board of your company, explaining from the legal aspect, the various ways of raising capital. *ICSA* (**4, 5, 12, 13**)

5. The directors of your company are considering making an offer of its shares to the public. Write a memorandum to them explaining what is meant by underwriting. Indicate any relevant statutory requirements. *ICSA* (**14**)

CHAPTER III

Application and Allotment

PROCEDURE

1. Opening the subscription lists. After the Prospectus has been issued (and a copy of it filed on or before the date of publication), the subscription lists may be opened, but not before the morning of the third day following the first issue of the Prospectus, or such later date as may be specified in the Prospectus: s.50.

NOTE: Although the company may legally proceed to allot shares at any time after the "time of the opening of the subscription lists", how early it can do so—if at all—will depend upon how successful or unsuccessful the issue proves to be.

That, too, will determine how soon the subscription lists can be closed. If the issue is obviously greatly oversubscribed when the lists open, they may be opened and closed within minutes. In any event, the lists are rarely kept open for more than a day; to do so would be tantamount to advertising the failure of the issue and would almost certainly lead to wholesale withdrawals of applications.

2. Maintain contact with the bank. As from the time of opening the subscription lists, regular contact should be maintained with the bank, which (it has been assumed) had been authorised to receive applications, and arrangements made for the collection from the bank of applications and application lists at frequent intervals, to enable the office staff to proceed with the work.

NOTE: There is usually a sense of urgency in handling applications and it is likely to be even more acute if there is a poor or rather lukewarm public response to the issue. In such a case, the aim will be to get the allotment letters posted before any of the applicants (suspecting failure, perhaps) withdraw their applications.

However, the company has some protection in this connection from s.50(5), which provides that applications are not revocable until after the expiration of the third day after the time of the opening of the subscription lists.

3. Check each batch of applications with the bank's application lists, prior to sorting the applications for distribution to various sections of the staff.

4. Recording applications. After applications have been sorted and distributed amongst the available staff, they are entered on Application and Allotment Sheets which, being loose sheets, are usually arranged either:

(*a*) alphabetically, i.e. according to applicants' names; or

(*b*) according to number of shares applied for.

5. Particulars entered on Application and Allotment Sheets. As the result of the issue may not yet be known at this stage (and no allotment having been made), only the following particulars can, so far, be entered on the Application and Allotment Sheets:

(*a*) Serial no. of application

(*b*) Name of applicant

(*c*) Address

(*d*) Occupation of applicant

(*e*) Number of shares applied for

(*f*) Amount paid on application

NOTE: Subscribers to the Memorandum and (where applicable) "firm" underwriters are usually entered first in the appropriate sheets.

6. Totals to a Summary Sheet. When all applications have been entered, totals of the appropriate columns so far completed are carried to a Summary Sheet, on which all information as to "number of shares applied for" and "amount paid on application" is aggregated.

7. The Summary Sheet is placed before the board. The Summary Sheet, having been totalled and thoroughly checked, can now be placed before a meeting of the board of directors (or allotment committee), to enable them to ascertain the final result of the issue, and—particularly in the case of a public company making its first offer to the public—to ensure that the "minimum subscription" has been subscribed.

8. Decisions of the board (or allotment committee) at this stage. Having considered the results of the issue, the decisions they must now make will depend upon whether the issue was oversubscribed or undersubscribed.

(*a*) *If oversubscribed*, they must decide upon a suitable basis for allotment of the shares, e.g. they may favour the "small" applicant, those applying for 100 shares or less being allotted in full; those from 100 upwards to be alloted on a reducing scale down to (say) 10 per cent of the number of shares applied for.

(*b*) *If undersubscribed*, it may reasonably be assumed that the deficiency will be taken up by underwriters; therefore, it will be merely a question of calculating rateably their respective liabilities. Even this is often unnecessary, as the company's contract is, more often than not, with the principal underwriter only, and the liabilities of sub-underwriters are his, not the company's, concern.

9. Further entries on Application and Allotment Sheets. Arising out of decisions made at the board (or allotment committee) meeting, the following further information can be added to the Application and Allotment Sheets:

(*a*) number of shares allotted, if any;
(*b*) total amount received in respect of shares allotted;
(*c*) total amount due on allotment.

10. Summary Sheet again placed before the board. Further totals can now be carried from the Application and Allotment Sheets to the Summary Sheet. The Summary Sheet is totalled and checked, and again placed before the board (or allotment committee) meeting.

11. Allotment procedure. At the board (or allotment committee) meeting, the following procedure may be followed.

(*a*) The chairman of the board (or allotment committee) signs or initials each Application and Allotment Sheet, for the purpose of identification.

(b) A resolution of allotment is put to the meeting and carried, for example:

RESOLVED: That 200,000 ordinary shares of £1 each, numbered 1 to 200,000 inclusive, be and they are hereby allotted to the applicants whose names and addresses are set out in the .... Application and Allotment Sheets now produced to the Board (or Committee) and initialled by the Chairman for the purpose of identification.

(*c*) The Secretary is then instructed to prepare and issue, with the least possible delay, letters of allotment and, where applicable, letters of regret. The latter must be sent to any applicants to whom no allotment has been made, together with their returned application moneys.

> NOTE: The Companies Act 1980, s.14, requires the authority of the company in general meeting or in the Articles of the company to give the directors the power to allot "relevant securities", i.e. shares in the company other than shares shown in the Memorandum to have been taken by the subscribers thereto or shares allotted in relation to an employee's share scheme, and any right to subscribe for, or to convert any security into, shares in the company other than shares so allotted. If such power is already contained in the company's Articles and expressed in general terms, the authority must be renewed every five years.

12. Dealing with letters of allotment and letters of regret. In order to ensure that the instructions he received at the board (or allotment committee) meeting are efficiently and expeditiously carried out, the Secretary must organise the work of allotment with as much care as was given to the handling of applications, bearing in mind that (unless there is any contrary arrangement) the posting of the letter of allotment is deemed to be valid acceptance of the application: *Household Fire Insurance Co. Ltd.* v. *Grant* (1879). He must, therefore, divide the staff into sections and put a responsible official in charge of each section.

Special arrangements must also be made, and the staff briefed, on the following important matters.

(*a*) *Stock exchange requirements.* If application has been, or will be made, for "permission to deal" on a stock exchange:

(*i*) letters of allotment must be serially numbered and autographically initialled by a responsible official;

(*ii*) all letters of allotment must be posted simultaneously, so as to afford equal treatment to all allottees;

(*iii*) letters of regret and refunded application moneys should, if possible, be posted at the same time as letters of allotment are posted. If that is not possible, give notice to the Press that allotment letters have been posted, the notice to appear on the following morning.

(*b*) *Organise a thorough system of checking* at each stage of the work.

(*c*) *Ensure compliance with* s.50, so that no allotment is made until the beginning of the third day after the first issue of the Prospectus or any later date specified in the Prospectus.

(*d*) *Organise a final check* by responsible persons—preferably persons who have done none of the earlier work—of the sealed envelopes with the Application and Allotment Sheets, to avoid misposting.

(*e*) *Obtain a certificate of posting* and ensure that a record of the posting is made on the final Application and Allotment Sheet, the entry being signed and dated by the person who was responsible for the posting.

13. Deal with letters of renunciation and split letters of renunciation. It may be assumed that allottees have been given facilities for renouncing the whole or part of their allotments of shares during a specified "renunciation period". If that is the case, the order of procedure must be changed, as the preparation of share certificates and the work of writing up the Register of Members must be delayed until the end of the renunciation period. The next stage is, therefore:

(*a*) to deal with letters of renunciation; and

(*b*) to attend to requests for split letters of renunciation.

The procedure for dealing with renunciation is dealt with later in this chapter (*see* **23**).

14. Preparation of share certificates. As already stated, this work must be delayed until the end of the renunciation period, after which the certificates are prepared from the Application and Allotment Sheets and from the separate sheets on which renunciations have been recorded. If, however, the amount payable on the shares goes beyond the allotment stage, the certificates may not be prepared until the shares are fully paid.

15. Write up the Register of Members. As soon as possible after the end of the renunciation period, i.e. when the names of the final allottees are known, their names must be entered in a Register of Members.

16. Return of Allotments. In compliance with s.52, *within one month* after allotment of the shares, deliver to the Registrar a Return of Allotments in the prescribed form, showing the following.

(*a*) In respect of shares allotted for cash:

    (*i*) number and nominal amount of the shares allotted;

    (*ii*) names, addresses and descriptions of the allottees;

    (*iii*) amount, if any, paid or due and payable on each share whether on account of the nominal value of the share or by way of premium.

(*b*) In respect of shares allotted for consideration *other than* cash:

(*i*) a written contract constituting the titles of the allottees, duly stamped;

(*ii*) any contract of sale (or for services or other consideration for the allotment) duly stamped; and

(*iii*) a return stating the number and nominal amount of shares allotted for consideration other than cash, the extent to which they are treated as paid up, and the consideration for which they have been allotted.

NOTE: If the contract referred to in (*b*)(*i*) above is *not* reduced to writing, particulars of the contract, stamped as though it had been a contract in writing, must be filed with the Registrar within one month after allotment.

(*c*) Section 24 of the Companies Act 1980 provides that a public company shall not allot shares as fully or partly paid up (as to their nominal value or any premium payable on them) otherwise than in cash unless, *inter alia*, a report with respect to its value has been made to the company by an expert appointed by the company during the six months immediately preceding the allotment of the shares. Where such a report has been delivered to the company it shall deliver a copy of the report to the Registrar for registration at the same time that it files the return of allotment of these shares under s.52 of the 1948 Act.

(*d*) The capital duty payable on an allotment (*see* I, **11**(*c*)) is paid as follows:

(*i*) Where shares are issued for a cash consideration—on a return of allotments (Form PUC2) delivered to the Registrar of Companies pursuant to s.52(1).

(*ii*) Where shares are issued wholly or partly for a consideration other than cash—on a return of allotments (Form PUC3) delivered to the Registrar of Companies pursuant to s.52(1).

RESTRICTIONS ON ALLOTMENT

17. Prohibition of allotment because of failure to obtain minimum subscription; s.47. In dealing with the procedure on application and allotment it was assumed that the public response was sufficient to warrant allotment or, failing that, that any under subscription would be taken up by the underwriters. Section 47, as amended by the

Companies Act 1980, s.16, legislates for the exceptional case where this does not apply by providing that:

(*a*) no allotment shall be made of any share capital of a public company offered for subscription unless:

(*i*) that capital is subscribed for in full; or

(*ii*) the offer states that, even if the capital is not subscribed for in full, the amount of that capital subscribed for may be allotted in any event or in the event of the conditions specified in the offer being satisfied; and

(*iii*) the sum payable on application has been paid to and received by the company, including any cheques received in good faith which the directors have no reason to believe will not be paid.

(*b*) If the above conditions are not fulfilled within 40 days after the first issue of the Prospectus:

(*i*) all application money must be repaid "forthwith", without interest; and

(*ii*) *if not repaid within a further eight days*, i.e. within 48 days after the first issue of the prospectus, the directors become jointly and severally liable to repay with interest at 5 per cent per annum after expiration of the 48th day.

(*c*) Any waiver of these requirements is *void*.

(*d*) Section 22 of the 1980 Companies Act provides that shares in a public company cannot be alloted unless at least one-quarter of the nominal value of the share and the whole of any premium on it have been received by the company.

18. Effect of irregular allotment: s.49. If shares *are* allotted before the minimum subscription has been subscribed, contravening the requirements of s.47:

(*a*) the allotment is *voidable* at the instance of the applicant and may be set aside within one month after the date of the allotment and not later (s.49 after amendment by the 1980 Act);

(*b*) any director who knowingly permits the allotment is liable to compensate the company and the applicant respectively for any loss, provided that proceedings are commenced within two years after the date of the allotment.

19. Summary. At this point it seems appropriate to summarise the restrictions imposed by the 1948 Act upon *public companies* as regards allotment of shares and to compare the effects of irregular allotment in each case.

CASE	EFFECT
(*a*) Section 47 prohibits the first allotment of shares until the minimum subscription has been received.	Allotment is voidable, at the insistance of the applicant, within one month: s.49.
(*b*) Section 50 imposes restriction as to time of allotment, i.e. no allotment of shares or debentures until the beginning of the third day after first issue of the Prospectus or such later date as may be specified.	Validity of allotment not affected, but company and every officer in default liable on conviction on indictment to a fine, or on summary conviction to a fine not exceeding the statutory maximum.
(*c*) Section 51 prohibits allotment of shares or debentures if a company fails to obtain "permission to deal", having stated in its Prospectus that application has been or will be made for such permission.	Allotment is *void* (s.51(1)) and the company and every officer in default are liable to fines: *see* Companies Act 1980, Schedule 2.

NOTE: The *full* effects of contravening ss.47 and 51 have already been stated, in this and earlier chapters. The object here has been mainly to draw attention to the comparative effects of *irregular* allotment upon the contract between company and applicant.

LETTERS OF RENUNCIATION

20. Renunciation is an important facility which is almost invariably given to allottees, whereby they are permitted to renounce shares allotted to them by completing a *letter of renunciation* (which accompanies the letter of allotment) in favour of another person, who is usually referred to as the "nominee".

21. Stock exchange regulations concerning letters of allotment require that, where the right of renunciation is given:

(*a*) a form of renunciation must appear on the back of the allotment letter, or be attached to it;

(*b*) facilities must be given to allottees for "splitting", i.e. by providing split letters of allotment, where an allottee wishes to renounce his allotment in favour of more than one nominee, or to retain part of his allotment and renounce the balance;

(c) the renunciation period must not exceed:

(i) *six weeks* for fully-paid shares, i.e. where the shares are to be paid in full on application;

(ii) *one month* (from date of the final call) for partly paid shares.

22. Advantages of facilities for renouncing and "splitting" allotments. There are particular advantages both for the company and for the allottees.

(a) For the company, it reduces the amount of work in its registration department in the two following ways.

(i) The original allottees can renounce all or part of the shares allotted to them without going through all the usual formalities of registering their transfers, so long as the renunciations take place during the renunciation period.

(ii) None of the original allottees will be recorded in the Register of Members until the end of the renunciation period; if during that period any of them have renounced their shares, the nominees' names will be recorded, and not the names of the original allottees. Thus, the number of entries in the Register of Members is cut down very considerably.

(b) For the allottee the main advantage is that he may renounce during the renunciation period, making a profit if the issue is a successful one. It is this feature which attracts the "stag" operator, who applies for shares with the intention of renouncing them if he can do so at a profit.

(c) Another advantage is the saving of transfer duty. No transfer duty is payable on shares renounced during the renunciation period—*a considerable advantage to the nominee*, as in the usual transfer procedure it is the transferee who is generally responsible for payment of transfer duty.

23. Procedure for dealing with letters of renunciation and "split" letters.

(a) *Renunciation by allottee.* Assuming that stock exchange regulations have been complied with, i.e. that the allotment letters included a form of renunciation and an undertaking to "split" letters of allotment:

(i) the allottee has the right to renounce in favour of a third party, by completing the form of renunciation and returning it to the company along with the Registration Application Form, completed by the nominee; or (*ii*) he may renounce to several nominees, or retain some of the shares for himself and renounce the balance, in which case he may return his allotment letter to the company and ask for two or more "splits" (i.e. split letters of allotment, or split letters of renunciation, to give them their alternative names) in whatever denominations he may require them to be "split".

(*b*) *Procedure on receiving letters of renunciation.*

(*i*) Number the completed letters of renunciation as they are received and check that both renunciation form and Registration Application Form have been signed and dated.

(*ii*) Record particulars of renunciations either on the Application and Allotment Sheets (if additional columns have been provided for that purpose) or on a separate List of Renunciations.

(*iii*) Send a receipt to each nominee, acknowledging receipt of his completed Registration Application Form.

NOTE: This receipt is important to the nominee, since it is usually accepted as "good delivery" on the stock exchange; in fact stock exchanges require that companies whose shares are "listed" shall certify transfers against the evidence of such a receipt, pending the issue of a share certificate.

(*iv*) Mark the Application and Allotment Sheets to indicate that renunciations have been received, e.g. a letter R may be made in red ink in a column provided for the purpose, against the name of any allottee who has renounced his allotment.

NOTE: At this stage it is *not* usual to cancel out the names of those who have renounced their allotments.

(*v*) Refuse to accept any letter of renunciation received after the closing date of the renunciation period, even if it had been signed before the closing date, as that is the last day for dealing free of transfer duty.

(*c*) *Procedure on receiving requests for split letters of allotment.*

(*i*) Ensure that the request is accompanied by the letter of allotment and a remittance for the appropriate fee for "splitting"—for example, at a rate of 10p per split letter.

(*ii*) Send the required number of split letters to the original allottee. These will be in whatever denominations he requires, and they are usually numbered in such a way as to facilitate cross-reference with the original letter of allotment.

(*iii*) Cancel the original allotment letter, e.g. by rubber stamp; and carefully file it, bearing in mind that it is the company's acceptance of the allottee's offer for shares.

(*iv*) Record the issue of the split letters. This can be done by marking the original entry in the Application and Allotment Sheet with a letter S in red ink and adding the serial numbers of the split letters in a column provided for the purpose. If, for example, the original letter of allotment is no. 100, the split letters may be numbered 100/1, 100/2, 100/3, etc., to simplify cross-reference.

NOTE: At this stage it is too early to cancel any of the original entries in the Application and Allotment Sheets.

(*v*) When the split letters are received, bearing the signatures of the nominees, signifying that they agree to accept the shares renounced in their favour:

(1) send a receipt to each nominee, acknowledging lodgment of his acceptance; and

(2) record particulars of the split letters received, either on the List of Renunciations (already being used for renunciations in full) or on a supplementary list, which may be referred to as a "Split Letters Record Sheet".

(*d*) *Procedure after the closing date for renunciations.*

(*i*) Cancel the appropriate entries on the Application and Allotment Sheets (i.e. those marked R or S) but only after ascertaining that the nominees concerned have agreed to accept the shares renounced in their favour.

(*ii*) If any of the shares renounced have not been accepted by the nominees, or if acceptances have been received *after* expiry of the renunciation period, the name of the original allottee will be allowed to remain on the Application and Allotment Sheet in respect of any shares for which he remains responsible.

(*iii*) Check Application and Allotment Sheets and any supplementary lists, such as the List of Renunciations and Split Letters Record Sheets, to ensure that the shares now remaining on all lists together equal the total number of shares originally allotted.

(*iv*) The Register of Members can now be written up from particulars on the Application and Allotment Sheets and where applicable, supplementary lists of renunciations.

(*v*) Share certificates may be prepared at this stage in favour of the original allottees and accepting nominees. It must be borne in mind that they are to be ready *within two months* after allotment of the shares (s.80) except where the conditions of issue provide otherwise, e.g. where the shares are to be paid for in full over a short period of, say, three months.

NOTE: In the case of "listed" shares, when the stock exchange regulations will apply, share certificates must be ready *within one month*; in the case of a new issue, that means within one month after the end of the renunciation period. However, as already indicated above, the conditions under which the shares are issued now alter the case, as it is not usual to issue share certificates until the shares concerned are fully-paid, and that may be several months or even years after the shares are first allotted. This point is dealt with more fully in VII.

24. Consolidation listing forms.

(*a*) In practice it is usually found that many of the original allottees renounce in favour of the same nominee.

(*b*) In order to save the nominee the trouble of completing several forms, the wording of the registration application form (or acceptance form, where that is used as an alternative) can be slightly altered and a consolidation listing form is added, for example:

I/We accept the shares .... comprised in the within allotment letter and in the attached allotment letters, the definitive numbers whereof and the number of shares comprised wherein are tabulated below:

No. of allotment letter	No. of shares	No. of allotment letter	No. of shares

(*c*) The nominee is required to complete only one of the allotment letters in the above manner; the other allotment letters renounced in his favour are stamped by the broker to link them up with the "parent" allotment letter bearing the signed acceptance form.

(*d*) Finally, the broker will return all the allotment letters to the company, where, having gone through the normal renunciation procedure, the nominee's name will be recorded in the Register of Members after expiration of the renunciation period, and a *single* share certificate will be prepared for *all* the shares renounced in his favour.

ALLOTMENT TO EXISTING MEMBERS

25. When a company wishes to make a subsequent issue of its authorised capital, it may decide, or be required by the Act of 1980 or its Articles to offer the shares of the new issue in the first place to existing shareholders (*see* **33** as regards the statutory pre-emption rights introduced by the 1980 Companies Act)—usually on terms advantageous to the shareholders, e.g. £1 shares may be offered at 112½p whereas the market price of the same class of shares at that time is 137½p.

26. As a rule the number of shares offered to each of the existing shareholders is *pro rata* to their present holdings, e.g. one new share may be offered for every five shares now held. This usually results in entitlement to fractions of shares, with consequent complications for the company. For that reason, fractions are frequently ignored.

27. Offers made to existing shareholders are known as "rights" issues. They may be made:

(*a*) *by provisional allotment letter*, in which the shareholder is informed that a certain number of shares have been "provisionally allotted" to him; or

(*b*) *by letter of rights*, in which a certain number of shares are offered to him.

28. Underwriting. As the existing shareholders are not bound to take up the shares offered to them, it is usual to underwrite a "rights" issue.

29. Procedure on a "rights" issue, using provisional allotment letters.

(*a*) Convene a board meeting to decide whether to make a "rights" issue and, having decided that it would be advisable to do so, to discuss the following important matters:

(*i*) the amount and terms of the proposed issue;

(*ii*) whether to underwrite the issue, and

(*iii*) if not, how to deal with any excess shares not taken up.

(*b*) Notify the stock exchange by phone, letter or telegram, as soon as possible after the meeting, i.e. assuming that it is intended to apply for permission to deal in the shares.

(*c*) Prepare lists, showing the number of shares to be offered to each shareholder, based upon his holding at a stipulated date.

(*d*) Convene another board meeting for the purpose of passing a resolution authorising the "rights" issue, and instructing the Secretary to:

(*i*) arrange for the preparation and printing of the necessary documents, e.g. provisional allotment letters, letters of renunciation, applications for excess shares, allotment sheets, share certificates, etc.;

(*ii*) arrange for the underwriting of the issue, unless other arrangements are being made for dealing with excess shares;

(*iii*) submit an application to the stock exchange, through the company's brokers, for a listing for the new shares.

NOTE: It has been assumed that a *board* meeting would be adequate to authorise the "rights" issue, and that the authority required by s.14 of the Companies Act 1980 (*see* 11 *above*) and/or any specific regulation in the Articles has been obtained.

(*e*) Notify the stock exchange of the above decisions.

(*f*) Approach underwriters and arrange for an underwriting contract after its terms have been approved by the board.

(*g*) Prepare all necessary documents referred to above.

(*h*) Submit an application to the stock exchange for a listing of the new shares, together with copies of all documents to be sent to shareholders; and specimen (or proofs) of the share certificate(s).

(*i*) Arrange for the closing of Register of Members (and Transfer Register, if any) and give notice of the proposed closing in the press.

NOTE: If this course is not adopted, it will be announced that the holders on a stipulated date will be entitled to the "rights" issue.

(*j*) File a copy of the provisional allotment letter with the Registrar.

(*k*) Send a provisional allotment letter to each shareholder so entitled, and obtain a certificate of posting.

(*l*) Deal with letters of renunciation and requests for "split letters".

(*m*) Record acceptances on provisional allotment lists. If, however, payment of the first instalment (or the full amount, if that is required) is not made to the company's bankers by the shareholder or his nominee(s) on or before the due date, the offer is deemed to have been declined.

(*n*) Applications for excess shares may be used to make up any deficiency. If there is still a deficiency, the shares undersubscribed will be taken up by the underwriters.

(*o*) Subsequent procedure will follow closely the usual allotment procedure already described in detail, briefly as follows.

(*i*) Board (or allotment committee) passes a resolution, authorising the allotment. Notify stock exchange.

(*ii*) After expiry of the renunciation period, write up the Register of Members and (if the shares are then fully paid) prepare and issue share certificates.

(*iii*) File a Return of Allotments in the prescribed form with the Registrar, in compliance with s.52.

30. Procedure on a "rights" issue, using a letter of rights.

(*a*) A letter of rights may be used as an alternative to a provisional allotment letter, and neither appears to have any important advantage over the other.

(*b*) The principal difference lies in the wording of the documents, i.e. the letter of rights invites the member to *apply* for a specified number of shares, whereas the provisional allotment letter informs him that a specified number of shares have been "provisionally allotted" to him and requests him to *accept* them by a certain date.

(*c*) Whichever document is used, the shareholder usually has the right to renounce the shares offered to him. In that case the document is of value, for even if the shareholder does not wish to take up the new shares he can sell his "rights" to do so on the market.

31. "Rights" not taken up by existing shareholders. Various ways have been suggested for dealing with excess shares, although several of them are wide open to criticism.

(*a*) Underwriting the issue is the most obvious method to adopt, but it may prove unpopular with those shareholders who would like the opportunity to apply for any excess shares.

(*b*) Excess shares may be offered to the remaining shareholders, or forms of "Application for Excess Shares" issued to shareholders along with the provisional allotment letter; any balance of shares still remaining to be taken up by the underwriters.

(*c*) Excess shares may be offered to the company's employees. This may be encouraged by those who favour the idea of employees entering into the field of investment, but might not have the support of those who contribute the bulk of the company's capital.

(*d*) Excess shares may be allotted to a trustee for those who failed to apply, who sells the shares for their benefit and distributes the proceeds (less expenses) to them. This method might lead to even greater apathy on the part of the shareholders; if they felt certain that the company would look after their interests in this way, they might be encouraged to ignore any future offers of shares.

(*e*) Excess shares may be sold, and the net proceeds utilised by the company to reduce the issue expenses.

(*f*) Excess shares may be offered as an alternative to commission for underwriting the issue. It would, of course, be necessary to ensure that this did not amount to an excessive rate or amount of commission, having regard to the provisions of s.53.

(*g*) Excess shares may be disposed of by the directors, usually amongst themselves. This method might be far from popular with the shareholders, unless they had already been given the opportunity to apply for the excess shares.

32. Allotment letters which are not surrendered in exchange for a new share certificate. When shares are offered, either in a Prospectus or on a "rights" issue and the shares are payable on application and allotment, e.g. 25p per share on application and the 75p balance on allotment, it is still the usual practice of many companies to require the surrender of the allotment letter in exchange for the new share certificate. If, however, a shareholder *fails* to surrender his letter of allotment, the course to be adopted by the company will depend upon whether the letter of allotment is of the "returnable" or "non-returnable" type.

(*a*) If it is of the *non-returnable* type, the company will, after a stipulated date, issue a share certificate to the allottee in any case, without any need for him to submit the letter of allotment, which then becomes valueless.

(*b*) If it is a *returnable* letter of allotment, the allottee's failure to surrender it may be due to inadvertence or to his failure to pay the allotment money; therefore, the company might adopt either or both the following courses.

(*i*) Write to the shareholder, requesting surrender of the letter of allotment. If this has no effect, record the fact in the Register of Members, so as to prevent any attempt to transfer the shares concerned against the letter of allotment, which is a valuable document and "good delivery" on the stock exchange.

(*ii*) Forfeiture of the shares may be carried out in accordance with the company's Articles, or, if applicable, Table A.

33. Pre-emption rights.

(*a*) The Companies Act 1980, s.17, provides that no equity securities may be allotted by a company for cash without first offering them to the holders of existing "relevant shares" and of "relevant employee shares" *pro rata* to their existing holdings; i.e. existing members of both private and public companies are entitled to the right of pre-emption in a new issue of equity shares on a *pro rata* basis.

(*b*) There are, however, many exclusions and exceptions and, in the case of a *private* company, any provision in its Memorandum or Articles which is inconsistent with the provisions of s.17 will override the Act.

(*c*) "Relevant shares", in relation to a company, are shares other than those which, in respect of dividends and capital, carry a right to participate only up to a specified amount in a distribution, and shares held, or to be held, under an employees' share scheme.

(*d*) "Relevant employee shares", in relation to a company, are shares of the company which would be relevant shares, but for the fact that they are held under an employees' share scheme.

ALLOTMENT OF BONUS SHARES

34. Authority to allot bonus shares. If the Articles permit, a company may allot fully paid bonus shares to its members:

(*a*) *out of undistributed profits*, in which case it amounts to a capitalisation of its reserves; or

(*b*) *out of a Share Premium Account balance*, i.e. out of the account created on allotting shares at more than their nominal value; or

(*c*) *out of a Capital Redemption Reserve*, created in connection with the redemption or purchase of its own shares.

35. Procedure. The procedure for making a bonus issue is similar in some respects to that for a rights issue, but there are many points of difference. A bonus issue procedure may be carried out in the following stages.

(*a*) Before attempting to carry out any of the necessary procedures, the following preliminaries must be dealt with.

(*i*) Ensure that the Articles permit the issue of bonus shares. If not, they must be altered by special resolution. (In this case, it has been assumed that the Articles give the necessary permission.)

(*ii*) Consult the Articles, also, to ensure that authority to make the issue will be given by the appropriate meeting. In this case, it has been assumed that the directors have power to recommend the issue but the company in general meeting must adopt the recommendation before it becomes effective. This is typical of most cases.

(*iii*) Ascertain that the company has sufficient unissued capital to cover the intended amount of the bonus issue. If not, an ordinary resolution must be passed to increase the company's authorised capital, and capital duty paid on the increased capital.

(*b*) Convene a board meeting, where, after discussion, the following business is carried out:

(*i*) a formal resolution is passed, recommending a bonus issue;

(*ii*) the basis of distribution, method of dealing with fractions and other details are settled;

(*iii*) the Secretary is instructed to convene a general meeting and, on the assumption that the directors' recommendation will be adopted, he will no doubt also receive instructions to arrange for the drafting and subsequent printing of the necessary documents; also, where applicable, to notify the stock exchange and, subsequently, obtain a listing for the shares to be issued.

(*c*) Notify the stock exchange of the board's decision, by letter or phone, as soon as possible after the meeting.

(*d*) Arising out of the board meeting, the Secretary will:

(*i*) convene an extraordinary general meeting, the notice giving brief particulars of the directors' recommendation;

(*ii*) draft, and obtain the board's approval of, the necessary documents, e.g. fully paid allotment letters, allotment lists, certificates, etc.

(*e*) An extraordinary general meeting is held, at which an ordinary resolution is passed, adopting the directors' recommendation to issue bonus shares. At that meeting, a trustee may be appointed for the shareholders entitled to participate in the bonus issue, and either then or at a subsequent board meeting a contract will be executed between company and trustee. (*See* (*l*) *below* for reference to the filing of a Return of Allotment.)

(*f*) A further board meeting will be held soon after the general meeting for the purpose of:

(*i*) passing a resolution allotting the bonus shares to members named in an allotment list produced by the Secretary; and

(*ii*) executing the contract between the company and the trustee for the shareholders, constituting the title of the allottees to the shares—unless, as stated above, it has already been executed at the general meeting.

(*g*) Submit an application for permission to deal in the shares, if it is intended to obtain a listing for the shares on the stock exchange. The application will be made through the company's brokers in the first place, but it will be necessary at a later date to submit copies of all documents to be sent to shareholders and a specimen (or proofs) of the new share certificate(s).

(*h*) File with the Registrar copies of notices, circulars, etc.

NOTE: It has been assumed that facilities for renunciation are being provided; therefore, although a full Prospectus is not required, it is still necessary to file copies of notices, circulars, etc., with the Registrar, as these documents collectively constitute a form of Prospectus within the definition of s.455.

(*i*) Post fully paid allotment letters, with accompanying letters of renunciation.

NOTE: Alternatively many companies now send renounceable share certificates in lieu of allotment letters.

(*j*) Deal with letters of renunciation and requests for "split" letters.

(*k*) After expiry of the renunciation period:
    (*i*) write up the Register of Members;
    (*ii*) prepare and issue new share certificates to original allottees and, where applicable, accepting nominees.

(*l*) File a return of allotments (Form PUC7) with the Registrar within one month, and, as a bonus issue amounts to an allotment for consideration other than cash, the return must be accompanied by the contract in writing, duly stamped, constituting the title of the allottees to the allotment: s. 52. Capital duty is not payable on the issue of bonus shares.

NOTE: This is the contract, referred to in (*e*) and (*f*)(*ii*) above between the company and a trustee for the shareholders. The contract is in the form of a deed, and bears a 50p impressed stamp. As a rule, the Secretary, Chairman or one of the largest shareholders is appointed trustee.

36. Methods of dealing with fractional entitlements. Both bonus and rights issues are likely to result in fractional entitlements; for example, where a company makes a bonus issue under which each shareholder is entitled to one new share for every three registered in his name, a member holding 100 shares would be entitled to $33\frac{1}{3}$ bonus shares. How to deal with these fractional entitlements is a matter which the directors must consider and deal with as fairly as possible to those concerned, since the company cannot allot fractions of shares. Various methods are available. The following are examples.

(a) Shares representing fractional entitlements may be sold, and any shareholder entitled to a fraction of a share will subsequently receive payment for the net proceeds of the sale of that fraction.

(b) All shares representing fractional entitlement may be allotted to a trustee for the shareholders affected, who has power to sell them on the open market for the benefit of the shareholders entitled to fractions.

(c) Fractional certificates may be issued to shareholders entitled to fractions of shares, enabling those who wish to do so to sell them to others who wish to buy sufficient fractional certificates to make up a whole share or shares.

(d) Shareholders may be invited to tender for shares, representing fractional entitlements, a trustee for the shareholders affected being responsible for distributing the proceeds.

(e) Fractions may be ignored entirely, a method which would certainly be unpopular if adopted in a bonus issue.

PROGRESS TEST 3

1. List the various stages in a procedure for receiving and handling application for shares, and for the preparation and despatch of allotment letters. It may be assumed that the issue is oversubscribed. (1–16)

2. State briefly the information to be given in a Return of Allotments. Within what period must it be filed? (16)

3. What statutory restrictions are imposed upon the allotment of shares by a public company? What is the effect (if any) of irregular allotment in each of the cases you mention? (17–19)

4. Briefly outline the procedure followed on receiving letters of renunciation and "split letters" at the company's office. (23)

5. Distinguish between each of the following:

(a) a capitalisation issue and a rights issue;
(b) high geared capital and low geared capital;
(c) an offer for sale and an advertised statement.
(I, 49; II, 13, 14; III)

6. Explain the meaning of the following terms used in connection with the issue of shares:

(*a*) brokerage;
(*b*) firm underwriting;
(*c*) a provisional allotment letter;
(*d*) a consolidated listing form.
ICSA   (II, **17, 18**; III)

7. A company whose shares are listed on the stock exchange is about to make a substantial issue of shares to be offered to existing shareholders with rights of renunciation. Describe the records that should be kept by the company in respect of such an issue.   (**29**)

8. What is a rights issue, and how is it effected? *ICSA*   (**25–32**)

9. On a new issue of shares to existing ordinary shareholders, what are the possible methods of dealing with:

(*i*) fractional entitlements;

(*ii*) rights not taken up;

(*iii*) allotment letters not surrendered in exchange for new share certificates?   (**31, 32, 36**)

CHAPTER IV

Calls and Instalments

PRELIMINARY CONSIDERATIONS

1. When shares are payable. When a company makes an issue of shares, they may be payable:

(*a*) *in full, on application*—although this is comparatively rare in the case of issues to the public;

(*b*) *on application and allotment*, for example 25p per share on application and the balance of 75p per share on allotment, for a £1 share issued at par; or

(*c*) *by calls or instalments*, for example, a £1 share issued at par may be payable:

    (*i*) 25p per share on application;

    (*ii*) 25p per share on allotment; and

    (*iii*) the balance of 50p by calls or instalments

NOTE: The Companies Act 1980, s.22, provides that a *public* company shall not allot any shares unless at least one-quarter of the shares' nominal value, and the whole of any premium on such shares, has been paid up. *Exception* is made, however, in the case of shares allotted under an employees' share scheme (*see* II, **17**).

2. A call is not an instalment, and any power given in the Articles to forfeit shares for non-payment of calls, or to charge interest on unpaid calls, does not apply to instalments—unless (as in Table A) the Articles provide that amounts due on allotment and instalments are deemed to be calls: Article 19.

3. An instalment differs from a call in the following respects.

(*a*) *An instalment* is due and payable on a fixed date specified in the conditions of issue; *a call* only becomes due as or if required.

(*b*) *An instalment* becomes due and payable without the passing of a resolution; *a call* only becomes due on the passing of a resolution to that effect—usually a resolution of the board of directors.

(*c*) *An instalment* is automatically due on the date fixed, without making any formal demand of the shareholder; *a call* must be made by the giving of proper notice in compliance with the provisions of the Articles.

4. Table A provisions as regards calls and the making of calls are as follows.

(*a*) The directors are authorised to make calls at a properly constituted board meeting: Article 15.

(*b*) A call is deemed to have been made at the time the directors' resolution was passed, and may be payable by instalments: Article 16.

(*c*) The resolution must state the amount, time and place of payment.

(*d*) The amount of the call is not to exceed one-fourth of the nominal value of the share: Article 15.

(*e*) The time for payment must be not less than one month from the date fixed for payment of the last preceding call: Article 15.

(*f*) At least fourteen days' notice must be given to the member, specifying time and place of payment: Article 15.

(*g*) A call may be revoked or postponed, as the directors may determine: Article 15.

(*h*) Joint holders are jointly and severally liable to pay calls: Article 17.

(*i*) Amounts due on allotment and instalments are deemed to be calls for the purpose of regulations as regards the charging of interest and forfeiture: Article 19.

(*j*) Interest may be charged on unpaid calls, after the date appointed for payment, at a rate not exceeding 5 per cent per annum: Article 18.

(*k*) Forfeiture of shares is permitted, under certain conditions, for failure to pay a call or an instalment: Article 33.

(*l*) Interest may be paid on calls paid in advance, but not exceeding 5 per cent per annum, unless the company in general meeting otherwise directs: Article 21.

(*m*) Power is given to differentiate between shareholders as regards the amount and time of payment of calls: Article 20.

NOTE: Section 59 permits differentiation, where authorised by the Articles, but the directors must use this power only for the benefit of the company and not of individuals: *Alexander* v. *Automatic Telephone Co.* (1900).

5. If a call is made improperly, a shareholder may be relieved of liability to meet the call, until such time as it is properly made, by application to the Court: *Re Cawley & Co.* (1889), where the call letter omitted the date of payment. It was held that the call was invalid until a resolution was passed fixing the date of payment.

PROCEDURE ON MAKING A CALL

6. Board meeting. The original decision to make a call will be made at a board meeting, after which the Secretary will be instructed:

(*a*) to prepare the necessary documents; and

(*b*) to arrange for the bank to receive call moneys.

NOTE: The directors *may* have to seek approval of the call by the company in general meeting, although this would be very unusual, as the Articles almost invariably vest the power to make calls in the directors.

7. Reference to the Articles. Before preparing documents or making any arrangements with the company's bankers, the Secretary would be well advised to refer to the Articles, to ensure that the call will be strictly correct as regards amount, notice, interval since last call, etc.

8. Preparation of documents.

(*a*) The Secretary's next step is to draft a form of *call letter*, which usually includes:

(*i*) *a form of receipt*, which the bank returns to the shareholder after he has paid his call money; and

(*ii*) *a detachable voucher*, which the bank returns to the company as advice of call money received.

(*b*) Other documents that may be drafted at this stage include a Call List and a formal letter of reminder for shareholders who fail to pay by the specified date.

(*c*) After obtaining board approval of the draft documents—but more particularly of the call letter—an order may be placed for the printing of the call letters, specifying that they must be numbered consecutively.

9. Arrangements with the bank can then be made, in particular:

(*a*) to receive payment of call moneys;

(*b*) to credit amounts received to a special Call Account;

(*c*) to return receipted call letters to shareholders; and

(*d*) to submit to the company, in due course, a list of call moneys received together with vouchers detached from call letters, referred to in **8**(*a*) above.

10. Convene a board meeting. Having received the printed call letters, a board meeting may now be convened (unless, as already explained, the Articles should make it necessary to hold a general meeting) to transact the following business.

(*a*) The call letter will be submitted to the board for approval.

(*b*) A resolution is passed, authorising the call, for example:

RESOLVED: That a call of 25p per share on the 200,000 ordinary shares of the Company, numbered 1 to 200,000, be and is hereby made; and that the holders of such shares be requested to pay the same on or before the .... day of .... 19......
to the Company's bankers, Town and Country Bank Plc, West-cheap, London E.C.5.

(*c*) The Secretary will be instructed to issue call letters.

11. Preparation of Call Lists. Having ensured that the Register of Members is written up-to-date, Call Lists can now be prepared for the Register, taking care, of course, to exclude any shareholders who may, by arrangement with the company, have paid calls in advance. The Call List may take the following form.

The Blank Company Plc

Call list

Second and final call of 25p per share on 200,000 ordinary shares of £1 each.

Call made ....19...... Payable on or before...............19......

No. of call letter	Folio in reg.	Shareholder		No. of shares held	Amount due on call at 25p per share	Paid			Out-standing	Remarks
		Name	Address			C.B. Folio	Date	Amount		
					£			£	£	

12. Preparation of call letters from Call Lists. After making a thorough check of the Call Lists, and reconciling the total number of shares with the total amount of calls payable, call letters are prepared from particulars on the Call Lists. Care must be taken to ensure that the call letters are strictly in accordance with the Articles, as failure to do so may invalidate the call. The following are the points requiring particular attention:

(*a*) amount of the call;
(*b*) interval since making the last call;
(*c*) length of notice;
(*d*) date fixed for payment;
(*e*) to whom cheques, etc., are to be payable;
(*f*) place of payment;
(*g*) capital duty.

As regards the last in the case of calls made on partly paid shares, the capital duty is paid on a statement (Form PUC5) delivered to the Controller of Stamps, Inland Revenue.

13. Post the call letters. After completion, the call letters should receive a final check prior to posting. A certificate of posting may be obtained.

14. Checking. Lists of all call moneys received will arrive in due course from the bank. They will be accompanied by the appropriate vouchers, and these should be checked against the list.

15. The Call Lists can now be completed from the particulars provided by the bank, and the share ledger written up from the Call Lists.

NOTE: The procedure, at this stage, will depend upon whether it has been the company's practice to issue share certificates for partly paid shares, or to issue certificates only after the shares are fully paid.

(1) If a share certificate had already been issued, the shareholder must return it to the company along with his receipted call letter. If it is the *final* call, the "partly paid" share certificate will be cancelled and a "fully paid" certificate issued to the shareholder. If it is *not* the final call, the company will merely record the payment in the space provided—usually on the back of the share certificate—and return the endorsed certificate to the shareholder.

(2) If a share certificate is issued only after shares are fully paid, no certificate will be issued at this stage, unless the call concerned is the *final* one.

16. Reminders. After a short interval, send reminders to shareholders who have failed to pay calls on or before the due date.

17. Calls still overdue. If the Articles permit, payment of interest may be demanded on overdue calls and, as a last resort, the necessary steps may be taken to forfeit the shares.

NOTE: If the shares referred to in the above procedure were "listed", the stock exchange would require notification of board decisions, and a specimen (or two advance proofs) of the share certificate would be submitted at the appropriate stage.

FORFEITURE

Forfeiture is a step, taken by a company only in the last resort, to expropriate the shares of a member who defaults in paying any part of the moneys due from him in respect of the shares declared forfeit.

It amounts to a reduction of capital, even though it may be only a temporary reduction in those cases where the forfeited shares are subsequently re-issued.

18. Limits imposed on the right of a company to forfeit shares.

(*a*) The Acts themselves do not expressly impose any limits, but because forfeiture amounts to a reduction of capital it can be carried out only:

(*i*) *then the Articles permit*, or where Table A applies (Articles 33–34 give the directors power to forfeit); or

(*ii*) *if the Articles are silent* and Table A has been excluded, by obtaining sanction of the Court: *Clarke & Chapman* v. *Hart* (1858).

(*b*) The directors of a company are not entitled to declare forfeit the shares of a member, unless:

(*i*) express power to do so is given to them in the Articles, or in Table A if their Articles are silent; and

(*ii*) as forfeiture is in the nature of a penalty, it must be carried out strictly in the manner prescribed in the Articles, or Table A where applicable; and

(*iii*) for the benefit of the company and not, for example, to relieve a shareholder of his liability on the shares: *Re Esparto Trading Co.* (1879); and

(*iv*) where the default arose in respect of non-payment of calls or other sums due from the member in respect of his shares, i.e. not for non-payment of *other* debts due to the company: *Hopkinson* v. *Mortimer Harley & Co.* (1917).

19. Summary of the legal effects of forfeiture.

(*a*) It amounts to a cancellation of the shares concerned and, therefore, to a reduction of capital, even though it may be only a temporary reduction.

(*b*) It cancels the membership of the shareholder concerned.

(*c*) It discharges the shareholder's liability in respect of the forfeited shares: *Ladies' Dress Association* v. *Pulbrook* (1900). But the Articles usually preserve the liability of the shareholder, as does Table A (Article 37).

20. Forfeiture under Table A. Table A permits forfeiture but sets out the necessary conditions and indicates the procedure to be followed.

(*a*) The directors may serve notice requiring payment with interest. If a call or instalment is unpaid on the due date, the directors may serve notice on the member in default, requiring payment with interest: Article 33.

NOTE: Non-payment may refer to default in paying a sum due on account of the nominal value of the share or on any sum due by way of premium: Article 39.

(*b*) The notice must name a further day (not less than 14 days after service of the notice) by which payment is to be made, failing which the shares concerned are liable to forfeiture: Article 34.

(*c*) In the event of failure to comply with the notice, the directors may by resolution declare the shares forfeited, for example:

RESOLVED: That the 200 ordinary shares of £1 each, numbered 301 to 500 both inclusive, on which the sum of 50p per share has been paid, and now registered in the name of Mr A. Blank of 15 Chetwynd Grove, Redpoole, Wessex, be and the same are hereby forfeited for non-payment of a second call of 25p per share, served on 1st November 19... in accordance with Minute No. 4 of the board meeting held on the 24th October 19... and for his failure to comply with requests for payment sent to him on 8th December 19... and 15th December 19...

(*d*) Forfeited shares may then be sold or otherwise disposed of, as the directors decide, but before sale or disposition the forfeiture may be cancelled, on terms decided by the directors: Article 36.

(*e*) Membership ceases on forfeiture, but liability for calls remains with the original holder until the company receives payment in full of all money due on the shares: Article 37.

(*f*) A statutory declaration in writing, stating that the declarant is a director or secretary of the company, and that a share (or shares) in the company has been duly forfeited on a given date, is conclusive evidence against all persons claiming to be entitled to the shares: Article 38.

NOTE: This provision is a protection for the company where the original holder refuses to return his share certificate, as the un-returned certificate can be rendered invalid by production of the statutory declaration.

(g) On re-issuing the forfeited shares: Article 38:

(i) the company may receive the consideration (if any) for shares sold or otherwise disposed of;

(ii) the company may execute a transfer of the shares in favour of the person to whom the shares are sold or disposed of;

NOTE: In order to comply with s.75 (which makes it illegal to register a transfer unless a proper instrument of transfer has been delivered to the company) the company will have to nominate some person to execute a transfer to the purchaser of the re-issued forfeited shares. Usually a member of the board will be empowered to do so.

(iii) the person to whom the shares are sold shall be registered as the holder of the shares;

(iv) he shall not be bound to see to the application of the purchase money, and his title to the shares will not be affected by any irregularity or invalidity of the procedure for forfeiture, sale or disposal of the shares.

21. Notice of forfeiture.

(a) It will be observed that Table A does not require the company to send notice to the shareholder to inform him that his shares have been forfeited.

(b) Nevertheless, it is usual to notify the shareholder by registered post that his shares have been declared forfeited, to prevent any misunderstanding.

(c) At the same time, it is customary to ask the shareholder to return his share certificate. In practice, shareholders seldom comply with such a request.

(d) The Secretary should, however, make every attempt to secure the return of the certificate; otherwise, if the shares are re-issued, there will be two share certificates in existence for the same set of shares.

NOTE: A provision similar to that in Table A, Article 38, referred to in **20**(*f*) above, will however enable the company to prove the invalidity of an unreturned share certificate.

22. Treatment of forfeited shares.

(*a*) *Reissue.* If forfeited shares are reissued, the price for which they are sold plus the amount already paid up by the original holder must not be less than the full nominal value; that is, the shares cannot be reissued at a price which would, in effect, amount to the issue of the shares at a discount (*see* II, **18**).

(*b*) *Disposal of shares forfeited* (or surrendered) to a *public* company. Such shares must be disposed of by the company, or cancelled, within three years from the date of forfeiture or surrender. If such cancellation reduces the company's issued share capital below the "authorised minimum", the company will then be obliged to re-register as a private company: Companies Act 1980, s.37.

23. Surrender of shares.

(*a*) In general, it may be said that *a surrender of shares is unlawful* because:

(*i*) it amounts to an unauthorised reduction of capital; and

(*ii*) the company's acceptance of the surrendered shares would make it a member of itself, which is illegal.

(*b*) But a surrender of shares is not always unlawful; for example:

(*i*) the directors may accept a surrender of shares and thus relieve the company of going through the formalities of forfeiture—if the Articles permit, and where the circumstances would justify forfeiture;

(*ii*) where the surrender does not involve a reduction of capital, e.g. a surrender of existing fully paid shares in exchange for new fully paid shares of the same nominal value: *Rowell* v. *John Rowell & Son* (1912).

(*c*) In any other circumstances, where a reduction of capital will result from the surrender of shares, application must be made for Court sanction.

(*d*) The effect of a *public* company's failure to dispose of shares surrendered to it is stated in **22**(*b*).

PROGRESS TEST 4

1. Explain precisely the differences between the following terms:

(*a*) rights and capitalisation issues;
(*b*) repayment of capital and a capital distribution;
(*c*) a call and an instalment.
ICSA   (III, 25–27, 35; IV, 2, 3)

2. When making a call, what are the important matters to be borne in mind? Is it permissible to differentiate between shareholders of the same class as regards the amount and time of payment of calls? If so, in what circumstances?   (**4, 7**)

3. Describe an office procedure for making a call, and prepare a call list suitable for the occasion.   (**6–13**)

4. "Forfeiture is a procedure that demands the utmost care." Explain, and suggest any precautions that ought to be taken in relation to forfeiture of shares and their reissue.   (**18, 20–22**)

5. The directors of your company wish to forfeit the shares of a member. Write a memorandum explaining the procedure. Assume that Table A applies. *ICSA*   (**20, 21**)

6. Distinguish between forfeiture and surrender of shares. Is a surrender of shares necessarily unlawful in all cases; if not, what are the exceptional circumstances?   (**18–19, 23**)

7. A final call has been made and has remained unpaid by a shareholder. Assuming Table A applies, explain in a memorandum to your board the action the company can take. *ICSA*   (**18–21**)

CHAPTER V

The Common Seal

REGULATIONS AS TO ITS USE AND CUSTODY

1. Every company must have a common seal, with its name engraved thereon in legible characters: s.108.

2. Regulations governing the use and custody of the seal are usually set out in a company's Articles of Association; they may, however, be prescribed by resolution of the board.

3. Table A provisions concerning the use and custody of the seal are set out in Article 113, as follows.

(*a*) The directors are to provide for the safe custody of the common seal.

(*b*) It is to be used only by the authority of the directors, or of a committee authorised by them.

(*c*) The instrument sealed must be signed by a director, and countersigned by the secretary, or by a second director or by some other person appointed by the directors for the purpose.

4. To ensure safe custody of the seal, and to prevent its misuse, various precautions are usually taken.

(*a*) The seal is usually kept in a suitable safe or in a strong room.

(*b*) It is often fitted with a double-locking device, with one key in the hands of the secretary, the other with the chairman or one of the other directors. This provides a form of internal check.

(*c*) Spare key(s) may be deposited with the company's bankers, with instructions to hand them over only to a specified person or against the written request of specified signatories.

(*d*) The use of an automatic sealing press has various "built-in" security measures, e.g. the die can be removed and locked away in a very small space, and the machine protected from unauthorised use by removing and locking away the electric plugging-in arrangement.

(*e*) If a "sealing committee" is appointed, e.g. to seal share certificates, make sure that any limitations to its power to use the seal are clearly ascertained.

(*f*) Supervision of sealing by the company's auditors, or transfer auditors, at regular intervals is an alternative method used in sealing large numbers of share certificates.

5. When the seal is required to be used.

(*a*) Although the seal is a company's official signature, it is not necessary to use it on all contract documents. Moreover, it is inadvisable to use it unnecessarily in matters of little importance or on any occasion where it is not legally required, as a contract under seal will in most cases be liable to a 50p deed stamp.

(*b*) According to the provisions of s.32, a company's contracts may be:

(*i*) *by word of mouth*, by any person acting under express or implied authority of the company;

(*ii*) *in writing*, signed by any person acting under express or implied authority of the company;

(*iii*) *in writing under common seal* of the company, where English law requires such forms of contract as between private persons.

(*c*) The seal is required on documents when demanded by:

(*i*) *the Companies Act 1948*, e.g.:

(1) share warrants to bearer: s.83;

(2) power of attorney to permit execution of deeds abroad: s.34;

(3) share certificates: s.81;

(*ii*) *the company's Articles of Association*, e.g. on debentures;

NOTE: Although debentures are not legally required to be under seal, in most cases the Articles and/or conditions of issue require them in that form.

(*iii*) *the law of contract*, e.g.:

(1) contracts without consideration;

(2) leases of land for more than three years;

(*iv*) *other statutes*, e.g.:

(1) powers of attorney: Powers of Attorney Act 1971;

(2) transfer forms: Stock Transfer Act 1963.

NOTE: The seal will be required on a transfer form where the transferor is a corporate body; it is no longer required in other cases to which the Stock Transfer Act 1963 applies.

6. Register of Documents Sealed (or Seal Register).

(*a*) This is not one of the statutory books; however, although there is no statutory obligation to keep such a register, most companies find it an advantage to do so.

(*b*) The particulars usually recorded are shown in the following suggested ruling for such a register:

Register of documents sealed

Minute No.	Date of Resolution	Description of documents sealed	Date of sealing	Names of persons present	Names of persons signing	Disposal of documents sealed

THE OFFICIAL SEAL

7. The official seal is a facsimile of the common seal of the company, but with the addition on its face of the territory, district or place where it is to be used.

8. Company's power to have an official seal. According to s.35, a company *may* have an official seal for use in any district, territory or place not situate in the United Kingdom:

(*a*) if the company's objects require or comprise the transaction of business in foreign countries; and

(*b*) if the company's Articles permit.

9. Provision as to use of official seal. If the official seal is used upon any deed or other document, it will be as binding upon the company as though its common seal had been used, provided that:

(*a*) the person affixing it had the company's authority in writing under seal;

(*b*) the deed or other document is one to which the company is party; and

(*c*) he is carrying out his authority in the territory, district or place in which the official seal was intended to be used: s.35(3).

10. Further provisions in the Articles regarding the official seal. In addition to authorising the use of an official seal, a company's Articles may also include some or all of the following provisions as to its use, security, attestation, etc.:

(*a*) Authority to use the official seal may be made, under the company's common seal, to a person or persons, e.g. to a sealing committee.

(*b*) The person or persons appointed are to affix the official seal and, by writing under hand, certify on the deed or other instrument to which the seal is affixed the date on which and the place at which it is affixed.

(*c*) Limits may be imposed upon the power of the person or persons appointed to use the official seal, as for example in the case of a sealing committee, and for revocation.

(*d*) Similar provisions may be made for custody and security measures as are made for the company's common seal, e.g. a double-locking device.

(*e*) Provision for attestation of signatures on documents on which the official seal is affixed.

SECURITIES SEAL

11. Stock Exchange (Completion of Bargains) Act 1976, s.2.

(*a*) Section 2 of the Stock Exchange (Completion of Bargains) Act 1976 permits a company to have an official seal for sealing securities issued by the company, and for sealing documents creating or evidencing securities so issued.

(*b*) The official seal so authorised must be a facsimile of the company's common seal with the addition of the word "Securities".

(*c*) A company incorporated before the coming into force of the Stock Exchange (Completion of Bargains) Act 1976 and already having an official seal may use it for sealing the securities and documents referred to above, notwithstanding anything stated to the contrary in the company's regulations or in any instrument (such as a trust deed) made before that date relating to any securities issued by the company.

PROGRESS TEST 5

1. What provisions does the Act make concerning the common seal of a limited company? What steps do you suggest ought to be taken to ensure (*a*) its safe custody, (*b*) that it is not misused?　**(1–4)**

2. The chairman of your company wishes to save the time consumed at monthly board meetings by the necessity to execute large numbers of documents under the common seal of the company. Prepare a memorandum, for consideration by him, setting out your proposals to remedy this situation. *ICSA* **(4)**

3. What do you understand by the term "common seal" as applied to a limited company? The articles of Zed Ltd. are silent on the subject of its common seal. What rules must the company apply as to (*a*) use and custody of the seal, (*b*) the signing of documents sealed? **(1–5)**

4. When is a contract effectively sealed? Give examples of documents which must be under common seal of the company in order to comply with statutory requirements, and of other documents where the necessity for sealing is dependent upon other considerations. **(5)**

5. Give a specimen ruling for a Register of Documents Sealed, and insert at least six different entries. Is there any statutory obligation to keep such a register? **(6)**

6. A company requires in the normal course of its business to execute documents under its common seal almost every day. The board of directors meets only once a month. Describe in detail the arrangements that should be made to deal with this position. **(4, 6)**

7. In order to give authenticity to a document or proceeding, is a company bound to use its common seal? Explain the position, and state your authority. Distinguish between a common seal and an official seal. **(1–3, 5, 7–9)**

8. Your directors have decided to make use of an official seal at one of the company's important overseas branches. You are required to report to them, suggesting any provisions that ought to be made for the effective and safe use of the official seal. **(9, 10)**

CHAPTER VI

The Register of Members

STATUTORY PROVISIONS AS TO FORM
AND CONTENTS, LOCATION, INSPECTION, ETC.

1. Contents: s.110. Every company must keep a Register of Members, showing:

(*a*) the name and address of each member;

(*b*) the date on which he was entered as a member and the eventual date on which he ceased to be a member;

(*c*) the number and, where the company has more than one class of issued shares, the class of shares which he holds (unless the company has no share capital) and the amount paid up on each share. If the shares have been converted into stock corresponding particulars of stock held are entered.

NOTE: Section 112 also requires particulars relating to the issue of any share warrants, where applicable (*see* VII, **12**).

Any entry relating to a former member of a company may be removed from the company's register of members after the expiration of twenty years from the date on which he ceases to be a member.

2. The form of the register.

(*a*) Section 436 provides that any register, index, minute book or accounting records required by the 1948 Act or the Companies Act 1980 to be kept by a company may be kept either by making entries in bound books or by recording the matters in question in any other manner. By s.3 of the Stock Exchange (Completion of Bargains) Act 1976 the power to keep a register or other record by recording the matters in question otherwise than by making entries in bound books, includes power to keep the register or other record by recording the matters in question otherwise than in a legible form, so long as the recording is capable of being reproduced in a legible form. This, in effect, legalises the use of a computer for the keeping of registers, books of accounts and other records.

(*b*) By s.111 if the membership of the company exceeds 50, there must be an alphabetical index, unless the register itself is in the form of an index. However, this requisite can be dispensed with, in any case, by utilising the provisions of s.436 and keeping the register in looseleaf form, provided adequate precautions are taken to prevent fraud and falsification.

(*c*) Failure to take adequate precautions against fraud and falsification renders the company and every officer in default liable to fines; therefore, it is usual to take the necessary security measures, for example:

(*i*) Fitting the register with a suitable locking device, and placing the keys in the custody of a responsible officer of the company.

(*ii*) Keeping the register in a fireproof safe or strongroom, a precaution to be taken whatever form the register may take.

(*iii*) The issue of new sheets to be carefully supervised, preferably by the officer who has custody of the keys.

(*iv*) Duplicate keys may be deposited with the company's bank and instructions given to hand them over only against instructions of authorised signatories.

(*v*) The loose sheets for the register may be specially watermarked and printed with the company's name, for purposes of identification.

(*vi*) The sheets may also be consecutively numbered, so that closer records can be maintained of sheets issued.

(*vii*) No unauthorised persons will be given access to the register(s) or to the loose sheets for the register.

(*viii*) The microfilming of loose sheets in use at regular intervals is a useful additional safeguard against loss of the records by fire or any other risk.

3. Advantages of using a looseleaf register. Although a bound register may be quite adequate for, say, a small private company with few shareholders and little or no share transfer activity, larger companies will usually derive great advantage, apart from being able to dispense with an index.

The principal advantages are as follows.

(*a*) The register can be split up, for example, when preparing dividend lists or the annual return, to enable the Secretary or registrar to distribute the work more evenly among the available staff.

(*b*) The shareholders' accounts can be kept in strict alphabetical order and are, therefore, more easily located.

(*c*) Closed accounts can be withdrawn entirely, i.e. after a suitable interval the accounts of any persons who have ceased to be members can be withdrawn and subsequently filed away in a safe place (*see* 1 *above*).

(*d*) Accounts of new members are easily inserted in their proper alphabetical order.

(*e*) Inspection is facilitated. If a member or other person demands to inspect the register, the fact that it is in looseleaf form would give greater facility for inspection and, moreover, as it could be inspected in sections, registration work could still proceed on the other sections.

(*f*) Microfilming of sheets is simplified. If, as indicated above, it is desired to microfilm the particulars in the Register of Members at regular intervals, it is much simpler to do so from loose sheets rather than from a bound book.

4. Location: s.110(2).

(*a*) It must be kept at the registered office of the company, or at any office of the company (or its agent) at which it is written.

(*b*) It must, however, be kept within the company's domicile, i.e. within the country in which the company was registered.

(*c*) The index (if any) must be kept at the same place as the register.

5. Alterations.

(*a*) Any alteration to the register must also be made within 14 days in the index, if any: s.111.

(*b*) Great care is essential in making alterations in the register; for example:

(*i*) an entry to be cancelled must on no account be erased;

(*ii*) to cancel an item it should be neatly ruled out and the correction typed or written above or alongside the cancelled entry;

(*iii*) any alteration must be initialled by the person who makes the alteration.

6. Inspection. Provisions as to inspection and the taking of copies of the register are set out in s.113.

(*a*) The register (and index, if any) must be available for at least two hours each business day:

(*i*) for inspection by any member, free of charge; and

(*ii*) for inspection by any other person, on payment of 5p, or less if the company so decides.

The obligation imposed on a company by the Companies Acts

1948 to 1980 to allow inspection, or to furnish a copy (*see* (*d*) *below*) of any register or other record shall under s.3 of the Stock Exchange (Completion of Bargains) Act 1976 (*see* **2** *above*) be treated as a duty to allow inspection of, or to furnish, a reproduction of the recording or of the relevant part of it in legible form.

(*b*) If, however, the company gives notice of its intention to close the register (by advertisement in a newspaper circulating in the district in which the registered office is situated), the register may be closed for any time or times not exceeding on the whole thirty days in each year: s.115.

(*c*) The register may be closed, for example, when dividends are paid, or when bonus or rights issues are made to existing members. On the other hand, some companies prefer not to close the register in such cases and simply declare that the dividend shall be paid (or the bonus shares issued) to members on the register at a specified date.

(*d*) Any person may demand a copy of the register (or any part of it) at a charge of 10p per 100 words (or less, if the company so prescribes) and the copy must be sent to the person requiring it *within ten days* of receiving the request.

(*e*) Refusal to grant inspection or default in supplying copies on request:

(*i*) renders the company, and every officer in default, liable to fines; and

(*ii*) the Court may compel inspection and order that the required copies be sent.

(*f*) Inspection cannot be refused on the grounds that it is desired for purposes hostile to the company: *Davies* v. *Gas Light & Coke Co.* (1909).

(*g*) The right of inspection ceases when a company goes into liquidation—but the Court can order inspection by creditors and contributories: s.266.

7. Rectification.

(*a*) Section 116 gives the Court power to order rectification of the Register of Members:

(*i*) if a person who has not agreed to take shares is included in the register, e.g. where he has been induced to take shares by misrepresentation; or

(*ii*) if his name is omitted or wrongfully removed from the register, e.g. by reason of an invalid forfeiture or forged transfer; or

(*iii*) if there has been default or unnecessary delay in recording the fact that a person has ceased to be a member, e.g. the directors may delay unduly the registration of a transfer which they have no power to reject.

(*b*) Application to the Court for rectification may be made by the person aggrieved, any member of the company, or the company itself, according to the circumstances.

(*c*) The Court may refuse the application, or order the rectification and payment of damages by the company to the aggrieved party: *Alabaster's Case* (1868).

(*d*) The section is not exhaustive of the Court's powers of rectification: *Burns* v. *Siemens Bros. Dynamo Works Ltd.* (1918) (*see* **9** *below*).

> NOTE: The register is only *prima facie* evidence of matters which the Act requires to be entered in it, but those who apply for its rectification must bear in mind that the onus of proof lies with the person who contests its accuracy. If, therefore, a person allows his name to remain in the register, he may be held liable as a member.

8. Notices to the Registrar: s.110(3).

(*a*) If the Register of Members is kept elsewhere than at the company's registered office, notice in the prescribed form must be sent to the Registrar, stating *where* the register is kept. The notice must be given *within fourteen days*; thus notice of its location is not required so long as it is kept at the registered office, but if it is removed to another place the Registrar must be notified within fourteen days of the change. Any subsequent change of place must also be notified within fourteen days of the change (*see also* **19** *below*).

(*b*) The company and any officer in default are liable to fines for non-compliance with the above requirements: s.110(4).

9. Joint holders.

(*a*) The joint holder first named in the Register of Members is, according to the Articles of most companies, entitled to receive payment of dividend and to exercise voting rights of the joint holding. As a rule, notices will be sent to him as the "senior" joint holder.

(*b*) For that reason, joint holders have the right to determine in which order their names shall be entered in the register.

(*c*) Alternatively, they are entitled to require the company to split their holding, so that each joint holder becomes the first named in the register for a part of the holding: *Burns* v. *Siemens Bros. Dynamo Works Ltd.* (1918).

(*d*) A limit may be imposed by the Articles as to the number of persons who may be registered in respect of a joint holding.

10. What constitutes membership? Entry in the Register of Members is only *prima facie* evidence of membership. A person may become a member in the following ways.

(*a*) By subscribing to the Memorandum of Association. This, according to s. 26, is sufficient to indicate agreement to become a member. Neither allotment nor registration is necessary in this case: *Evans' Case* (1867).

(*b*) In other cases, a person becomes a member by:

(*i*) *agreement* to become a member; and

(*ii*) *entry* of his name in the Register of Members: s.26.

NOTE: A person improperly entered in the register may *constructively* agree to his name remaining there, by exercising the rights of a member; in that case he may be estopped from denying his membership.

11. Notice of trust.

(*a*) Section 117 provides that: "No notice of any trust, express, implied or constructive, shall be entered on the register, or be receivable by the Registrar, in the case of companies registered in England."

(*b*) A person entered in the Register of Members is the person legally entitled to deal with the shares, but some person or persons may possess an equitable or beneficial interest in them, e.g.:

(*i*) the registered member may have borrowed money from a banker, or other person, on the security of the shares; or

(*ii*) he may be merely a nominee of a person or persons entitled to the beneficial interest in the shares, e.g. the nominee of a limited company.

(*c*) However, by virtue of s.117, the company is unable to take notice of these outside interests, and is entitled to regard the person named in the register as the beneficial owner of the shares in his name, even if he gives notice that some other person has a lien on, or equitable interest in, the shares concerned.

NOTE: A company is, nevertheless, bound to accept certain documents, such as probate of a will, as sufficient evidence of a legal representative's powers to deal with shares: s.82.

(*d*) On receipt of a "notice of trust", the usual procedure is as follows.

(*i*) Write a letter in reply, stating that the company is unable to recognise the trust or to act upon it in any way. The notice may be returned with this letter, which ought to be sent by registered post or recorded delivery, to the person submitting the notice.

(*ii*) Keep an unofficial record of the contents of the notice, but not in the Register of Members.

NOTE: Although s.117 enables the company to treat the registered holder of shares as the beneficial owner, it cannot ignore the notice as regards fixing priorities in respect of a lien: *Bradford Banking Co.* v. *Briggs* (1886). An unofficial note will warn the company that notice of a lien has been received which will, should the occasion arise, have priority over their own lien on the shares concerned.

12. Stop notice.

(*a*) Although, as stated above, a company cannot recognise notice of a trust, under the Charging Orders Act 1979, s.5, and the Rules of the Supreme Court, Order 50, Rules 11–14, any person claiming to be beneficially interested in shares of a company who wishes to be notified of any proposed transfer of those shares may serve a stop notice on the company.

(*b*) To obtain such the person concerned must file with the Central Office of the Supreme Court (or a district registry) an affidavit identifying the shares in question and describing his interest in them together with the notice, being served. The copy of the notice served on the company must be sealed with the seal of the Central Office (or district registry) and must be accompanied by an office copy of the affidavit.

(*c*) On receipt of such notice, the company is restrained from accepting any transfer of the shares included in the notice for a period of fourteen days after giving notice of lodgment of the transfer to the person indicated in the notice as having an interest in the shares.

(*d*) During the fourteen-day period, the interested party must take whatever steps are necessary to prevent the company from accepting a transfer of the shares.

(*e*) If, after fourteen days, no further instructions have been received by the company, it can then proceed to register the transfer of the shares affected.

13. Designated accounts.

(*a*) The increasing amount of work done by banks and insurance companies as executors and trustees in recent years, has resulted in a corresponding increase in the number of requests which company registrars receive to open "designated accounts", e.g. a banking company acting as trustees for many persons may ask to have several accounts opened in its name, so that the separate holdings of its clients can be easily distinguished by letter or number.

(*b*) Some companies refuse to permit designation of accounts, as they consider that in acting upon such instructions they would be taking notice of a trust, contrary to the requirements of s.117 of the Act.

(*c*) It appears to have been unofficially established that the designation or "earmarking" of accounts does not of itself constitute notice of a trust. Nevertheless, it has been suggested that companies acting upon instructions to designate accounts might protect themselves by:

(*i*) reserving the right to treat all the designated accounts as one account if at any time they should think fit to do so; and

(*ii*) making it clear to the sender of the notice that they are *not* recognising a trust.

(*d*) Despite such precautions, the method used to designate accounts in the Register of Members also requires careful consideration.

(*e*) The Stock Exchange listing agreement requires listed companies to permit members to have designated accounts.

THE DOMINION REGISTER

14. What companies may keep a Dominion Register? Section 119 permits the keeping of a Dominion (or Branch) Register by any company:

(*a*) having a share capital; and

(*b*) whose objects authorise the transaction of business in the British dominions outside Great Britain, the Channel Islands or the Isle of Man.

It should be noted that the Act does *not* compel a company to keep a Dominion Register.

15. Provisions. If a Dominion Register is kept, it is subject to the following regulations, which are set out in ss.119 and 120.

(*a*) *Form.* It must be kept in the same manner as the principal register, of which it is deemed to be part.

(*b*) *Contents, inspection and taking of copies.* In these respects too, it is subject to the same regulations as the principal register.

(*c*) *Situation*. Notice in the prescribed form must be given to the Registrar within fourteen days of:

(*i*) the situation of the office in which it is kept;

(*ii*) any change of its situation;

(*iii*) discontinuance of the office.

(*d*) *Notice of closing* the Dominion Register must be advertised in the district of the dominion in which it is kept.

(*e*) *Rectification* of the register may be ordered by any competent court in that part of HM dominions in which the register is kept.

(*f*) *A duplicate* of the Dominion Register must be kept at the place where the company's principal register is kept.

(*g*) *A copy of every entry* in the Dominion Register must be sent as soon as possible to the company's registered office for entry in the principal register.

NOTE: In practice, entries for the principal register are notified on transmission sheets, and the duplicate register reconciled with the Dominion Register at regular intervals.

(*h*) *Distinguishing prefix*. Shares in a Dominion (or Branch) Register must be distinguished from those in the principal register. For this purpose, a distinctive prefix to the serial number of share certificates may be used on all certificates issued by the dominion office.

(*i*) *Discontinuance*. If a Dominion Register is discontinued, the shares hitherto registered in it must be transferred either to some other Dominion Register in the same part of HM dominions or to the principal register.

16. Other provisions. So long as the above regulations are complied with, a company may include any other provisoins in its Articles with regard to the keeping of a Dominion Register, e.g. members may be given the right to transfer to a Dominion Register and to re-transfer back to the principal register, on request in writing.

17. The advantages of opening a Dominion Register.

(*a*) Shareholders resident in the dominion concerned are able to register transfers locally, and thus avoid much of the delay involved if transfers had to be sent to the company's registered office in the United Kingdom.

(*b*) Dividends may also be paid from the dominion office, and earlier payment is ensured.

(*c*) Transfers registered and executed in the dominion concerned are exempt from UK transfer duty. Dominion shareholders may, therefore, benefit by a saving in transfer duty.

(*d*) The above factors make the shares more attractive—at least to shareholders in the dominion concerned—and that is an advantage to the company itself, particularly when it requires more capital.

18. Transfer of shares to a Dominion Register. When a shareholder who is already entered in the principal register wishes to transfer his holding to the company's Dominion Register, the usual procedure is as follows.

(*a*) A request in writing is usually required by the Articles. This should be lodged at the company's registered office, together with his share certificate(s).

(*b*) The share certificate(s) are cancelled and carefully filed; a note to this effect is made in the principal register.

(*c*) A Dominion (or Branch) Removal Receipt is then sent to the shareholder by way of receipt for the certificate(s) he has lodged with the company.

(*d*) The shareholder will receive a Dominion (or Branch) Share Certificate on producing his removal receipt at the branch office in the dominion.

NOTE: The share certificate he receives will probably be of distinctive design and (if the Articles permit) may bear the company's official seal. As already indicated, the shares must, in any case, be distinguished from those registered in the principal register: s.120.

(*e*) The necessary entry is made in the Dominion Register from particulars on the removal receipt.

(*f*) Notice of the entry is recorded on a Transmission Sheet containing particulars of all transfers to the Dominion Register over, say, one month. At the end of the month the Transmission Sheet will be sent to the registered office and the transfer particulars recorded in the duplicate register.

THE ANNUAL RETURN

19. Annual Return to be made by a company *having* a share capital: s.124.

(*a*) *When it must be made.* Every company having a share capital must make an Annual Return once at least in every year (that is, calendar year and not financial year); *except* that a return need not be made:

(*i*) in the year of its incorporation; nor

(*ii*) in the following year (if the company is excused under the provisions of s.131 from holding an annual general meeting in that year).

(*b*) *Contents*. These are prescribed in the Sixth Schedule to the Act:

(*i*) address of the registered office;

(*ii*) situation of Register of Members and Register of Debenture Holders (if any), if not kept at the registered office;

(*iii*) summary of share capital and debentures, giving particulars of:

(1) *nominal* share capital;

(2) *issued* share capital and debentures;

(*iv*) particulars of indebtedness, giving the total amount of indebtedness in respect of all mortgages and charges requiring registration under the Act;

(*v*) list of past and present members, giving:

(1) a list of names and addresses of members, as at the fourteenth day after the date of the annual general meeting;

(2) a list of persons who have ceased to be members since the date of the last return or, where applicable, since incorporation;

(3) the number of shares held by each existing member at the date of the return;

(4) the number of shares transferred since the date of the last return (or incorporation) by persons who are still members and by persons who have ceased to be members; also the date of registration of transfer in each case;

(*vi*) particulars of directors and secretaries; that is, of those persons occupying the respective positions at the date of the return.

(*c*) *Further provisions* affecting a company having a share capital are as follows.

(*i*) Where any of the company's shares have been converted into stock, particulars required in the List of Members will relate to stock instead of shares.

(*ii*) If full particulars of members and their holdings have been given in one year, it will only be necessary to include in the next two returns the required particulars relating to persons who have ceased to be members or become members since the last return, and of shares transferred since that date.

(*iii*) If particulars from a Dominion Register are received at a company's registered office after the Annual Return has been made, such particulars must be included in the next or a subsequent annual return.

20. Annual Return to be made by a company _not_ having a share capital: s.125.

(*a*) *Requirements.* Every company not having a share capital must make an Annual Return once at least in every calendar year, but subject to the same exceptions as those applied to a company having share capital.

(*b*) *Contents:*

(*i*) address of the registered office;

(*ii*) the situation of the Register of Members and Register of Debenture Holders (if any), if not kept at the registered office;

(*iii*) particulars of directors and secretaries; i.e. of those persons occupying the respective positions at date of the return.

NOTE: Particulars of indebtedness are also required but in the form of a statement annexed to the Annual Return.

21. Time for completion of the Annual Return: s.126.

(*a*) The Annual Return must be completed within 42 days after the annual general meeting for the year.

(*b*) A copy of the Annual Return, signed both by a director and by the Secretary, must be sent forthwith to the Registrar.

22. Registration fee.

The fee payable on registration of an annual return is £20.

PROGRESS TEST 6

1. Enumerate the main requirements of the Act as to the contents of a Register of Members. Is it permissible to use a looseleaf register? If so, what precautions are necessary, and why?   (**1, 2**)

2. What are the provisions of the Act in regard to the form of the Register of Members? What are the advantages of using a looseleaf register?   (**2, 3**)

3. State briefly the Act's requirements concerning (*a*) location of the Register of Members, (*b*) right of inspection and the taking of copies, and (*c*) the company's power to close it.   (**4–6**)

4. What practical difficulties might the secretary of a large public

company encounter in affording inspection of the Register of Members and providing copies of its contents, in accordance with statutory requirements? (6)

5. You have been appointed secretary of a company shortly after incorporation and subsequent to the allotment of 100,000 shares of £1 each. All transactions have been properly carried out and recorded, except that the Register of Members has not been opened. Explain the steps you would take to open the Register and bring the entries up-to-date. (1–4; 8)

6. In what different ways can a person become a member of a company, and with what documents is the secretary concerned in each case? (10)

7. The Act states that no notice of any trust shall be entered on the Register of Members. What is the purpose and effect of this statement? As secretary of a company receiving such a notice, what steps would you take, and why? (11)

8. Describe the various precautions normally taken in a registrar's office to minimise the risk of a company being affected by notice of a trust. (11–13)

9. Draft a report to your board, setting out the advantages to the company and members concerned of opening a Dominion Register, explaining the statutory requirements, and recommending a procedure for satisfying them. (14–18)

10. Set out briefly the contents of an annual return. What would you do if the Accounts were not ready by the latest date for holding the annual general meeting? *ICSA* (19–21, 24)

CHAPTER VII

Share Certificates

LEGAL EFFECTS

1. Definition. A share certificate is a document bearing the common seal of the company and which, when issued to a member, indicates the extent of his interest in the company's capital.

2. Effect of certificate. A certificate under the common seal or securities seal of a company is only *prima facie* evidence of title (s.81, as amended by s.2(3) of the Stock Exchange (Completion of Bargains) Act 1976), that is, the holder is *not* given an absolute title to the shares included in the certificate.

Nevertheless, at common law, a company is estopped from denying the validity of a certificate issued under seal both as to the *title* of the holder and as to the *amount paid* on the shares, e.g.:

(*a*) a company will be liable to any person who, in good faith, suffers loss through relying on the certificate, where the company has denied that he is the registered holder: *Balkis Consolidated Co. v. Tomkinson* (1893);

(*b*) where the company has denied that shares included in a certificate are fully paid: *Bloomenthal v. Ford* (1897).

3. Holder's remedies. The holder's remedy in such cases is to sue the company for damages; i.e. for the value of the shares at the date of the breach. He is *not* entitled to the shares, as the true owner cannot be deprived of them; nor can he compel the company to enter his name in the Register of Members.

4. Where estoppel does not operate. The holder's right of estoppel against the company is lost in the following circumstances.

(*a*) If the certificate upon which the holder relied had been issued fraudulently and without the company's authority: *South London Greyhound Racecourses v. Wake* (1931).

(*b*) Where the the certificate issued was a forgery: *Ruben v. Great Fingall Consolidated* (1906).

(*c*) Where it can be shown that the holder knows that the amount stated on the certificate as paid has not in fact been paid.

NOTE: The right of estoppel is also lost where a person has not relied upon the certificate; if, for example, he had not required the transferor to produce a certificate.

PREPARATION AND ISSUE

5. Preparation. In preparing share certificates, the following matters must be borne in mind as regards their form and contents.

(*a*) *Form.* The form of the certificate may vary, but approval of the stock exchange must be obtained if the shares are "listed" (*see* (*f*) *below*).

(*b*) *Distinguishing types.* Certificates covering different classes of shares are often distinguished by the use of different styles or colours. The form may also vary according to whether the shares are fully or partly paid, the latter usually having space on the back of the certificate in which to record payments of calls.

(*c*) *Book form or loose?* Certificates printed in book form are still favoured by some companies. When this method is used the certificates are in three parts, comprising the counterfoil (which remains in the book), certificate, and receipt of the certificate. For a small company, this method will probably prove quite adequate but larger companies—particularly those which are highly mechanised—will probably prefer certificates on loose forms, so that several members of the staff can enter particulars on the certificates simultaneously from the Register of Members or direct from the Allotment Sheets.

(*d*) *When under seal.* Share certificates must, by implication, be under seal of the company, s.81 stating that "a certificate under seal shall be *prima facie* evidence of title". In the case of listed shares, stock exchange regulations expressly provide that share certificates *must* be under seal but a company is permitted to have an official seal for sealing securities issued by the company, and for creating or evidencing securities so issued. This must be a facsimile of the common seal with the addition on its face of the word "Securities": Stock Exchange (Completion of Bargains) Act 1976, s.2 (*see* V, 11).

(*e*) *Contents.* The share certificates of most companies follow a similar pattern, and the following contents are common to most:

(*i*) name of the company;

(*ii*) act under which the company was incorporated;

(*iii*) authorised capital and its division into shares;

(*iv*) class of shares to which the certificate relates;

(*v*) number of shares included in the certificate;

(*vi*) distinctive numbers of the shares, unless dispensed with under s.74;

(*vii*) name and address of the holder and a statement that he (or she) holds the shares subject to the company's Memorandum and Articles;

(*viii*) notice to the effect that no transfer of the shares can be registered unless accompanied by the certificate;

(*ix*) signature (as required by the Articles) and seal.

(*f*) *Stock exchange requirements.* The principal stock exchange regulations affecting contents of share certificates are as follows.

(*i*) The authority under which the company is constituted must be stated.

(*ii*) The authorised capital and the nominal amount and denomination of each class (if there is more than one class of shares) must also be stated.

(*iii*) Conditions as to capital, dividends and redemption (if any) under which the security is issued must be stated (preferably on the face of the certificate) if it represents a preference security, such as preference shares and redeemable preference shares.

(*iv*) The number of shares the certificate represents, or if an application is to be made to deal in units of stock the amount of stock and the number and denomination of the units, must be stated in the top right-hand corner of the stock certificates.

(*v*) The minimum amount and multiples thereof in which the stock is transferable must be stated (where applicable) on the face of the stock certificate.

(*vi*) A notice that no transfer of the security can be registered without production of the certificate must appear as a footnote.

(*vii*) The company's seal must be affixed under authority of the directors (but *see* **5**(*d*) *above*), and the certificate must be dated. Further, and with the aim of achieving standardisation, the overall size of a certificate should not exceed 225 mm × 200 mm.

(*g*) *Mechanical signatures on share certificates.* Because of the considerable time involved in autographic signing of share certificates by the directors and secretaries of large companies, many of them use mechanical signatures in place of the autographic signatures of directors; others have dispensed entirely with signatures on share certificates.

(*h*) In order to facilitate the operation of the TALISMAN

settlement system (*see* VIII, **4**), s.1 of the Stock Exchange (Completion of Bargains) Act 1976 provides that a company is exempted from the obligation imposed by s.81(1) of the 1948 Act to prepare certificates in consequence of shares, debentures or debenture stock allotted or transferred to a stock nominee.

6. Issue of certificates. The preparation and issue of share certificates following a *transfer* of shares is dealt with in VIII, **4, 5** and **6**. At this stage it is intended to deal with matters affecting the issue of certificates by a company following the usual application and allotment procedure already described in III, **1–16**.

(*a*) *The first certificate* is usually given free of charge to every member whose name is entered in the Register of Members. Table A entitles a member to one free certificate for *all* his shares, with the proviso that if he requires more than one, each certificate after the first will cost him $12\frac{1}{2}$p, or less if the directors so determine: Article 8.

NOTE: The stock exchange regulations forbid any charge for a first share certificate, but permit a charge not exceeding 5p for a replacement.

(*b*) *Time limit for delivery*. It should be borne in mind that certificates must be ready for delivery:

(*i*) *within two months* after the shares have been allotted, unless the conditions of issue otherwise provide: s.80; or

(*ii*) *within one month* after the expiration of the renunciation period, in the case of certificates covering shares which are listed on the stock exchange.

NOTE: For non-compliance with s.80, the Court may, on application of the person entitled to the certificate, direct the company and any officer of the company to make good the default within a specified time. It may also order that the costs of the application be borne by the company and any officer responsible.

(*c*) *After the expiration of the renunciation period*, and assuming that allotment letters and bankers' receipts for the allotment money have been received either from original allottees or their accepting nominees, the Register of Members is written up and, unless the conditions provide to the contrary (e.g. if further calls or instalments are to be paid on the shares, certificates may not be issued until the shares are fully paid) share certificates are prepared.

(*d*) *Checking the certificates*. After preparation of the certificates, they should be thoroughly checked by the company's auditors, or, if possible, by responsible officials of the company who have played no part in preparing the certificates.

NOTE: As the company is estopped from denying that the person named in a share certificate is the legal owner of the shares to which it refers, and as to the amount paid up on them, great care must be exercised in preparing all share certificates.

(e) *Authorisation by the board*. At a board meeting especially convened for the purpose, the share certificates (perhaps supported by a report in which the auditors vouch for the accuracy of the documents) are submitted to the board by the Secretary. The board then authorise the signing and sealing of the certificates in the words of a resolution such as the following:

RESOLVED: That share certificates, numbered .... to ...... both inclusive, in respect of .... ordinary shares of £1 each, allotted by resolution of the Board dated .... be sealed under the common seal of the Company and signed by .... and .... and counter-signed by the Secretary.

NOTE: The wording of the resolution must, of course, depend upon the degree of relaxation permitted by the stock exchange (in the case of listed shares) as regards directors' and Secretary's signatures.

(f) *Recording the resolution*. After the certificates have been signed and sealed, the resolution is recorded in the minute book of board meetings, and an entry made in the Register of Sealed Documents.

(g) *Final steps*. The certificates can now be prepared for posting and a final check made by a responsible official before posting. When they are posted, it is advisable to send them by registered post or recorded delivery.

NOTE: In some cases, the company advises the shareholders when certificates are ready, stating that the documents may be collected at the company's registered office in exchange for the allotment letter and receipt for the allotment money.

Another alternative is to write to the shareholders, informing them that their certificates will be posted to them on receipt of their written requests to do so. In that way the company puts the onus upon the shareholder in the event of his certificate going astray after posting.

(h) *Receipts*. Whichever method is used, i.e. whether the certificates are sent through the post or collected by the shareholders, a receipt for the certificate should be asked for, and this should bear the usual signature of the shareholder. In this way the company ensures that it has a specimen of each shareholder's signature.

7. Lost certificates.

(*a*) A duplicate share certificate must not be issued without taking adequate precautions. Companies frequently receive requests for replacement of certificates which have been lost, destroyed or mislaid; therefore, the Articles usually give the directors the necessary power to protect the company against any loss it may incur by reason of its issuing a replacement certificate.

(*i*) The company may require the shareholder to make a *statutory declaration* that he has lost the certificate and the circumstances of the loss.

(*ii*) *A letter of indemnity* may be demanded from the shareholder in which he undertakes to compensate the company for any loss it may suffer as the result of the issue of a duplicate certificate.

(*iii*) *A guarantee* given by a bank or person of sound financial standing may be accepted by the directors as an alternative, or in addition to, a letter of indemnity.

NOTE: Table A permits the directors to require evidence, indemnity and the payment of the company's out-of-pocket expenses: Article 9.

(*b*) A further precaution that may be taken before issuing a replacement certificate is to examine the Register of Members and ensure that no "stop notice" has been received in respect of the shares concerned. It has been known for a shareholder to deposit the original certificate by way of security for a loan, and then make a fraudulent attempt to obtain a duplicate.

(*c*) If a duplicate certificate is issued, it should be marked conspicuously with the word DUPLICATE across the face of the certificate, preferably in a distinctive colour or spelt out by perforation.

(*d*) Note of the loss and issue of a duplicate certificate should then be made against the shareholder's name in the Register of Members. If the member himself, or some unauthorised person, presents the original certificate at some later date, the entry in the Register will draw attention to the loss. In that event, an explanation would be demanded and transfer of the shares permitted only on production of the duplicate certificate.

(*e*) A charge is usually made for a duplicate certificate. As already stated in this chapter, Table A permits a charge of $12\frac{1}{2}$p for renewal of a certificate, but the directors may charge less, if they think fit. Stock exchange regulations permit a maximum charge of only 5p.

8. Damaged, worn or mutilated certificates. In cases where a certificate has been damaged, badly worn or mutilated, any request for replacement must be accompanied by the original certificate, if possible; if it is not produced when the original request is made, the shareholder must be asked to surrender it, after which the necessary procedure may be followed.

(*a*) If the certificate is badly damaged or mutilated it must be thoroughly examined and identified. If it is not identifiable as a share certificate, or if there is any doubt, it may be decided to treat it as though it were a "lost" certificate and to require a letter of indemnity from the shareholder.

(*b*) In any case, when a duplicate certificate has been prepared, the original must be clearly marked CANCELLED across its face, and then carefully filed.

NOTE: If the mutilated condition of the "document" will not permit this treatment, the only alternative is to place what remains of the document in a suitable envelope and (having stated on the outside of the envelope what it contains) keep it in a safe place pending any later developments.

(*c*) The issue of the duplicate certificate must then be recorded in the Register of Members, and the duplicate sent to the member on receipt of evidence (where necessary), letter of indemnity and/or letter of guarantee, and of any charge for the replacement certificate permitted by the Articles.

SHARE WARRANTS

9. Authority to issue share warrants.

(*a*) A company limited by shares may issue share warrants under its common seal:
　　(*i*) if authorised to do so by its Articles, and
　　(*ii*) only in respect of fully paid shares: s.83.

10. Principal features of a share warrant.

(*a*) It must be issued under common seal of the company.

(*b*) It states that the bearer is entitled to certain fully paid shares in the company named in the warrant.

(*c*) It is a negotiable instrument; that is, it is transferable by mere delivery, so that anyone who takes it in good faith and for value acquires a good title to it, even if he received it from someone who had no title to it.

NOTE: Because of its intrinsic value as a negotiable instrument the warrant itself must be made as proof against forgery as possible. In the case of a listed company the Stock Exchange regulations require its submission and approval at proof stage and provide that its printing must be undertaken by recognised security printers on first-class bond or banknote paper, having a watermark of the printer, the company or the issuing house. Further, each series must be clearly numbered sequentially.

(*d*) It may be issued with coupons attached, by means of which the holder is able to claim any dividend to which he is entitled.

(*e*) It must be stamped at the time of issue, the stamp duty being based upon the *market* value of the shares included in the warrant. (As the transfer of a warrant is free of stamp duty, the duty payable at issue is three times the *ad valorem* duty which would be payable on a transfer of the shares at their market value.) In the case of a share warrant the payment of the duty is not indicated by an impressed stamp, but by a "denoting" or adjudication stamp.

11. Issue procedure.

(*a*) If the Articles do not authorise the issue of share warrants, they must be altered by special resolution to give the necessary authority. (It is, of course, being assumed that the company concerned is one permitted to issue share warrants under s.83, and that the shares to be included are fully paid).

(*b*) Printed application forms are made available to all shareholders affected, on which they are entitled to apply for share warrant(s) in exchange for share certificate(s).

(*c*) On receipt of application forms:

(*i*) ensure that they are fully completed;

(*ii*) see that they are accompanied by the share certificate(s) and a remittance to cover stamp duty plus any small fee charged by the company;

(*iii*) check the particulars against the Register of Members;

(*iv*) issue a carefully worded receipt to the applicant, signifying that the receipt must be produced on or after a specified date in exchange for the "document(s)" for which he has applied—without specifying the nature of the documents.

(*d*) Having arranged for the printing of share warrants in fixed denominations of (say) 1, 5, 10, 25, etc.:

(*i*) select warrants of the denominations applied for, and present them for stamping at the Inland Revenue office, as they must be stamped *before* being completed and signed;

(*ii*) complete the warrants, i.e. other than signing and sealing;

(*iii*) cancel the relative share certificate(s);

(*iv*) strike the member's name out of the Register of Members and enter the following particulars:

(1) a statement that the warrant has been issued;

(2) the date of the issue;

(3) particulars of shares included in the warrant, with distinguishing numbers (if any), as required by s.112;

(*v*) record the exchange of share warrants for share certificates in a separate register kept for that purpose;

(*vi*) write up the Share Warrants Register (or Registers). A separate book, or part of the Register, is usually kept for *each* denomination of share warrant, so that a separate record can be kept of stock and issues of all warrants for (say) five shares; another for ten-share warrants, and so on.

NOTE: Obviously, great care must be taken in the preparation and issue of the warrants, as they are negotiable instruments; for example, the printers may be required to certify that they have printed only the exact number ordered, and all unused forms ought to be securely locked away and issued only by a responsible official (*see* **10** *above*).

(*e*) A thorough check of the warrants can now be made and the particulars on the warrants reconciled with entries in the Registers already mentioned. If this work is done by the company's own registration department staff, it must obviously be done by persons who had no part in preparing the warrants. In most cases, however, the checking of warrants is done by the company's internal audit staff or by the transfer auditors, in which event they will prepare an audit certificate if they find everything in order.

(*f*) At a meeting of the board the completed warrants are produced, supported (where applicable) by the audit certificate, and a resolution passed, authorising the signing, sealing and issue of the share warrants.

(*g*) The warrants are signed and sealed, and appropriate entries made in the minute book of board meetings and in the Register of Documents Sealed.

(*h*) Finally, the share warrants are issued in exchange for the appropriate receipts. It must, however, be borne in mind that in the case of a listed company the warrants ought to be ready for issue within fourteen days of deposit of the share certificates in order to comply with stock exchange regulations.

12. The effects of issuing share warrants.

(*a*) Unless the Articles so provide, the holder of a share warrant is no longer a member of the company, as his name does not appear in the Register of Members: s. 112(5).

(*b*) In most cases the Articles, supported by the conditions of issue, give him most, if not all, the normal rights of a member; for example:

(*i*) on deposit of his share warrant at the registered office of the company, he may be entitled:

(1) to sign a requisition for calling a meeting or give notice of intention to submit a resolution to a meeting; or

(2) to attend and vote in person or by proxy, and to exercise any other privilege of a member at a meeting;

(*ii*) on delivering up a "coupon" (detachable from the warrant by perforation) bearing the appropriate serial number, in accordance with instructions published in one or more specified newspapers, he will be entitled to receive the dividend payable on the shares specified in his share warrant;

NOTE: An additional coupon, usually referred to as a "talon", can be detached from the warrant and exchanged for a new set of coupons for dividend as and when required.

(*iii*) on surrendering his share warrant to the company for cancellation, to have his name entered as a member in the Register of Members;

NOTE: He has a statutory right to do this, subject to the Articles: s.112(2).

(*iv*) on application, he may be able to arrange for the company to furnish him with a copy of the annual reports and accounts at a specified address.

(*c*) The holding of a share warrant is not sufficient qualification to allow the holder to act as a director, where a share qualification is required by the Articles: s.182(2).

13. Lost share warrants.

(*a*) The Articles and/or conditions of issue of the warrants usually authorise the directors to issue a new warrant to replace one which has been lost or destroyed, if satisfactory evidence and adequate indemnity are provided.

(*b*) Some or all of the following precautions are usually taken to safeguard the company:

(*i*) to insist that the applicant advertises his loss and offers a reward;

(*ii*) to demand proof of loss or destruction (this is, in fact, a stock exchange requirement);

(*iii*) to require a statutory declaration from the applicant as to the circumstances of the loss (or evidence of destruction) and as to his title to the shares included in the warrant;

(*iv*) to demand a substantial guarantee and/or letter of indemnity.

(*c*) If a share warrant or dividend coupon is destroyed or defaced, the directors must insist upon surrender of the document for cancellation.

(*d*) The applicant must also pay the necessary stamp duty in respect of the new warrant, and any fee which the company normally charges for a replacement.

14. Surrender of share warrants for share certificates. The procedure is as follows.

(*a*) On receipt of the prescribed form of request for reconversion together with the share warrant and registration fee:

(*i*) issue a transfer receipt to the applicant;

(*ii*) check particulars of the documents against the Register of Share Warrants;

(*iii*) record the exchange of share certificates for share warrants in a separate register kept for that purpose;

(*iv*) write up the Share Warrants Register, noting the fact that the warrants have been surrendered;

(*v*) cancel the share warrant(s) surrendered and file them;

(*vi*) prepare the new share certificate in favour of the applicant. Check thoroughly.

(*b*) At a meeting of the board (or transfer committee), the share certificates are produced, supported (where applicable) by an audit certificate, and a resolution is passed, authorising the signing, sealing and issue of the share certificates.

NOTE: The board or transfer committee will deal with the certificates as for ordinary transfer procedure.

(c) The share certificates are signed and sealed, and appropriate entries made in the minute book of board meetings, and in the Register of Documents Sealed.

(d) The Register of Members is amended to restore the applicant's name.

(e) Finally, the share certificate(s) are issued in return for the transfer receipt.

PROGRESS TEST 7

1. Define a share certificate. Explain its functions, and mention any statutory provisions affecting it.   (**1, 2**)

2. Discuss the legal effect of a share certificate and explain the doctrine of estoppel in relation to that document. In what circumstances might the right of estoppel be lost?   (**2–4**)

3. What are the usual contents of a share certificate? To what extent might the transferability of the shares be affected by the contents of the certificate?   (**5**)

4. The stock exchange regulations permit the use of mechanical signatures on share certificates as an alternative to the autographic signatures of directors. Under what conditions is the alternative form of signature permitted? Draft a specimen article authorising the use of mechanical signatures.   (**5**)

5. What particulars must be given on documents of title of a company with stock exchange listing? *ICSA*   (**5**)

6. Describe the preparation and issue of a share certificate.   (**5, 6**)

7. Suggest a procedure to be adopted for dealing with requests from shareholders for the replacement of lost or damaged share certificates.   (**7, 8**)

8. What are the principal features of a share warrant? In what circumstances, and by what authority, is a company permitted to issue share warrants?   (**9, 10**)

9. Enumerate the advantages and disadvantages of a share warrant. What are the respective purposes of (a) a "coupon", and (b) a "talon", when used in connection with a share warrant?   (**10, 12**)

10. Describe fully the methods by which a person may become a member of a company. Is the holder of a share warrant to bearer a

member of the company which has issued it? Give reasons for your answer.   (VI, **10**; VII, **12**)

11. Write full notes on (*a*) placing of shares, and (*b*) share warrants. *ICSA*   (III, **1–20, 25–31, 34–36**; VII, **9–14**)

CHAPTER VIII

Transfer and Transmission of Shares

TRANSFER OF SHARES

1. Form of transfer.

(*a*) Section 73 provides that shares (or any other interest of any member in a company) are personal estate, as distinct from real estate, and transferable in manner provided by the Articles.

(*b*) The Stock Transfer Act 1963 has made radical changes in the form and contents of a transfer instrument and, despite the provisions of s.73 (referred to above), overrides any special provisions contained in the Articles governing the form in which securities subject to the Act are to be transferred, including (*inter alia*) *fully paid up* registered securities issued "by any company within the meaning of the Companies Act 1948, except a company limited by guarantee or an unlimited company": s.1(4), Stock Transfer Act 1963.

(*c*) It is unlawful to register a transfer of shares (or debentures) unless a proper instrument of transfer is delivered to the company: s.75 (*see Re Greene* (1949)).

(*d*) Section 6 of the Stock Exchange (Completion of Bargains) Act 1976 has extended the powers of the Treasury under s.3 of the Stock Transfer Act 1963, to prescribe alternative stock transfer forms, and thus enabled the Treasury to prescribe new transfer forms to meet the requirements of the Stock Exchange TALISMAN settlement system. The "TALISMAN sold transfer", as it is designated, is based on the usual stock transfer form though in a more computer-orientated format, with the name of the designated stock exchange nominee, SEPON Ltd, preprinted as the transferee.

2. Right of transfer.

(*a*) Shareholders have a *prima facie* right to transfer their shares to whomsoever they please, even to a pauper: *De Pass's Case* (1859). But the company's regulations may give the directors the power to restrict a member's right of transfer.

(*b*) Private companies may, by their Articles, restrict the right of transfer, but are no longer compelled to do so as Part II of Table A and s.28 of the 1948 Act were repealed by the Companies Act 1980.

(c) Notice of refusal to register a transfer must be given to the transferee within two months after lodgment of the transfer: s.78.

(d) Table A provides that the directors may decline to register a transfer of *partly paid* shares to a person of whom they do not approve. They also have power to decline registration of a transfer of shares on which the company has a lien: Article 24.

(e) In the case of listed shares, i.e. where stock exchange regulations apply, the power of refusal to register a transfer must be restricted to *partly paid* shares.

(f) The power of refusal to register a transfer must be exercised by the directors in the interests of the company. Any abuse of this power may justify rectification of the register by the Court, e.g. on proof of bad faith on the part of the directors: *Smith* v. *Fawcett Ltd.* (1942).

(g) The directors' refusal to register a transfer does not affect the contract between transferor and transferee, unless there was agreement between them to that effect. The transferor remains as registered holder of the shares, and will hold them "in trust" for the transferee.

(h) Power of refusal in the Articles does not extend to letters of renunciation, nor does it apply to letters of request submitted by executors and administrators. These are not "transfers" within the meaning of the Act; if, therefore, the power of refusal is to be extended to them, there must be special provision to that effect in the company's Articles.

3. Transfer procedure. Although the Secretary (or his registrar) is not concerned with transfers of his company's shares until the transfer forms are actually received in the registration department, it might be well to give a brief outline of the procedure which has already taken place on the stock exchange and in the brokers' office.

(a) A shareholder wishing to sell instructs his broker—a member of the stock exchange concerned—to get a quotation for his shares, or he may give instructions to sell so long as he can obtain a specified minimum price.

(b) The broker then acts as "middleman" between his client and a jobber (or dealer), who specialises in a particular "market", such as oil shares or industrial shares, and actually operates on the floor of the stock exchange.

(c) Having obtained a quotation from the jobber which appears to be a fair one (and not less than the minimum price which his client may have specified), the broker will either sell or report back to his client for further instructions.

(*d*) The deal between jobber and broker having been completed, each makes a brief note of the transaction in his notebook. However, as stock exchange transactions are settled at fortnightly intervals—on "account days"—the shares in the transaction just described may be bought and sold several times between the date of the original purchase and the next account day.

(*e*) All of these intermediate transactions are processed within the clearing department of the stock exchange, using the new TALISMAN settlement system which came into operation in 1979, and, finally, the seller's broker is advised of the name and address of the last purchaser.

(*f*) The seller's broker is then in a position to prepare a form of transfer, ready for his client's signature, if required.

NOTE: The form of transfer required to be completed at this stage is referred to in the Stock Transfer Act 1963, as a *Stock Transfer Form* although a subsidiary form (a Broker's Transfer Form) may also be required (*see* 6).

(*g*) After the seller (who will now be referred to as the transferor) has signed the Stock Transfer Form, his broker places his own stamp and date on the form (in a "box" beside the transferor's signature) and then has it stamped by the Inland Revenue for the appropriate transfer duty.

(*h*) The Stock Transfer Form, together with the relevant share certificate, is now passed to the purchaser's broker.

NOTE: It is being assumed that the *whole* of the shares included in the certificate are being transferred to a *single* buyer, otherwise a more complicated procedure becomes necessary.

(*i*) The purchaser's (transferee's) broker places his stamp on the Stock Transfer Form in the place provided and sends the form, now fully completed, together with the share certificate, to the company for registration.

NOTE: It will be noted that the Stock Transfer Act 1963 has removed the need for the transferee's signature on the transfer instrument, i.e. in those cases to which the Act applies.

4. The TALISMAN settlement system.

(*a*) In the mid-1970s the Stock Exchange decided to introduce a computerised settlement system to replace the then existing ticket system. The new system, Transfer Accounting, Lodgement for Investors, and Stock Management for Jobbers, termed by the abbreviation TALISMAN, provides for all market transactions in the securities of companies to be executed through the agency of a Stock Exchange "pool" account. Towards this end a nominee company, Stock Exchange Pool Nominees (SEPON Ltd.) was established and an account opened in its name in the register of members and debenture-holders of every company with listed securities.

(*b*) To facilitate the introduction of the system the Stock Exchange (Completion of Bargains) Act 1976 was passed. The terms of this Act have already been noted, but by way of summary the main changes in the law introduced by the Act may be tabulated as follows:

(*i*) A company shall be exempted from the present obligation imposed by s.80(1) of the 1948 Act to prepare share or stock certificates in respect of securities allotted or transferred to the Stock Exchange nominee, SEPON Ltd.

(*ii*) A company shall be empowered to have an official seal for use in sealing share or stock certificates. Such seal shall be a facsimile of the common seal with the addition of the word "securities".

(*iii*) The power conferred on a company by s.436(1) of the 1948 Act in regard to registers and records kept other than in bound books shall include power to keep those registers and records otherwise than in legible form, so long as the recording is capable of being reproduced in a legible form.

(*iv*) The power of the Treasury under the Stock Transfer Act 1963 shall be widened to enable new transfer forms to be prescribed for transfers to or from a Stock Exchange nominee, i.e. SEPON Ltd.

(*c*) The TALISMAN system does not, as yet, extend to all stock exchange transactions and thus the documentation introduced by the Stock Transfer Act 1963 (the Stock Transfer Form and the Broker's Transfer Form) is still in use, though to a much reduced extent, and the procedure outlined in **3** above is still applicable where the TALISMAN system is not operative. The Stock Transfer Form can, in any case, be used generally for non-listed shares and/or debentures.

(*d*) A market transaction carried out utilising the TALISMAN system involves the following:

(*i*) The selling broker concerned and the jobber involved both report the bargain struck to the Stock Exchange Settlement Centre (SESC) which records and keeps accounts of acquisitions and disposals of securities on behalf of jobbers and brokers.

(*ii*) The SESC will then forward a sale docket to the selling broker.

(*iii*) The selling broker forwards to SESC the certificate relating to the securities involved accompanied by a TALISMAN sold transfer form signed by the seller and made out in favour of SEPON Ltd.

(*iv*) SEPON Ltd., which acts as a depository of securities throughout the settlement period, submits through SESC both documents to the company whose securities are involved.

(*v*) The company will effect a transfer of the holding concerned into the name of SEPON Ltd. There is no need for a share certificate to be made out in favour of SEPON Ltd.; and in order that the interposition of transfers into and out of the nominee account do not result in double stamp duty being paid, such transfers are exempt from stamp duty.

(*vi*) On account day SESC effects delivery to buyers by debiting the account of sellers (whether brokers or jobbers) and crediting the accounts of the buyers (whether brokers or jobbers) before commencement of business on account day. Sellers and buyers are informed what is due to and from them and settlement is made later on account day.

(*vii*) Once credited to his account the jobber is able to deliver them by having his account debited and that of the buyer (broker or jobber) credited.

(*viii*) The buyer's broker communicates the relevant information concerning a purchase of an amount of shares to SESC.

(*ix*) SESC acting on behalf of SEPON Ltd. prepares a TALISMAN bought transfer form and submits it to the company involved.

(*x*) The company will effect a transfer of the shares concerned from SEPON Ltd.'s account to the buyer and prepare a new share certificate in the buyer's name.

(*xi*) The company will forward the new share certificate to SESC and the latter will pass it on to the buyer's broker.

(*xii*) On account day, the buyer's broker will conclude the transaction by payment of the agreed price for the shares to SESC.

5. Duties of Secretary.

(*a*) *Check validity of transfer.* The first duty of the Secretary (or registrar) on receiving transfer form and share certificate at the company's registered office is to check them as regards form of transfer etc. as follows:

(*i*) *Form of transfer*. Ensure that the form of transfer is in accordance with that prescribed for the occasion in the Stock Transfer Act 1963.

(*ii*) *Transferor's name*. Check the name given in the transfer instrument with that on the share certificate and in the Register of Members. Any discrepancy must be referred back to the transferor or his broker.

NOTE: The transferor's address is not essential. If it is not stated, the address shown against his name in the register can be used. If, however, an address is given which *differs* from that in the register, the matter should be investigated.

(*iii*) *Transferor's signature*. Compare the signature of the transferor on the transfer form with his name as stated in the body of the form (e.g. the addition or omission of an initial) and with his specimen signature, if available.

NOTE: Where the transferor is a corporate body having a common seal, execution under seal is necessary.

(*iv*) *Transferee's name and address* should be clearly stated. This must not be left blank.

NOTE: As already stated, the transferee's signature is no longer required on a transfer to which the 1963 Act applies.

(*v*) *Particulars of the shares transferred*, i.e. number, distinctive numbers (if any) and class, as stated in the transfer form, must be checked with those stated in the Register of Members and on the share certificate.

(*vi*) *Consideration*. Compare the consideration stated in the transfer form with the current market price of the shares, to ensure that it is "reasonable".

(*vii*) *Transfer duty*. Check the adequacy of the transfer duty in relation to the consideration stated in the transfer form. In doubtful cases it is advisable to get it passed by an Inland Revenue marking officer or return it to the broker.

(*viii*) *Transfer fee*. Ascertain that the appropriate transfer fee (if specified in the Articles) has been received.

(*xi*) *Stamps*. The stamps of both transferor's and transferee's brokers should be looked for, in the case of a stock exchange transaction. In non-market transactions, the stamp of an agent or other person acting for transferor and transferee, respectively, will replace the brokers' stamps.

(*x*) *Check the Register of Members* to ensure that there is no legal impediment to the transfer, such as a stop notice.

(*xi*) *Partly paid shares*. If the transfer form relates to partly paid shares, it might be considered advisable to make enquiry concerning the transferee, to prevent the shares passing (for example) to an infant who might be able to repudiate liability either before or within a reasonable time of his coming of age.

(*b*) *Endorse the transfer form by rubber stamp* or small adhesive label, with a list of the various stages of the registration procedure. As each stage of the procedure is completed, an appropriate entry is made in the space provided on the panel and, in some cases, the person who carried out the work initials the entry and records the date. A specimen panel is shown below:

NOTE: Although the transfer register is not a statutory book, some companies use it for the purpose of recording the above particulars.

TRANSFER No.		RECEIPT TO TRANSFEREE	
DATE RECEIVED		CHECK	
OLD CERT. No.		SELLER'S FOL.	
NEW CERT. No.		BUYER'S FOL.	

(*c*) *Transfer advice*. A transfer advice may be sent to the transferor, in a "plain, opaque envelope". This advises him of the lodgment of the transfer and states that, if the company receives no intimation to the contrary by return of post, it will be assumed that the transfer is in order and that the registration of the transfer can be proceeded with.

NOTE: As most companies insure against forged transfers, the practice of sending these advices is becoming comparatively rare. In any case, it has been held that if the transferor fails to reply, he is *not* thereby prevented from denying the validity of the transfer: *Barton* v. *L.N.W. Rly. Co.* (1889).

(*d*) *Transfer receipt*. As the transfer form and contents appear to be in order, a transfer receipt is prepared and issued to the transferee or his broker. This acknowledges receipt of the transfer documents and (where applicable) transfer fee. If it is of the *returnable* type, it will state that, if the transfer is approved, the new certificate can be obtained on or after a certain date, in exchange for the transfer receipt. If, on the other hand, the *non-returnable* form of transfer receipt is used, it merely acknowledges the transfer form and transfer fee, and informs the transferee that the certificate will be sent to him (or his broker) if or when the transfer is approved, by ordinary post at his risk.

(*e*) *Cancellation*. Cancel the old share certificate and prepare a new one in favour of the transferee.

(*f*) *Record* on the back of the old certificate the number of the *new* certificate, then file the old one.

(*g*) *Preparation for board meeting*. Convene a meeting of the board (or transfer committee), unless meetings are held automatically at (say) weekly or monthly intervals. Prior to the meeting, all transfer forms and new certificates must be given a final check. In some cases this is done by the company's auditors, who prepare an audit certificate. Transfer forms, share certificates, and (where applicable) audit certificate are then placed before the board or transfer committee; if approved, the following resolution will be passed:

RESOLVED: That share transfers nos. .... to .... both inclusive in respect of £1 ordinary shares be and they are hereby approved, and that the corresponding share certificates nos. .... to .... inclusive be signed, sealed and issued.

(*h*) *Signing and sealing*. The share certificates are then signed and sealed, following the passing of the above resolution.

NOTE: According to s.2, Stock Exchange (Completion of Bargains) Act 1976, an official seal with the addition on its face of the word "Securities" may be used (*see* V, 11).

(*i*) *Record the sealing of the certificates* in the Register of Sealed Documents.

(*j*) *Adjust the Register of Members* from particulars on the transfer forms, to show:

(*i*) *in the transferor's account*, the date on which membership ceased (if applicable); the transfer number, number of shares transferred, distinctive numbers of shares, name of transferee, balance (if any) now held;

(*ii*) *in the transferee's account*, date of entry in the register, transfer number, number of shares acquired, name and address, distinctive numbers of shares acquired, and amount paid up.

(*k*) *The new share certificates are issued* after a thorough check of the certificates and of entries in the register of members, i.e. they will be sent by post, and a certificate of posting should be obtained. If, however, a *returnable* transfer receipt had been issued to the transferee, the certificate will be issued on production of the receipt.

NOTE: Care must be taken to ensure that the certificates are ready for delivery within two months of lodgment of the transfer unless the conditions of issue provide to the contrary, s.80. But the time limit is reduced by the stock exchange to *one month* from the date of expiration of any right of renunciation, and to *two weeks* from the date of lodgment of a transfer in the case of a company with listed shares.

(*l*) *The transfer forms are securely filed*, as they must be retained for inspection by the Inland Revenue authorities.

(*m*) *Receipts.* File the signed receipts for the new share certificates, i.e. if the new certificates were issued originally with receipt forms attached. As an alternative, the receipts may be posted, or stapled to their corresponding counterfoils where the certificates had been in book form.

(*n*) *Notice of refusal.* It has been assumed that all transfers have been approved by the board or allotment committee; if any transfer is *not* approved, notice of refusal must be sent within two months of lodgment of the transfer, unless the conditions of issue provide to the contrary.

6. Certification of transfers.

(*a*) *Certification is necessary:*

(*i*) where the shareholder wishes to split the sale of his shares, e.g. A has a share certificate for 1000 shares, and wishes to transfer (say) 500 to B, 300 to C and 200 to D;

(*ii*) where the shareholder wishes to sell part of his holding and retain the balance, e.g. A, with a share certificate for 1000 shares, wishes to transfer 700 to B and retain the 300 balance;

(*iii*) where the shareholder has not yet received a share certificate for the shares he wishes to transfer and can produce only a "temporary" document, such as a transfer receipt (of the returnable type), an allotment letter or a balance receipt.

(*b*) *Procedure.* In the above circumstances, the seller (or his broker) lodges the transfer form and the relevant share certificate (or a temporary document) with the company for certification. However, if the shares are listed, they may be lodged with the stock exchange, which will undertake the work of certification against share certificates, but *not* against temporary documents.

Assuming that certification is to be carried out by the company, the procedure is as follows.

(*i*) On receipt of the transfer form and share certificate (or temporary document), ensure that the shares referred to in the transfer form are in fact those included in the certificate or temporary document.

NOTE: The new Stock Transfer Form, introduced by the Stock Transfer Act 1963, is suitable for *all* transactions, whether through the medium of a stock exchange or otherwise, but a separate *Broker's Transfer Form* must also be lodged in favour of each buyer where a holding is being sold to more than one buyer as the result of stock exchange transactions.

(*ii*) Check the transfer form(s) and in particular:

(1) ensure that the appropriate form, or forms, are being used for the occasion—Broker's Transfer Forms must *not* be accepted for "non-market" deals;

(2) where Broker's Transfer Forms are received, they must be linked up with the Stock Transfer Form to which they relate, e.g. as regards name of the transferor, stamp of the selling broker, etc.;

(3) other points to be checked at this stage are the transferor's signature, the name of the transferee(s), consideration money, and particulars of the shares transferred;

NOTE: In the case of "market" transactions, the stock exchange suggests that the name of the transferee need *not* be given to the Registrar at the time of the certification.

(4) if transfers are stamped for transfer duty (though this is not legally necessary at this stage), ensure that they are properly stamped in relation to the consideration stated; that also means ensuring that the latter is reasonable.

(*iii*) If the transfer documents are in order, the transfer forms are endorsed by rubber stamp with the following certificate, which must be signed (not merely initialled) by the Secretary:

Certificate/Documents of title for .... shares/stock has/have been lodged at the Company's office.
Date ....   Blank Company Limited
Moorgate, ... Secretary London, E.C.2.

NOTE: Where certification is carried out by the stock exchange, the secretary of the Quotations Department of the stock exchange concerned sends the certificate(s) to the company and gives advice of certification. The subsequent procedure carried out by the company will then depend upon whether the shareholder is transferring his holding to two or more buyers, or transferring to one buyer and retaining the balance.

(*iv*) After certification, or after advice of certification from the stock exchange concerned, a transfer advice *may* be sent to the transferor (as already indicated in 5(*c*), this practice has been abandoned by most companies). If this procedure is followed, it will, of course, be unnecessary to send a transfer advice when the transfer is subsequently lodged for registration.

(*v*) Endorse particulars of the certification on the back of the share certificate (or temporary document of title) and file the latter after cancellation.

(*vi*) Return the transfer form to the seller (or his broker) and, if he is selling only *part* of his holding, a balance receipt will be sent at the same time or as soon as possible afterwards.

NOTE: Where certification is effected by a stock exchange, a balance receipt is *not* sent by the stock exchange, but the company is advised of the certification and asked to send a balance certificate to the selling broker—unless any other instruction is included.

(*vii*) A new certificate, or certificates, will be issued to the transferee(s) and, where applicable, to the transferor; i.e.:

(1) on receipt of transfers for registration from the transferees (or their brokers); and/or

(2) on receipt of a balance receipt from the transferor (or his broker).

NOTE: If the stock exchange suggestion is followed, and a non-returnable balance receipt is used, the company will send a balance certificate to the transferor (or his broker) without awaiting production of documents.

7. The effects of certification.

(*a*) The buyer (or his broker) accepts the certification as evidence of the seller's title to the shares concerned, and certified transfers are accepted by common custom as "good delivery" on the stock exchange.

(*b*) Legally, however, certification is *not* a warranty that the seller has any title to the shares; it is merely a representation by the company that the documents have been produced which purport to give the seller a *prima facie* title to the shares.

(*c*) If a false certification is made negligently, the company is under the same liability as if it had been made fraudulently: s.79; thus the company will be liable to compensate any person who acts on the faith of a false certification.

(*d*) A company is deemed to have certificated an instrument of transfer and is, therefore, liable upon it if:

(*i*) the act of certification is performed by a person duly authorised by the company to do so; and

(*ii*) the certification is signed by a person authorised to certify transfers on the company's behalf, or by any officer or servant, either of the company or of a body corporate so authorised: s.79(3).

(*e*) Where the stock exchange undertakes the certification of transfers, the company cannot be held liable on a false certification, as the stock exchange is not authorised by the company to carry out the work.

8. Stamp duty.

(*a*) Transfers of shares or other marketable securities, including debentures, are subject to stamp duty, which is based on the consideration passing from the transferee to the transferor. The current rate of *ad valorem* stamp duty is £2 per cent of the consideration, with a graduated scale where the consideration is less than £100.

(*b*) In suitable cases, however, the transfer form may be stamped at less than the full *ad valorem* rate of £2 per cent; these are as follows.

(*i*) *Transfers for a nominal consideration* where there is no actual sale of the securities and the consideration stated in the transfer form is a nominal one of (say) 25p. In such cases a fixed duty of 50p only is payable. The following are some of the cases listed on the back of a transfer form where, subject to completion of the relevant certificate by both transferor and transferee (or by some person or persons acting on their behalf), the fixed duty of 50p is applicable:

(1) transfers vesting the property in trustees, e.g. on appointment of a new trustee;

(2) transfer by way of security for a loan, or retransfer to the original transferor on repayment of a loan;

(3) transfer to a beneficiary under a will of a specific legacy of stock, etc.;

(4) transfer to a residuary legatee of stock, etc., forming part of the residue divisible under a will;

(5) transfer by the liquidator of a company of stocks, etc., to

persons who were shareholders, in satisfaction of their rights on a winding-up.

NOTE: A gift made during the lifetime of the donor, i.e. a "gift *inter vivos*", is chargeable with *ad valorem* stamp duty calculated on the value of the securities concerned. In this, and in the cases listed above, the stamp duty must be adjudicated; that is, the transfer form must bear the stamp of the Inland Revenue marking officer. If it has not been passed by the marking officer, or if there is any doubt as to the adequacy of the stamp duty, it should be returned for adjudication.

(*ii*) *Domestic transfers.*

(1) Where a shareholder transfers shares to himself and another jointly (e.g. a huband may wish to have his shares registered jointly in the names of himself and his wife), this is known as a "domestic transfer".

(2) In such cases, as there is no consideration, a nominal consideration is stated in the transfer form and the stamp duty is calculated on *half* the market value of the shares concerned.

NOTE: This must not be confused with a "gift *inter vivos*"; the difference lies in the fact that the transferor in a domestic transfer *retains* an interest in the securities transferred, whereas the donor in a gift *inter vivos* does not.

(3) When transfer documents are submitted in respect of domestic transfers, it is essential to ensure that they bear the Inland Revenue adjudication stamp to indicate that the reduced rate of duty is justified.

(*iii*) *Transfer under s.42 of the Finance Act 1920.*

(1) A temporary transfer of a marketable security *to* a stock exchange jobber in the ordinary course of his business is subject to a maximum duty of 50p only, under the provisions of the above Act.

(2) To benefit by this concession, the jobber undertakes either to transfer the securities concerned within two months after the date of the transfer or to pay the difference between the full *ad valorem* duty and the duty already paid.

(3) Transfers received must bear an Inland Revenue "supplementary stamp", marked "Finance Act 1920, Section 42". Neither Secretary nor Registrar is under any liability, so long as a 50p duty stamp has been impressed.

9. Blank transfers.

(*a*) A blank transfer is frequently given as security for a loan and operates as a mortgage of the shares included in the transfer form.

(*b*) The borrower completes a transfer form, but leaves the name of the transferee blank. Transfer form and share certificate are then deposited with the lender in return for the loan.

(*c*) If the borrower fails to repay the loan on the date arranged, the lender may insert his own name as transferee and get the transfer registered in his own favour; or he may sell the shares to a third party, after giving reasonable notice of his intention to the borrower.

(*d*) As the Stock Transfer Act 1963 provides that registered securities may be transferred by means of an instrument under hand, the position of the lender is strengthened as it is now a comparatively simple matter to enforce his security. Hitherto there had been various legal complications when a transfer was required to be under seal.

10. Forged transfers.

(*a*) No rights can be acquired by the transferee under a forged transfer as it is *void*.

(*b*) The rights and liabilities of the company on a forged transfer are as follows.

(*i*) It must restore the "transferor" (i.e. the true owner) to the register and compensate him for dividends due to him.

(*ii*) It must remove the transferee's name from the register, and recover from him any dividends he may have received as the result of the forgery.

(*iii*) It must compensate a second transferee (if any) who has received a share certificate and has been entered in the Register of Members.

NOTE: In this case the company is estopped from denying the title of a second transferee, *if* he had relied on the share certificate and had acted in good faith.

(*iv*) It may claim compensation for all losses suffered as a result of the forgery from the person who lodged the transfer.

NOTE: That person, by lodging the transfer for registration, gave an implied warranty that it was genuine and that he would compensate the company if the transfer should prove to be a forgery.

(*c*) The rights of the "*transferor*", i.e. the true owner, are as follows.

(*i*) He can compel the company to restore his name to the Register of Members and make good any dividends he may have lost as the result of the forgery.

(*ii*) His right of action lies *only* against the company.

(*d*) The *transferee*, even though he may have acted innocently:

(*i*) obtains no title to the shares included in the transfer;

(*ii*) is liable to repay any dividends he may have received, as the results of the forgery, to the company; and

(*iii*) is liable to indemnify the company for any loss it may have suffered.

The transferee will, of course, have a claim against the forger.

(*e*) A *second* transferee, acting in good faith, who has relied upon the share certificate:

(*i*) is entitled to compensation from the company, as the company is estopped from denying his title to the shares; or

(*ii*) as an alternative, the company may procure an equivalent number of shares and have them transferred into his name, and so replace those which must be restored to the true owner.

11. Forged Transfers Acts 1891 and 1892.

(*a*) A company may, by its Articles or by *special* resolution, adopt these Acts, which prescribe methods for providing compensation for persons who suffer loss as the result of forged transfers, or forged powers of attorney.

NOTE: There is no compulsion to adopt these Acts.

(*b*) The methods prescribed are as follows:

(*i*) The company may charge an additional fee on each transfer, but not exceeding 5p per £100 transferred.

(*ii*) Creating a fund by reservation of capital, accumulation of income or any other method which the company may decide upon.

(*iii*) Covering the risk by taking out a forged transfers insurance policy—the method which is most commonly adopted.

TRANSMISSION OF SHARES

12. Transmission signifies a change in the ownership of securities otherwise than by ordinary transfer; that is, either:

(*a*) by death; or

(*b*) by operation of law, as in bankruptcy.

13. Member's death.

(*a*) The following provisions are of assistance to the legal representatives of a deceased member.

(*i*) Section 75 provides that a transfer of shares or debentures must not be registered except on production of an instrument of transfer, but it is made clear that the section does not prevent a company from registering as shareholder or debenture-holder a person to whom the shares or debentures are transmitted by operation of law.

(*ii*) Section 76 states that a transfer of the shares of a deceased member made by a personal representative shall, although the personal representative is not himself a member, be as valid as if he were.

(*iii*) Section 82 provides that the production to a company of any document which is by law sufficient evidence of probate or letters of administration shall be accepted by the company as sufficient evidence of the grant.

(*b*) The courses open to a personal representative in dealing with the shares (or debentures) of a deceased member of a company will be determined by various considerations, namely:

(*i*) whether the deceased had held the shares solely or jointly;

(*ii*) whether he died testate or intestate; and

(*iii*) whether, having died testate, he appointed an executor who was able and willing to act as his executor.

(*c*) Assuming that the deceased had held the shares *solely*:

(*i*) if he left a will, and appointed an executor, his executor must produce probate of the will to the company;

(*ii*) if he left a will, without naming an executor, or

(1) appointed an executor who refused to act, or

(2) appointed an executor who predeceased him,

his legal representative will be an administrator who must produce letters of administration with the will annexed (*cum testamento annexo*) to the company as evidence of his appointment as administrator of the deceased;

(*iii*) if he died intestate, i.e. without leaving a will, his next of kin (or other person or persons so entitled) may apply to the Court for, and produce to the company, General Letters of Administration, as evidence of his appointment as administrator of the deceased.

NOTE: If the deceased had *no* next of kin, the Crown, any creditor, or a Consul (in the case of a foreigner) may apply for letters of administration.

(*d*) After production of the appropriate document(s) by the legal representative of the deceased in the above cases, the procedure is as follows.

(*i*) The documents must be accepted by the company as sufficient evidence, despite anything in the Articles to the contrary: s.82.

(*ii*) The executor or administrator cannot be treated

automatically as holder of the shares, and the name of the deceased must be allowed to remain in the Register of Members.

(*iii*) If, however, the Articles permit, the executor or administrator may request the company to place his name on the register. In that case, if his request is approved, he will be treated as shareholder in his own right and responsible for any liability attaching to the shares.

(*iv*) The company's Articles will decide the method to be adopted for registering the legal representative; that is:

(1) whether a formal transfer is required, to transfer from (say) the executor of X to the executor in his own private capacity; or

(2) whether a Letter of Request will suffice, as in Table A: Article 31.

(*v*) In some cases (as in Table A, Article 32) the Articles permit the directors to compel the legal representative either:

(1) to have the shares registered in his own name; or

(2) to transfer the shares within a stipulated period (Table A allows him 90 days);

failing which, dividends, bonuses or other moneys payable in respect of the shares may be withheld until the legal representative complies with the company's requirements.

(*e*) Assuming that the deceased had held the shares *jointly*:

(*i*) the shares vest in the survivor or survivors of the joint holding;

(*ii*) the company will require evidence of death, in the form of a death certificate; if probate of the will or letters of administration are accepted instead, the document produced should be endorsed in such a way as to make it quite clear that it was accepted as evidence of death only.

NOTE: The Articles usually provide, as in Table A, Article 29, that the estate of the deceased joint holder is not released from any liability remaining on the shares which had been jointly held by him with other persons.

(*f*) Where the estate of a deceased shareholder does not exceed £1500 the deceased's representatives may take advantage of the provisions of the Administration of Estates (Small Payments) Act 1965 and adopt a less formal course of action than that outlined above. In such circumstances it is usual to call for:

(*i*) a death certificate;

(*ii*) a letter from the Capital Taxes Office agreeing that, on the information furnished to it, no duty arises;

(*iii*) the share certificate;

(*iv*) a statutory declaration to the effect that the person claiming to deal with the shareholding is entitled to do so;

(*v*) a letter of indemnity from the same person, indemnifying the company against any loss or liability it may incur as a result of dealing with the shareholding informally, and undertaking to obtain formal probate or administration if called upon by the company to do so.

14. Member's bankruptcy.

(*a*) On becoming bankrupt, a member's shares vest in his trustee in bankruptcy.

(*b*) The trustee must, however, prove to the company that he is entitled to deal with the bankrupt's shares, by producing:

(*i*) an office copy of the Court's order by which he was appointed, *or* the company may accept a copy of the *London Gazette* advertising his appointment; and

(*ii*) an authenticated copy of his signature.

(*c*) Production of the above documents permits the trustees to deal with the bankrupt's shares in the course of realising his property. He may elect to deal with the shares in any of the following ways.

(*i*) He may transfer the shares, as the Bankruptcy Act 1914, s.48, gives him the same right of transfer as the bankrupt himself had formerly possessed.

(*ii*) He may have the shares registered in his own name, where the articles permit or require him to do so; if, however, there is any liability on the shares, he is unlikely to do so as he would then become personally liable, and, moreover, he would also lose his right to disclaim the shares.

(*iii*) He may disclaim the shares if they are partly paid and so long as he had not had them registered in his own name; in which case, the company will be entitled to prove in the bankruptcy for the amount unpaid on the shares.

(*d*) If the bankrupt is a joint holder, the above procedure still applies; that is, the shares pass to the trustee in bankruptcy and *not* to the surviving joint holder(s).

15. Insanity of a member.

(*a*) The Court may appoint a Receiver to administer the affairs of a shareholder who is of unsound mind.

(*b*) The Receiver must produce to the company the Court order, or an office copy of it, confirming his appointment, and this must be accepted by the company as sufficient evidence of the appointment.

(*c*) The Receiver is then able to deal with the shares concerned, in accordance with the authority given in the order, e.g. to transfer the shares, or merely to receive dividends due to the insane member.

(*d*) If the mental patient is a joint holder, his interest does *not* pass to the surviving joint holder(s) but to the Receiver.

16. Liquidation of a corporate member.

(*a*) When a corporate member is wound up, the liquidator must produce evidence of his appointment before he becomes entitled to deal with the shares concerned. The evidence required depends upon the mode of winding-up adopted, i.e. whether it is a compulsory liquidation or a voluntary liquidation.

(*b*) In a *compulsory* liquidation, the liquidator will be required to produce the Court order by which he was appointed, or a copy of the *London Gazette* in which his appointment was advertised.

(*c*) In a *voluntary* liquidation, the liquidator must produce certified copies of the resolutions for winding up and authorising his appointment.

17. Chain of transmission.

(*a*) If the sole legal representative of a deceased member, i.e. executor or administrator, has the shares of the deceased registered in his own name, then in the event of his own death *his* personal representative (whether executor or administrator) can deal with the shares as part of his estate.

(*b*) If, however, the sole legal representative of a deceased member had allowed the shares to remain in the name of the deceased, a chain of transmission (or chain of representation) may be formed, and from that point:

(*i*) there will be an unbroken chain of transmission, provided the legal representative dies testate; that is, his right of representation will pass by operation of law to his executor, and so on from executor to executor, until one of them dies intestate;

(*ii*) the chain of transmission might also be broken if an executor in the "chain" died testate, but failed to appoint an executor, or appointed one who refused to act or had predeceased him.

(*c*) It is important to note that the chain of transmission cannot be continued by an administrator, as he is not a person appointed by the deceased executor as being capable of administering the estate of the original deceased shareholder.

NOTE: As already explained earlier in this chapter, most companies require legal representatives either to transfer the shares of the deceased shareholder or to have them registered in their own names, as in Table A, Article 32; therefore, the chain of transmission and the legal complications which it might entail are usually avoided.

PROGRESS TEST 8

1. What are the statutory provisions affecting a shareholder's right to transfer his shares and the form of the transfer instrument? **(1, 2)**

2. Describe an office procedure for dealing with transfers lodged with a company for registration, paying particular attention to the points which should be borne in mind when scrutinising the transfer forms and accompanying documents. **(3, 5)**

3. Explain what is meant by certification of transfers? *ICSA* **(5)**

4. Discuss the merits and disadvantages of the adoption by a company of a system of non-returnable transfer receipts and balance receipts. **(5, 6)**

5. A holds 1,000 shares in a public company. He instructs his broker to sell 400 of the shares. They are sold through the Stock Exchange as to 300 to a broker acting for B and as to 100 to a broker acting for C. Describe the documents you, as Company Secretary, should receive as a result of these sales, and from whom; and the action to be taken in the Registration department to complete the transactions. *ICSA* **(3, 5, 6)**

6. Outline the procedure involved in a market transaction utilising the TALISMAN settlement system. **(3, 4)**

7. Describe the following and explain in what circumstances they are used:

(*a*) an offer for sale;

(*b*) brokers transfer forms or (in countries outside the United Kingdom) transfer deeds;

(*c*) consolidated listing forms.
ICSA **(II, 13; III, 24; VIII, 6)**

8. Explain the purpose and legal effect of certification of transfer. Discuss the legal effect where certification is carried out by the stock exchange. **(6, 7)**

9. Explain (*a*) transfer receipt, (*b*) transfer advice, (*c*) transfer for a nominal consideration. When can a transfer for a nominal considera-

tion be accepted with only a 50p transfer duty stamp? **(5–8)**

10. Is the secretary responsible for the proper stamping of a share transfer? When may he safely accept a transfer bearing nominal stamp duty? How should he deal with the stamping of a transfer between a parent and subsidiary? *ICSA* **(5, 8)**

11. How should the following documents be stamped, if at all, and how should a company registrar satisfy himself as to the adequacy of the stamping?

(*a*) A transfer of shares by way of gift *inter vivos*.

(*b*) A transfer from an executor to the sole legatee under a will.

(*c*) A transfer where the transferor is a subsidiary of the transferee.

(*d*) A power of attorney.

(*e*) A form of proxy, valid for a specified meeting and any adjournment of that meeting. **(VIII, 8; IX, 6)**

12. You are the registrar of a listed public company. Would you accept the following documents for registration? If not, give your reasons for rejection:

(*a*) a probate granted overseas;

(*b*) a transfer not previously certified of 500 ordinary shares accompanied by a certificate for 750 ordinary shares;

(*c*) a transfer with a material alteration thereon;

(*d*) a transfer stamped 50p but without the stamp of a marking officer to indicate that it has been passed for payment of the fixed 50p duty. **(VIII, 6; IX, 4, 10)**

13. What do you understand by a "blank" transfer? For what purpose(s) might it be used? **(9)**

14. Describe the various ways in which ownership of shares in a company may change, outlining the procedure to be followed in each case, including any necessary action by directors. **(3, 12)**

15. What courses are open to a personal representative in dealing with the shares of a deceased member of a company? In what respect (if any) would the position be altered if the deceased member had held his shares jointly with another? **(13)**

16. What do you understand by "transmission" of shares? Which provisions of the Act are of assistance to the legal representatives of a deceased member? **(12)**

17. Distinguish between (*a*) transfer and transmission; (*b*) executor and administrator: (*c*) probate and letters of administration. **(VIII, 12; IX, 4, 5)**

18. Explain (*a*) "chain of transmission", (*b*) letter of request. Prepare a specimen letter of request. **(13, 17)**

CHAPTER IX

Registration of Documents

DOCUMENTS RECEIVED FOR REGISTRATION

1. The registration department of a large company is usually in the charge of the company registrar, who is directly responsible to the company secretary.

2. The work of the registration department.

(*a*) Registration of transfers of shares and debentures.

(*b*) Preparing and filing returns with the Registrar of Companies.

(*c*) Payment of dividend and, where applicable, debenture interest.

(*d*) Registration of miscellaneous documents, other than those received in connection with certification and registration of transfers.

(*e*) Maintaining, and keeping up to date, various registers, including the Register of Members, Register of Directors' Interests, Register of Charges, Register of Directors and Secretaries, Register of Interests in Shares, Register of Debenture Holders (if any), and various non-statutory registers kept for the purpose of registering the miscellaneous documents referred to in (*d*) above.

3. Miscellaneous documents requiring registration, other than those concerned with transfer procedure:

(*a*) probates,

(*b*) letters of administration,

(*c*) powers of attorney,

(*d*) court orders, e.g. appointments of trustee in bankruptcy, receiver in case of insanity, liquidator,

(*e*) certificates, e.g. of death, marriage, etc.,

(*f*) statutory declarations, e.g. of identity.

4. Probate.

(*a*) The probate of a will is an official copy of the will, sealed by the Court of Probate after it has been proved.

(*b*) It is one of the first duties of the executor appointed in the will to obtain probate to enable him to administer the estate of the deceased.

(*c*) When he presents the probate (or a photostat copy of it) to a company, the company is bound to accept it as evidence of the executor's right to deal with the property of the deceased, including his shares and debentures: s.82.

(*d*) It is, however, important to ensure that the probate bears the seal of the appropriate Court.

5. Letters of administration.

(*a*) This is the Court's official appointment of an administrator, giving him authority to administer the estate of a deceased person, usually because the deceased died without leaving a will or, having left a will, failed to appoint an executor.

(*b*) Letters of administration are usually granted to a person (or persons) interested in the real or personal estate of the deceased, e.g. the next of kin, or a legatee if there was a will but no executor appointed. If there are no next of kin, the grant may be made to:

(*i*) the Crown,

(*ii*) a creditor, or

(*iii*) a consul, in the case of a foreigner.

(*c*) Having been granted letters of administration and produced the document (or a photostat copy of it) to the company, the administrator is then entitled to deal with the property of the deceased, including his shares and debentures; the company is, in fact, bound to accept the document as evidence of his authority: s.82.

NOTE: This document, like the probate, must be sealed by the appropriate Court; if not, it must be re-sealed or a fresh grant (an ancillary grant) taken out.

(*d*) Letters of administration may take various forms, the form being determined by the circumstances in each case.

(*i*) A general grant of administration is made where the deceased died intestate. This is, of course, the commonest form of grant.

(*ii*) Letters of administration *cum testamento annexo* (i.e. with the will annexed) are granted where the deceased died testate but failed to appoint an executor, or where the executor appointed refuses to act or pre-deceased him.

(*iii*) Letters of administration *de bonis non*, granted where an administrator is appointed to take over the administration of an estate because the original executor or administrator had died without completing the administration of the estate.

(*iv*) Letters of administration *durante absentia*, granted to an administrator who is appointed to act during the absence abroad of the executor or administrator.

(*v*) Letters of administration *pendente lite*, granted to an administrator appointed to act pending the result of litigation concerning validity of the will.

(*vi*) Letters of administration *durante dementia*, granted to an administrator appointed to carry on the administration of the estate during insanity of an executor or administrator.

(*vii*) Letters of administration *durante minore aetate*, granted where an administrator is appointed to take over administration of an estate during the infancy of a sole executor named in the will.

6. Power of attorney.

(*a*) A power of attorney is the actual authority or instrument embodying an authorisation to one person, the attorney (grantee or donee), or to two or more persons either jointly, or jointly and severally, to act on behalf of the principal (grantor or donor).

(*b*) Section 1 of the Powers of Attorney Act 1971 provides that such an instrument shall be signed and sealed by or by direction of and in the presence of the donor, and that where it is not signed by the donor himself but by some other person on his behalf in his presence and at his direction, two other persons shall be present as witnesses and shall attest the instrument. This confirms the view that the term "power of attorney" is properly restricted to an authority given under seal.

(*c*) A power of attorney may be general giving the attorney wide power as regards the grantor's business, or may be special, specifying a limited number of actions or even the execution of a single document.

(*d*) A photocopy of a power of attorney, certified by the donor or by a solicitor or stockbroker, and any copy of a photocopy, similarly certified, shall be sufficient proof of the existence and contents of the power: Powers of Attorney Act 1971, s.3.

(*e*) A power of attorney should be stamped 50p.

(*f*) By s.4 of the Powers of Attorney Act 1971 a power of attorney whenever created, which is created to secure a proprietary interest of the donee, or the performance of an obligation owed to the donee, shall not be revoked, so long as the donee has that interest or the obligation remains undischarged, either by the donor without the donee's consent, or by the reason of death, incapacity, or bankruptcy of the donor or, if the donor is a body corporate, by reason of its dissolution.

(*g*) Where the donee of a power of attorney acts in pursuance of the power at a time when it has been revoked he shall not incur any liability (either to the donor or to any other person) if at that time he did not know of the revocation; and where a person, without knowledge of the revocation, deals with the donee the transaction shall be as valid as if the power had then been in existence: Powers of Attorney Act 1971, s.5.

(*h*) Section 7 of the Powers of Attorney Act 1971 provides that the donee of a power of attorney may execute any instrument with his own signature and, where sealing is required, with his own seal, and do any other thing in his own name, by the authority of the donor of the power; any document so executed or thing so done has the same effect as if executed or done by the donee with the signature or seal, or in the name of the donor.

7. Registration of miscellaneous documents.

(*a*) In large companies, where requests for alteration of the Register of Members for various reasons (apart from transfers) are numerous, it may be found convenient and time-saving to have a separate register in which to record the receipt of the more important documents. Thus, separate registers may be kept for, say:

(*i*) probates and letters of administration;
(*ii*) powers of attorney;
(*iii*) court orders, notices and certificates.

(*b*) Specimen rulings for two of these registers are illustrated below:

Register of probates and letters of administration

No.	Date regd.	Particulars of deceased		Date of death	Executor/Administr.		Folio in Register	Remarks
		Name	Shares held		Name	Address		

Register of powers of attorney

No.	Date regd.	Shareholder		Particulars of power of attorney		Attorney		By whom presented	Folio in register
		Name	Address	Date	Description	Name	Address		

(*c*) It may, however, be sufficient in many cases to keep a single register, which might be named "Register of Important Documents" and either ruled to record every type of document received for registration, or divided into sections, such as (1) Probates and letters of administration, (2) Powers of attorney, (3) Death certificates, (4) Marriage certificates, (5) Notices and orders, (6) Miscellaneous.

(*d*) Some companies have already dispensed with "registers" in book form, and many will now favour the use of computers. This they are entitled to do with the coming into operation of the Stock Exchange (Completion of Bargains) Act 1976, s.3, so long as their computerised recordings are capable of being reproduced in a legible form.

(*e*) On receiving documents for registration, it is advisable to have them checked and endorsed (usually by means of a rubber stamp), after which the endorsement is signed by the Secretary, registrar or other responsible official. Where a registration fee of (say) $12\frac{1}{2}$p is charged, the endorsement will serve as an acknowledgment of the document and as a receipt for the registration fee.

The usual registration stamp is as follows:

Registered

For and on behalf of

EXCHANGE TRADING CO. LTD.

....Registrar

Received fee .... Date ....

(*f*) On receipt of Probate or Letters of Administration for registration, the relevant share certificate should be endorsed with the following particulars:

Probate/Letters of administration

of the Will of .... who died on ....19......
has this day been presented by the persons undermentioned, and
registered in the Company's books.

Name(s) .... Executor/Administrator

Address(es)...

....

| | For and on behalf of |
| Dated this | EXCHANGE TRADING CO. LTD. |

| ....day | Secretary |
| of.............19...... | ....Registrar |

---

8. Photographic copies of documents.

(*a*) Photographic copies of documents are presented for registration as common practice. In many cases such copies are generally acceptable; in other cases, the Secretary (or registrar) must use his discretion, and in any doubtful case it is always advisable to insist on production of the original document.

(*b*) Present practice regarding the acceptance of photographic copies of documents for registration may be summarised as follows.

(*i*) *Probates and Letters of Administration.* A photostatic copy may be accepted with safety if it bears the impressed seal of the probate office. A privately produced copy, photographic or otherwise, should *not* be accepted.

(*ii*) *Powers of attorney.* A photocopy of a power of attorney, certified by the donor or by a solicitor or stockbroker, and any copy of a photocopy, similarly certified, shall be sufficient proof of the existence and contents of the power.

(*iii*) *Death and marriage certificates.* Certified copies issued by the appropriate registrar are generally acceptable. Privately photographed copies should not be accepted unless fully authenticated by a responsible person.

(*iv*) *Court orders.* Courts orders appointing a liquidator, receiver in insanity, trustee in bankruptcy, etc., are commonly presented as "office copies". These are quite acceptable, so long as they bear the seal of the appropriate Court. Copies in any other form should not be accepted.

(*v*) *Certified copies of resolutions*, such as the resolution appointing a liquidator in a voluntary winding-up, are acceptable, so long as they are fully authenticated in manner provided in s.36 of the Act, i.e. actually signed by a director, secretary or other authorised officer of the company. The same may be said of certified extracts from a company's Articles, minutes, etc.

9. Circumstances in which documents are submitted for registration. Apart from alterations due to transfer of shares, the following are some of the circumstances in which documents are presented to a company for registration.

(*a*) *Member's death*, where deceased had held shares:
    (*i*) solely,
    (*ii*) jointly.

(*b*) *Registering power of attorney*, where the attorney wishes to establish his authority to deal with shares, etc.

(*c*) *Member's bankruptcy*, where the trustee in bankruptcy produces evidence of his appointment.

(*d*) *Member's insanity*, the Receiver appointed by the court, proving his appointment and entitlement to deal with the estate of the insane member.

(*e*) *Liquidation of a corporate member*, the liquidator producing evidence of his appointment.

(*f*) *Change of name*, from various causes, e.g.
    (*i*) marriage of a female shareholder;
    (*ii*) shareholder's elevation to the peerage;
    (*iii*) corporate member changes name by special resolution;
    (*iv*) change by deed poll;
    (*v*) combination of various accounts under one name.

(*g*) *Change of address*, either by letter or on any standard form for the purpose.

10. Procedure on receipt of documents for registration

Circumstances	Document(s) produced or required to be produced	Procedure
1. Member's death	Probate/Letters of Administration (or acceptable copy) and share certificate.	(1) Ensure probate (or letters of administration) is correctly sealed by English Court of Probate. (2) Enter in Register of Probates. (3) Endorse probate/letters of administration with "registration stamp" *(see illustration in 7).* (4) Endorse share certificate with the general "registration stamp" (also illustrated in 7). (5) Record member's death in Register of Members; e.g.: *"Probate of the will of John Blank (deceased) registered at Company's office ....19....* *Executor/Administrator:* *Name.............Address............."* (6) Return share certificate and any other document not to be retained. If equipment is available, the latter may be photocopied before return. (7) Carefully file any copies retained. (8) Prepare new address plate in favour of legal representatives.

2. Registering power of attorney	Power of attorney (or acceptable copy).	(1) Carefully examine the power, to ensure that it is:
		  (a) correct in form;
		  (b) adequately stamped and witnessed;
		  (c) still in force; and
		  (d) correctly signed and sealed by appointer.
		(2) Enter in Register of Powers of Attorney.
		(3) Particulars of the power of attorney should not, as such, be recorded in the Register of Members for they are essentially the private concern of the grantor and grantee. However, the existence of the power could be noted as an *aide memoire* through the use of some code indication against the appropriate entry in the register.
		(4) Carefully note exact powers given to attorney and/or copy document; file copy.
		(5) If in doubt as to power being still in force, obtain statutory declaration of non-revocation.
		(6) Endorse the power with registration stamp, and return.
		(7) Prepare new address plate in favour of attorney.

3. Member's bankruptcy	Bankruptcy order (or acceptable copy). NOTE: A copy of the *London Gazette*	(1) Record receipt of document in Register of Important Documents or special register (if any). (2) Record particulars of appointment in Register

Circumstances	Document(s) produced or required to be produced	Procedure
3. Member's bankruptcy (contd.)	containing notice of appointment is sometimes accepted.	of Members, e.g.: "Notice of appointment of Trustee in Bankruptcy, dated .... registered Company's office (date) .... Trustee's name/address ...." (3) Endorse the order (or copy) with "registration" stamp. (4) Return the order (or copy) to trustee, usually after taking a copy. (5) Prepare new address plate in favour of the trustee.
4. Member's insanity	Protection Order (or acceptable copy). NOTE: The order may give only limited power to the Receiver.	(1) Record receipt of document in Register of Important Documents or special register (if any). (2) Record particulars of appointment in Register of Members, e.g.: "Order appointing Receiver dated .... registered at Company's office .... (date) .... Receiver .... name/address"

		(3) Endorse the order (or copy) with "registration" stamp. (4) Return the order (or copy) to Receiver, usually after taking a copy. (5) Prepare new address plate in favour of the Receiver.
5. Liquidation of corporate member	In *compulsory* winding-up: Court order (or acceptable copy) appointing liquidator. In *voluntary* winding-up: certified copies of the resolutions: (*a*) for winding up (*b*) appointing the liquidator.	(1) Record receipt of document(s) in Register of Important Documents or special register (if any). (2) Record particulars of appointment in Register of Members, e.g.: "*Order of Court for compulsory winding-up dated .... registered at Company's office .... (date) .... Liquidator(s) .... and ....*" (3) Return document(s), usually after taking copy. (4) Prepare new address plate in favour of liquidator.
6. Change of name due to marriage of female shareholder	Marriage certificate (or acceptable copy) and share certificate.	(1) Send member a special request form (if any) for completion in her new name. (2) Record request in Register of Important Documents, or any special register. (3) Amend entry in Register of Members.

Circumstances	Document(s) produced or required to be produced	Procedure
6. Change of name due to marriage (contd.)		(4) Prepare new share certificate or endorse the old certificate. (5) Endorse marriage certificate (or copy) with "registration" stamp. (6) Return marriage certificate (or copy) and new share certificate (or old one, suitably endorsed). (7) File the request form. (8) Prepare new address plate.
7. Change of name due to shareholder's elevation to the peerage	Copy of London Gazette notifying change of name and share certificate usually accepted.	(1) Record in Register of Important Documents or any special register. (2) Amend Register of Members, e.g.: "*Copy of Gazette, dated .... registered at Company's office (date) ....*" followed by detail of the change. (3) Prepare new share certificate or endorse the old one. (4) File copy of the *Gazette*. (5) Prepare new address plate.

8. Change of name by corporate members	Certified copy of special resolution authorising the change. Share certificate. Impression of the company's new seal. Certified extract of company's articles as to use of seal.	(1) Record receipt of documents in Register of Important Documents, or any special register. (2) Amend Register of Members, i.e. alter name of the company, and note production of documents. (3) Prepare new share certificate, or endorse the old one with the change of name. (4) Return any documents whose return is requested (after photocopying) together with amended (or new) share certificate. (5) File copies of any documents retained and (if applicable) cancelled share certificate. (6) Prepare new address plate.
9. Change of name by deed poll	Deed of poll, or copy of *London Gazette* notifying the change of name and share certificate.	(1) Send member a special request form (if any) for completion in new name. (2) Record receipt of documents in Register of Important Documents, or special register. (3) Amend entry in Register of Members, e.g. *"Deed of Poll dated .... registered at Company office .... date ...."*. (4) Prepare new share certificate, or endorse the old one, showing change of name.

Circumstances	Document(s) produced or required to be produced	Procedure
9. Change of name by deed poll (*contd.*)		(5) Return the deed of poll (after taking a copy) together with either new share certificate or the old one suitably endorsed.
		(6) File letter of request and, where applicable, cancelled share certificate and copy of *London Gazette*.
		(7) Prepare new address plate.
10. Shareholder's request to have shares in various names combined under his true name	Statutory Declaration of Identity and share certificates.	(1) Record receipt of documents in Register of Important Documents.
		(2) Make necessary amendments in the Register of Members, transferring from accounts in fictitious names into true name of the member.
		(3) Prepare new share certificate in shareholder's true name.
		(4) Send new share certificate to member, after cancelling and filing old certificates.
		(5) File the Statutory Declaration.
		(6) Prepare a new address plate.

11. Change of address	Notice of change of address. NOTE: It is not usually necessary to produce share certificate.	(1) If a standard form is provided, ensure that it bears signature of shareholder. (2) Acknowledge the notice, to both old and new addresses, if in doubt. (3) Amend the Register of Members. (4) File the shareholder's notice. (5) Prepare new address plate.

PROGRESS TEST 9

1. Give specimen rulings for the following:

(a) Register of probates and letters of administration; and

(b) Register of powers of attorney.

To enable your company to dispense with these and other registers of this type, what alternative measures would you suggest? (7)

2. Discuss the growth of documentary photography in so far as it concerns documents presented to a company for registration. Summarise the type of documents of which photographs might be presented, and state which of these, in your opinion, should be accepted, giving reasons for your answer. (8)

3. How would you deal with the following documents submitted to you for registration:

(a) bankruptcy order; (b) deed poll; (c) notification of member's elevation to the peerage; (d) notice of change of name of corporate member; (e) court order appointing liquidator of corporate member. (10)

4. (a) X is a shareholder in the public company of which you are secretary. Probate is lodged by the executors of X. What alterations would you make in the company's register of members? You return the probate to the executors enclosing the usual "letter of request" for completion by them but, before this is returned to the company, the executors sell part of the holding and the necessary documents of transfer are lodged. Detail the action you would take.

(b) What action would you take on receipt of probate of the will of a deceased member whose shares were held by him jointly with his wife? *ICSA* (4, 9, 10)

5. What action should be taken by the secretary of a public company upon receipt of the following documents:

(a) letters of administration granted by Bermuda;

(b) death certificate of A, who holds shares jointly with B;

(c) letter from a solicitor advising that a shareholder has died and asking for a valuation of the company's shares on the date of his death. The company does not have an official quotation. *ICSA* (5, 9, 10)

6. Some months ago a power of attorney was submitted to you, as secretary, and after examination was registered in the usual manner. Subsequently several transfers of shares took place, the attorney signed on behalf of the transferor. A further transfer, similarly signed, is now submitted, but on this occasion the attorney is named as transferee. What action would you take and what advice would you

give to the board in reference to this transfer? **(6, 10)**

7. As secretary of a public company you receive the following letters. You are required to draft appropriate letters in reply:

(*a*) A shareholder, Miss C. Dee, writes to tell you that she has married and her name is now Wye. You reply in the usual form requesting a sight of the marriage certificate. You receive an indignant reply, refusing to send the certificate as she considers that you should accept her written advice.

(*b*) The widow of a shareholder, A. Bee, writes enclosing the death certificate of her husband who had 15 shares in your company having a market value of £27. In a covering letter Mrs Bee explains that the total value of her husband's estate is only £180 and, to save the cost of a grant of administration she asks if you will transfer the shares to her name. *ICSA* **(5, 10)**

8. Outline the circumstances in which the following documents may be lodged with the secretary of a company;

(*a*) letters of administration *de bonis non*;

(*b*) a garnishee order absolute;

(*c*) a stop notice.

What action should the secretary take on each document? **(VI, 12; IX, 5, 9, 10)**

9. Explain:

(*a*) the difference between a stock transfer form and a broker's transfer form;

(*b*) the action you would take on receiving advice of a change of address from a shareholder;

(*c*) what the Stock Exchange requires to be shown on the face of a share certificate;

(*d*) how you would deal with a probate lodged for registration. *ICSA* **(VII, I; VIII, 6; IX, 4, 10)**

CHAPTER X

Dividends

GENERAL RULES—PROFITS AVAILABLE FOR DISTRIBUTION

1. Definition. A dividend is that part of a company's net profit which is distributed to its shareholders in proportion to their respective shareholdings.

2. The chief rules relating to declaration and payment of dividends are as follows.

(*a*) *Power to declare dividends.* In most cases the power to declare a dividend and other provisions relating to declaration and payment of dividends are set out in a company's Articles.

(*b*) *Provisions of Table A* relating to dividends are as follows.

(*i*) *Power to declare dividends* is given to the company in general meeting, but the dividend must not exceed the amount recommended by the directors: Article 114.

(*ii*) *Interim dividends.* The directors have power to pay interim dividends, where it is justified by the profits: Article 115.

(*iii*) *Source of dividend.* No dividend or interim dividend shall be paid otherwise than in accordance with the provisions of Part III of the Companies Act 1980 which apply to the company: Article 6 (*see* **3** below).

(*iv*) *Power of directors to create reserves.* Before recommending a dividend, the directors are empowered to set aside sums out of profits as reserves, or to carry forward any profit which they consider should not be distributed: Article 117.

(*v*) *Calculation of dividend.* Unless shares have special rights, dividends are to be calculated on the amounts paid, or credited as paid, on the shares: Article 118.

(*vi*) *Calls in advance.* Dividends will not be paid on calls paid in advance: Article 118.

(*vii*) *Unpaid calls* may be deducted from dividend due to a member: Article 119.

(*viii*) *Permitted forms of payment*. Dividend (or bonus) may be paid wholly or partly in the form of specific assets, such as shares or debenture stock of another company, and the issue of fractional certificates is permitted in regard to such distribution: Article 120.

(*ix*) *Method of payment*. Dividend, interest or other moneys payable in cash may be paid by cheque or warrant sent through the post to a shareholder's registered address: Article 121.

(*x*) *Dividend, etc., due to joint holders* will be sent to the address of the joint holder first named in the register, unless the joint holders direct otherwise in writing: Article 121.

(*xi*) *Delay in payment of dividend* does not entitle a shareholder to claim for interest against the company: Article 122.

(*c*) *If, however, Table A is expressly excluded* and the Articles make no provision to the contrary, dividend will be calculable on the *nominal* value of the shares concerned, i.e. irrespective of the amount paid up: *Re Bridgewater Navigation Co.* (1891).

(*d*) *Unclaimed dividends*. In some cases, Articles provide that unclaimed dividends shall be forfeited after a specific period. Where Stock Exchange regulations apply, forfeiture of unclaimed dividend *is* permitted, but only after the claim becomes statute-barred, i.e. twelve years after the date of declaration of the dividend.

NOTE: It must be realised, however, that the appearance of "unclaimed dividends" in a company's balance sheet may constitute sufficient acknowledgment of the debt to permit its revival: *Jones* v. *Bellgrove Properties* (1949).

3. Profits available for distribution. In order to ensure that a company's capital fund was not reduced by payments of capital masquerading as payments of dividend the courts declared that "dividends could only be paid out of profits and not out of capital". This rule simple enough to state in the abstract in practice became clouded and subject to potential abuse as the judiciary sought to establish what for this purpose was to be regarded as profit and what was to be regarded as capital.

Happily, however, the Companies Act 1980 in implementation of the EEC Second Directive on the Harmonisation of Company Law, while continuing and giving statutory effect to the basic principle established by the judges, lays down specific detailed rules to give effect to that principle and in so doing overrides the decisions of the courts in so far as they are inconsistent with the legisliation.

The law as established by the Companies Act 1980 may be summarised as follows:

(*a*) A company must not make a distribution except out of profits available for the purpose, which, broadly interpreted, means its accumulated realised profits so far as not previously utilised by distribution or capitalisation less its accumulated realised losses, in so far as they have not previously been written off in a reduction or reorganisation of capital duly made: Companies Act 1980, s.39.

(*b*) In the case of a *public* company, it may only make a distribution at any time:

(*i*) if at that time the amount of its net assets is not less than the aggregate of the company's called-up share capital and its undistributable reserves; and

(*ii*) if, and to the extent that, the distribution does not reduce the amount of those assets to less than that aggregate.

NOTE: For this purpose "undistributable reserves" include the share premium account, capital redemption reserve and any other reserve which the company is prohibited from distributing by any enactment, or by its articles or memorandum: Companies Act 1980, s.40.

(*c*) The right to make, and the amount of, any distribution is, however, dependent upon the company being able to produce "relevant accounts", and this applies to an interim as well as to a final distribution; that is, in all cases, a distribution must be demonstrably justified by the accounts.

NOTE: The "relevant accounts" in the case of a particular distribution are the last annual accounts which were laid or filed in respect of the last preceding accounting reference period; or such interim accounts as are necessary to enable a proper judgment to be made as to the amounts of any of the relevant items: Companies Act 1980, s.43.

(*d*) The consequences of making an unlawful distribution are stated but do not impose any criminal sanction. If, however, a member knows (or has reasonable grounds for believing) that a distribution to him was in contravention of the Act, he will be liable to repay to the company a sum equal to the value of any distribution unlawfully made to him: Companies Act 1980, s.44.

NOTE: The above sections do not refer to investment companies. Provisions relating to distributions made by such companies are dealt with separately in the Companies Act 1980, s.41.

DIVIDEND PROCEDURE AND DOCUMENTS

4. Procedure on declaration and payment of dividends.

(*a*) Consult the Articles. When profit available for dividend has been determined, it may be necessary to consult the company's Articles so as to ensure that the dividend rights of the various classes of shareholders are understood and that the distribution will be properly made.

(*b*) A board meeting is convened at which the directors decide what dividend (if any) they recommend for each of the various classes of shares, and a resolution is passed, recommending the payment of dividend(s) and stating the rate(s) and date of payment.

NOTE: Where applicable, i.e. in the case of a company whose shares are listed, the stock exchange will require notification of the date of the above meeting and, following the resolution recommending the payment of dividend (or the decision to pass any dividend or interest payment), must be notified of the decisions by letter or telephone. Similar notification may be given simultaneously to press agents.

(*c*) Further resolutions may be passed at the same meeting, on the assumption that the directors' recommendation concerning the payment of dividends will be approved, namely:

(*i*) that the Register of Members (and Transfer Register, if any) be closed and the fact advertised;

NOTE: In practice, many companies do not close the books but announce payment of dividends to all persons appearing in the Register of Members on a specified date prior to the date fixed for payment.

(*ii*) that the bank be authorised to deal with the payment of dividends, and to open a special dividend account or accounts;

(*iii*) that the draft of the directors' report be approved;

(*iv*) that copies of the directors' report and accounts, together with auditors' report and the balance sheet, be distributed to those so entitled;

(*v*) that the annual general meeting be convened, the notices to be accompanied by copies of the report and accounts, and sent not less than 21 days before the meeting.

(*d*) Convene the annual general meeting, ensuring that the notices are accompanied by copies of the directors' report and accounts, and that adequate notice is given.

NOTE: Notice should also be sent to the company's auditors and, where applicable, copies of the report and accounts *only* should be sent to any members who are not entitled to attend the meeting, and to debenture holders.

Where stock exchange regulations apply, four copies of the report and account should be sent simultaneously to the stock exchange concerned, and copies may also be handed to the company's press agents for circulation.

(*e*) Give notice in the Press as to the closing of the Register of Members, if that is intended.

(*f*) The Register of Members is brought up to date. Transfers received on or before the date fixed for closing the register (and Transfer Register, if any) will be the subject of another board meeting (or meeting of the transfer committee), at which a resolution will be passed authorising transfers.

(*g*) Once the Register of Members has been brought up to date, the dividend lists can be prepared from the register. These lists are usually on loose sheets to facilitate distribution of the work. A specimen ruling is shown.

Dividend list

Shareholder		No. of shares	Gross dividend	*Less* tax	Net amount	Warrant no.	Remarks, dividend mandates, etc.
Name	Address						
			£	£	£		

(*h*) At the annual general meeting, it may be assumed that the dividend(s) recommended by the directors are approved by the shareholders.

(*i*) Dividend warrants, having already been printed and serially numbered, are now prepared from the dividend lists (in practice this work is often done even before the holding of the annual general meeting).

(*j*) Check dividend warrants and reconcile them back to the dividend list total(s), after which the bank may be supplied with a dividend list and instructed to transfer the list total to a special dividend account or accounts.

(*k*) The Secretary may now sign the warrants or, alternatively, in a large company, either of the following methods may be employed:

(*i*) by resolution of the board, the signing may be delegated to several responsible officials: or (*ii*) if permitted by the Articles, mechanical signatures may be used.

NOTE: If this method is used, the bank must be notified and special precautions must be taken to minimise error or fraud.

(*l*) Dividend warrants can now be made ready for posting. After they have been folded, inserted in addressed envelopes (or window envelopes), sealed and franked, they should be given a final check and the total number of envelopes agreed with the dividend lists.

NOTE: At this stage, it may be necessary to prepare vouchers and "strip lists", ready for despatch to "listed" (or "bulk") banks, referred to in (*m*) below.

(*m*) Finally, the dividend warrants are posted. At the same time, where applicable, post vouchers and "strip lists" to the "listed" banks.

(*n*) Subsequently, the bank will return the "cheque" portion of the warrants as they are presented for payment by the shareholders. After checking them against the bank statement they should be securely filed and retained for at least twelve years, to satisfy the Limitations Act 1980.

NOTE: It is also advisable to retain the dividend lists, for the same reason.

5. Dividend warrants.

(*a*) A dividend warrant is an important document, as it serves two main purposes.

(*i*) The "notice" or "counterfoil" portion informs the shareholder of the gross amount of the dividend, the rate and amount of tax deducted, and the net amount of dividend to which he is entitled. It also states that tax has been or will be paid. This must be carefully preserved as evidence of the tax deducted.

(*ii*) The "warrant" or "cheque" portion must be presented to the bank upon which it is drawn—usually within a specified period of, say, six months—otherwise it becomes "stale".

(*iii*) The following is a simple form of dividend warrant.

BLANK PLC

Transfer Office _____ London _____ 19 _____

ORDINARY SHARES

FINAL DIVIDEND for the year ended _____19___of _____ % less Income Tax.

I certify that the Income Tax deducted from this dividend will be accounted for to the proper officer for the receipt of taxes. This voucher should be retained by the shareholder and will be accepted by the Inland Revenue as evidence of payment of tax by deduction.

(signed) _____ Secretary

Standard rate of Income Tax	Holding (Units)	Gross Amount	Income Tax @ _____	NET AMOUNT

Name and address of Shareholder

Voucher No. _____

- - - - - - - - - - - - (Perforation) - - - - - - - - - - - - -

Ordinary Share Dividend _____19 ___

BLANK PLC

POUND BANK PLC

Pay _____ or Order

_____ £ _____

(Authorised signature)

Warrant No. _____

(*b*) To prevent fraud during the preparation of dividend warrants:

(*i*) there must be strict control, by a responsible official, on the issue of blank warrants to the staff engaged in completing them;

(*ii*) only the exact number of blank warrants should be issued by him, and spoilt warrants must be returned to him for replacement and cancellation.

(*c*) Even stricter security measures are necessary when facsimile signatures are used on the dividend warrants, whether the "signing" is done by machine in the company's own offices or by the printers who were responsible for the printing of the warrants. In the latter case, the measures suggested are as follows.

(*i*) Notify the company's bankers that it is intended to use facsimile signatures on dividend warrants, and provide them with specimens of the signatories (if, as is usual in most cases, the warrants are to be initialled for the purpose of identification, the bank will also require specimens of the initials of persons so authorised).

(*ii*) Instruct the printers to supply a specified number of warrants bearing facsimile signatures. The number specified should include a small number of spares, to allow for spoilt warrants.

NOTE: It is usually necessary to order a small supply of warrants *without* signature, to replace any which may be lost after using up all of those bearing facsimile signatures. These must be signed manually as and when they are needed.

(*iii*) When the warrants are received from the printers they must be strictly controlled by a responsible official as regards issue, replacement in exchange for spoilt warrants, and cancellation of the latter.

(*iv*) After completion of the warrants, they should be thoroughly checked, and then initialled in the space provided. The checking must be carried out by members of the staff who had no part in preparing the warrants, or by the company's auditors.

(*v*) Notify the bank of the number of warrants to be issued and serial numbers of the warrants.

(*vi*) Any "signed" warrants in excess of requirements must be cancelled as soon as ever possible. If any replacements are subsequently required, the unsigned warrants (already referred to) must be used, after hand signature.

(*vii*) The printers' "blocks" of facsimile signatures should be returned, and carefully stored in safe or strong room.

(*viii*) Obtain a certificate from the printers:

(1) as to the number of warrants printed by them;

(2) that they have "broken type" and cancelled or destroyed any warrants used by them in trial prints.

6. Dividend mandates.

(a) *Definition*. A dividend mandate is an instruction, given to a company by one of its shareholders, to pay any dividend to which he is entitled to his bank, broker or other person. The instruction may, of course, refer to the payment of interest on, say, debentures.

(b) *Forms*. A shareholder is usually entitled to this facility, and most large companies provide printed forms for the purpose; if not, the official mandate form (or Dividend Request Form, as it is called) recommended by the Committee of the London Clearing Bankers is obtainable from banks in the clearing house system.

(c) *Joint holders*. A mandate in respect of dividend payable to a joint holding must be signed by *all* the joint holders, and the death of any one of them automatically revokes the instructions. A fresh mandate should then be obtained from the surviving joint holder(s).

(d) *"Listed" banks.*

(*i*) Where, as often happens, a bank is named in a large number of mandates, labour and stationery can be saved if only one warrant is prepared for the total dividend payable to all the shareholders who have mandated in favour of that particular bank.

(*ii*) This one "cheque" portion of the warrant is then sent to the head office of the bank concerned, together with a list of the shareholders affected, showing the dividend due to each and the branches at which they have their respective accounts. A "counterfoil" portion is also sent for each shareholder included in the list.

(e) *A specimen of a dividend mandate* is shown opposite.

7. Outstanding dividends.

(a) These are a source of trouble and expense. It may surprise many to learn that there should be any difficulty in getting shareholders to claim the dividend to which they are entitled. Nevertheless it is a fact that many large public companies regard this as a serious problem, as a great deal of time is taken in marking off paid warrants as they are received from the company's bank and, in the last resort, recording those warrants which remain outstanding.

(b) To ensure that the number of outstanding warrants is kept to a minimum, companies introduce all manner of devices, on the principle that "prevention is better than cure"; of these, the following are typical.

Dividend request form

To the Secretary,
Blank Company Plc,
Finsbury Square, E.C.2.

I/We, the undersigned, request and authorise you to pay, unless and until you receive further notice, all interest and dividends now due, or from time to time falling due and becoming payable, on any stock, shares or other securities now or hereafter registered in my/our name(s) in the books of the above company to ....at .... or to any branch of that bank to which my/our account may be transferred, whose receipt shall be your full and sufficient discharge.

Signature(s) ....

Address ....

Dated ....

Note: In the case of *joint* accounts, this form requires the signatures of *all* joint holders.
The Company cannot undertake to make warrants payable to a particular account with the banker named; such instructions must be given *direct* to the banker concerned.

(*i*) The attention of shareholders is drawn to the many advantages, to themselves as well as to the company, of completing a dividend mandate. This may be done by circular letter to the shareholders.

(*ii*) As an alternative to the sending of circular letters, some companies print a memorandum on the back of their dividend warrant counterfoils, in which they bring to the shareholders' notice the advantages of dividend mandates, and provide a form of mandate on each warrant.

(*iii*) In the case of new members, a letter of welcome might be sent which would include a recommendation to make use of a dividend mandate (enclosed with the letter).

(*iv*) As warrants frequently become outstanding following a shareholder's death, it is often a good plan to draw the attention of the legal representative(s) to the current dividend position and, where applicable, to any outstanding dividends as soon as possible after probate or letters of administration have been presented.

(*v*) A footnote printed on all dividend warrants, reminding shareholders that the warrant becomes "stale" after (say) six months, is another method employed by many companies, but it is doubtful whether it has the desired effect with the more troublesome cases.

(c) If, despite all the above preventive measures, the number of un-claimed dividends continues to mount, then some system of record-ing the unclaimed sums must be devised, for example, as follows.

(i) Mark off paid warrants against the dividend list as the warrants are received from the bank after payment. Check also against the bank statement concerned with the dividend account.

(ii) Prepare a list of outstanding warrants (i.e. those which had not been marked off against the dividend list) giving brief particulars, including warrants numbers and their respective amounts.

(iii) Amend the list if, during (say) the next six months, any of the outstanding warrants are cashed and the paid warrants received from the bank.

(iv) At the end of the period of (say) six months, outstanding warrants having become "stale", require re-dating, and shareholders are usually required to present them at the company's office for re-dating and vertification. A footnote on the warrant usually emphasises this. If, however, a large number of warrants are still out-standing, a letter to the shareholders concerned along the following lines might serve a useful purpose.

Dear Sir (or Madam),

We note from the Company's dividend account that the dividend warrant(s) described below, issued to you on ....19......, do(es) not appear to have been presented for payment.

As the warrant is now out of date, we should be obliged if you would return it to us for verification and re-dating. It will be returned to you as soon as possible, after which you may present it to your bank for early payment.

If you have lost or destroyed your warrant, please let us know by return. We shall then provide you with the necessary form for completion, to enable us to supply you with a duplicate warrant.

Please return this letter with your reply.

Yours faithfully,

Date .... Secretary.

Particulars of outstanding warrant(s)

Date payable	Dividend No.	Warrant No.	Amount	
			£	p

(*v*) The dividend account is closed at the end of the (say) six-month period and any balance transferred to an Outstanding Dividends Account.

(*vi*) An "Outstanding Dividend Register" may be prepared, if warranted by the number of unclaimed dividends. It is usually advisable to use a looseleaf register for this purpose.

(*vii*) A separate account is kept in the register for each dividend, in which a record will be made whenever unclaimed dividends are transferred to the Outstanding Dividends Account. As outstanding dividends are cashed from time to time and the paid warrants received from the bank, an entry will be made in the appropriate account or accounts and, where applicable, any "closed" account will be removed from the register.

(*viii*) A Summary Account is kept in the register. If this is kept up to date, the running total of this account ought to agree, or be reconcilable with, the Outstanding Dividends Account at the bank.

8. Loss or destruction of dividend warrants. A large company often receives letters from its shareholders stating that a dividend warrant has been lost, mislaid or destroyed. In such cases, it is obviously necessary to safeguard the company against false statements and against the fraudulent conversion of the original warrant if the company issues a duplicate. A typical procedure on receipt of a shareholder's request for a duplicate warrant is as follows.

(*a*) Notify the bank at once and give instructions to stop payment on the original warrant (if the shareholder has delayed his request, it may be found that someone has already fraudulently cashed the warrant!).

(*b*) Acknowledge the shareholder's letter and send him a form of indemnity, requesting him to return the completed form and (if permitted by the Articles) a nominal replacement fee of, say, $12\frac{1}{2}$p.

(*c*) On receipt of the completed form of indemnity and remittance of the replacement fee (where applicable, supply a copy of the warrant, taking care to mark it DUPLICATE

(*d*) If the counterfoil portion of the warrant is also to be replaced, the copy must also be marked DUPLICATE, as this is a requirement of the Inland Revenue authorities.

(*e*) Authorise the bank to honour only the *duplicate* warrant.

(*f*) Record the issue of the duplicate warrant on the dividend list.

NOTE: Some companies demand a banker's counter-indemnity in addition to the shareholder's own indemnity. If the amount of the warrant is large, such a demand may be justifiable, but it may seem somewhat harsh to the small shareholder, as the bank charge for a counter-indemnity might be at least $52\frac{1}{2}$p.

9. Department of Trade and Industry powers under s.174 to impose restrictions, including (*inter alia*) the withholding of payment of dividend, are as follows.

(*a*) Where the Department of Trade and Industry is having difficulty in finding out the relevant facts concerning shares which are the subject of an investigation owing to the unwillingness of the persons concerned to assist the investigation, it has power to direct that no payment shall be made on any sums due from the company on those shares, whether in respect of capital or otherwise.

(*b*) An aggrieved person may, however, apply to the Court to remove the restriction imposed by the Department of Trade and Industry.

(*c*) In order to obtain information from a person on whom a notice is served under s.74 of the Companies Act 1981 (power of company to require information with respect to interests in its voting shares), s.77 of the 1981 Act gives the company rights to apply to the court for an order directing that the shares in question shall be subject to the restrictions imposed by s.174 of the 1948 Act relating to the transfer, voting or dividend rights in respect of such shares.

PROGRESS TEST 10

1. Define the term "dividend" and state the chief rules to be applied by a company as regards the payment of dividends to its shareholders. **(1, 2)**

2. Outline the procedure for paying a dividend on ordinary shares, commencing with the board's decision to recommend a distribution. **(4)**

3. Prepare a programme covering the procedure for paying a dividend to a large number of shareholders. The programme should be set out in chronological order so that each item can be marked off as it is completed. *ICSA* **(4)**

4. Owing to a large increase in the number of shareholders of the public company of which you are secretary, it is intended to print future dividend warrants with a facsimile signature. Detail the precautions which should be taken in connection with the issue of these warrants and draft a form to be used to ensure that every warrant printed is accounted for. *ICSA* **(5)**

5. Write brief notes on (*a*) dividend warrant, (*b*) dividend mandate, (*c*) interim dividend, (*d*) listed banks. (**2–6**)

6. On being appointed secretary of a public company incorporated thirty years ago, you find that a considerable number of dividend warrants have remained unclaimed from time to time. The company has regularly paid two dividends annually, but no composite record of the outstanding dividends has been maintained. Discuss the advantages and disadvantages of endeavouring to trace and pay the persons entitled to the outstanding dividends and state how you would keep a record of the unclaimed sums so that a continual reference to individual dividend sheets could be avoided. Assuming that the directors instructed you to make every effort to pay the outstanding dividends, how would you deal with the matter? (**7**)

7. As secretary of a company, you are informed in writing by a shareholder that a dividend warrant for £50 recently received by him has been accidentally destroyed. Explain in detail the office procedure involved in connection with the lost warrant and also write a letter in reply to the shareholder. (**8**)

8. In certain circumstances the Department of Trade and Industry is empowered by s.174 of the Companies Act 1848 to subject shares or debentures to certain restrictions. You are asked to assume that this power has been exercised in regard to a holding which is registered in your company's books and you are required to write to the member concerned explaining why you are unable to pay to him a dividend which has been declared. (**9**)

CHAPTER XI

Alterations of Share Capital

ALTERATION OF CAPITAL UNDER s.61

1. Permitted forms of alteration. For various reasons a company may find it necessary to alter its share capital, and s.61 provides that a company limited by shares, or a company limited by guarantee and having a share capital, may, *if its Articles permit*, alter the conditions of its Memorandum in order to effect any of the following alterations.

(*a*) *Increase* the share capital by new shares of such amount as the company thinks necessary.

(*b*) *Consolidate and divide* all or part of the share capital into shares of larger amount.

(*c*) *Convert* all or any of its paid up shares into stock.

(*d*) *Re-convert* stock into paid up shares of any amount.

(*e*) *Subdivide* all or part of its shares into shares of smaller denomination, but maintaining the proportion between the amount paid and the amount (if any) unpaid on each reduced share.

(*f*) *Cancel* shares which have not been taken up, and thus reduce the whole or part of the company's unissued authorised capital

NOTE: This form of cancellation must not be confused with a reduction of capital under s.66.

2. Consent of general meeting. The above alterations can be effected only by the company in general meeting; that is, the power to make the alteration *cannot* be delegated to the directors.

3. Form of resolution required.

(*a*) *An ordinary* resolution is adequate, unless the company's Articles demand another form of resolution.

(*b*) Where the Articles give no power to alter the capital, *one* special resolution is sufficient both to alter the Articles for the purpose and to alter the share capital: *Campbell's Case* (1873).

4. Notice must be given to the Registrar of the passing of the resolution to give effect to any of the above resolutions:

(*a*) *within 15 days* after passing the resolution to *increase* the capital: s.63;

(*b*) *within one month* after passing the resolution in all other forms of alteration of capital permitted under s.61.

5. Increase of capital.

(*a*) *The need for increased capital* is usually the result of expanding business. If, for example, the whole of a company's authorised capital has been issued and paid up, further capital may be needed for purposes of development, and the directors may prefer to increase the authorised capital and issue further shares rather than issue debentures or apply to the bank for an overdraft.

(*b*) *Procedure.*

(*i*) Convene a general meeting of the company, giving notice required by the Articles—but not less than 14 days' notice of an extraordinary general meeting.

NOTE: If the Articles require a special resolution to increase capital, not less than 21 days' notice is required.

(*ii*) The necessary resolution is passed; e.g.:

RESOLVED: That the capital of the Company be and is hereby increased from £50,000 in shares of £1 each to £100,000 by the addition to the authorised capital of 25,000 £1 shares, to rank *pari passu* in all respects with the aforementioned £1 shares, and 25,000 6% preference shares of £1 each.

(*iii*) If a listed company, send four copies of the resolution to the stock exchange as soon as possible. Subsequently, it will be necessary to submit:

(1) a specimen, or printer's proof, of any new shares certificates, and a statement as to when the certificates will be ready; and

(2) application for a fresh listing if the increased capital is in a new form of security.

(*iv*) Within 15 days of the passing of the resolution, file with the Registrar of Companies:

(1) *notice of Increase in Nominal Capital* on the special form provided for the purpose;

(2) *statement of Increase of Nominal Capital*, bearing a stamp for capital duty at the rate of £1 per £100 calculated as stated in I, 11.

(3) *a copy of the resolution* authorising the increase of capital.

(4) A copy of the memorandum as amended.

(*v*) Amend all copies of the Memorandum to ensure that every copy subsequently issued shows the increase of capital. Failure to comply renders the company, and every officer of the company in default, liable to fines for each occasion on which copies are issued after the date of the alteration.

6. Consolidation and division into shares of larger denomination.

(*a*) *When desirable.* Although consolidation alone is now a comparatively rare occurrence, when used in conjunction with a division it enables a company to even out shares of odd nominal values; where, for example, a company has on some previous occasion created shares of $7\frac{1}{2}$p for each as the result of a repayment of capital under s.66, ten $7\frac{1}{2}$p shares may be consolidated into one 75p share and the latter sub-divided into three 25p shares.

(*b*) *Procedure.*

(*i*) Convene a general meeting of the company, giving notice appropriate to the form of resolution required by the articles.

(*ii*) The necessary resolution is passed, i.e. an *ordinary* resolution (unless the Articles provide to the contrary), for example:

RESOLVED: That the 300,000 fully-paid ordinary shares of $7\frac{1}{2}$p each be consolidated into 30,000 fully-paid ordinary shares of 75p each, and that the said 30,000 fully-paid ordinary shares of 75p each be divided into 90,000 fully-paid ordinary shares of 25p each.

(*iii*) If a listed company, send four copies of the resolution to the stock exchange as soon as possible and ensure compliance with other requirements if it is intended to obtain a fresh listing.

(*iv*) Within one month of the passing of the resolution, file with the Registrar of Companies a Notice of Consolidation on the special form provided for the purpose accompanied by an amended copy of the memorandum.

NOTE: If an ordinary resolution is adequate to authorise the consolidation, it will *not* be necessary to file a copy with the Registrar; if, however, a special resolution is required by the Articles, it will be necessary to file a copy of it within 15 days.

(*v*) Amend all copies of the Memorandum in stock, so that the effect of the consolidation is clearly shown: s.25.

7. Conversion of fully paid shares into stock, and reconversion.

(*a*) *The advantages claimed* for conversion of shares into stock—namely, that it enables a company to dispense with distinguishing numbering of its shares and permits transfer in irregular amounts or fractions—are now less apparent, if they exist at all. This may be judged from a consideration of the following points.

(*i*) Section 74 permits a company to dispense with the numbering of its shares, subject to conditions laid down in that section (*see* I, **47**).

(*ii*) The Articles of most companies require stock to be transferred in fixed multiples.

(*iii*) Where stock exchange regulations apply, transfer is restricted to multiples of £1.

(*b*) *Procedure.*

(*i*) As a preliminary, ensure that the Articles give the necessary power to effect the conversion, and that the shares *are* fully paid.

(*ii*) Convene a general meeting of the company, giving notice appropriate to the form of resolution required.

(*iii*) The necessary resolution is passed—an ordinary resolution, unless the articles require any other form of resolution; for example:

RESOLVED: That the 2,000,000 ordinary shares of 25p each forming part of the Company's capital, already issued and fully-paid, be and are hereby converted into stock, to be known as Ordinary Stock.

(*iv*) If a listed company, send four copies of the resolution to the stock exchange as soon as possible and, either then or subsequently, submit:

(1) a specimen, or printers' proof, of the new stock certificate, and a statement as to when the new certificates will be ready; and

(2) an application for a fresh listing for the new security.

(*v*) Within one month of the passing of the resolution, file with the Registrar of Companies a Notice of Conversion (or, where applicable, of re-conversion) accompanied by an amended copy of the memorandum.

NOTE: If an ordinary resolution is adequate to authorise the conversion (or re-conversion), it will *not* be necessary to file a copy with the Registrar; if, however, the Articles require a special resolution, it will be necessary to file a copy of it within 15 days.

(*vi*) Amend all copies of the Memorandum in stock, so that the effect of the conversion is clearly shown: s.25.

8. Subdivision of shares into shares of smaller denomination, e.g. £1 shares subdivided into 20 5p shares.

(*a*) *When desirable.* This is usually done because of the increasing popularity of shares of small denomination and the wider section of the public they appear to attract.

(*b*) *Procedure.*

(*i*) Convene a general meeting of the company, giving notice appropriate to the form of resolution required.

(*ii*) The necessary resolution is passed—an ordinary resolution, unless the Articles require any other form of resolution; for example:

RESOLVED: That the capital of the Company, comprising 100,000 ordinary shares of £1 each fully paid up, be subdivided into 2,000,000 ordinary shares of 5p each fully paid up.

(*iii*) If a listed company, send four copies of the resolution to the stock exchange as soon as possible and ensure compliance with other relevant stock exchange requirements.

(*iv*) Within one month of the passing of the resolution, file Notice of Subdivision on the official form for the purpose accompanied by an amended copy of the memorandum.

(*v*) Amend all copies of the Memorandum in stock, so that the effect of the subdivision is clearly shown: s.25.

9. Cancellation of shares which have not been taken up; e.g. a company with authorised capital of £100,000 and issued capital of £50,000 may cancel (say) £30,000 of its *unissued* authorised capital, thereby reducing the authorised capital to £70,000.

(*a*) *The effect* is to reduce the capital which the company is by its Memorandum authorised to issue, and can only be effected under s.61 where the authorised capital exceeds the issued capital.

(*b*) *Not a reduction of issued capital.* It is not to be confused with a reduction of capital such as can be effected under the provisions of s.66 (*see* **11–15**).

(*c*) *Loss of capital duty.* Cancellation of authorised capital under s.61 seldom occurs in practice, as capital duty has already been paid on the original authorised capital and there is no provision in the Act for repayment of capital duty.

(*d*) *Avoiding loss of capital duty.* Cancellation may, however, be effected simultaneously with an increase of capital, so that there would be no loss of capital duty; for example:

(*i*) 50,000 £1 deferred shares with heavy voting rights may be cancelled because the rights attaching to the shares are set out in the company's Memorandum and that document makes no provision for variation of shareholders' rights.

(*ii*) Simultaneously, the capital may be increased to its original amount by the addition of (say) 200,000 25p ordinary shares with restricted voting rights, or none at all.

(*e*) *Procedure.*

(*i*) Convene a general meeting of the company, giving notice appropriate to the form of resolution required.

(*ii*) The necessary resolution is passed, i.e. an ordinary resolution unless the Articles require any other form of resolution; for example:

RESOLVED: That the unissued 50,000 deferred shares of £1 each forming part of the Company's authorised capital, be and they are hereby cancelled, and that the capital of the Company be and is hereby increased by the addition of 200,000 ordinary shares of 25p each.

(*iii*) If a listed company, send four copies of the resolution to the stock exchange as soon as possible, and ensure compliance with other relevant stock exchange regulations.

(*iv*) Within one month of the passing of the resolution, file Notice of Cancellation on the official form for the purpose, such to be accompanied by an amended copy of the memorandum.

NOTE: If the cancellation is effected simultaneously with an increase of capital, so long as there is no increase beyond the registered capital of the company, it will *not* be necessary to file any other documents.

(*v*) Amend all copies of the Memorandum in stock, so that the effect of the cancellation (and simultaneous increase, where applicable) is clearly shown: s.25.

10. Additional work entailed in connection with the above procedures. According to the form of alteration, some or all of the following matters may have to be dealt with by the Secretary and/or registrar:

(*a*) preparation of new share certificates;

(*b*) closing the Register of Members if it is intended to call in share (or stock) certificates;

NOTE: In practice the certificates are *not* usually called in, i.e. they continue to be accepted on the stock exchange as good delivery, and the exchange of a new certificate for the old one is effected if or when a transfer is subsequently lodged for registration.

(c) alteration of the Register of Members, e.g. in cases of consolidation or sub-division;

(d) transfer from Share Register to Stock Register, in case of a conversion to stock.

REDUCTION OF CAPITAL UNDER s.66

11. When reduction is allowed. Section 66 permits a company limited by shares, or a company limited by guarantee and having a share capital, to reduce its share capital in any way:

(a) if the articles permit,

(b) by special resolution, and

(c) with Court sanction.

NOTE: Power given in the Memorandum alone is *not* sufficient: *Re Dexine Patent Packing Co.* (1903).

12. Statutory methods. The Act mentions the following particular methods of capital reduction, but these are not to be regarded as exhaustive and do not affect the generality of the power.

(a) Extinguishing or reducing the unpaid liability on any of the company's shares; for example:

(i) a £1 share with 75p paid up to rank as a 75p share fully paid, i.e. *extinguishing* the liability of 25p per share; or

(ii) a £1 share with $37\frac{1}{2}$p paid up to rank as a 50p share with $37\frac{1}{2}$p paid up, i.e. *reducing* the liability.

(b) With or without extinguishing or reducing liability on any of the company's shares, cancelling any paid up share capital which is lost or unrepresented by available assets; for example:

(i) a fully paid £1 share to rank as a fully paid 50p share, i.e. *without reducing liability*; or

(ii) a £1 share with 75p paid up to rank as a 50p share fully paid, i.e. *extinguishing* liability.

(c) With or without extinguishing or reducing liability on any of the company's shares, paying-off any paid up share capital which is in excess of the wants of the company; for example:

(i) each holder of £1 fully paid shares to be repaid 25p per share, and the shares then to rank as 75p fully paid shares, i.e. *without extinguishing or reducing* liability;

(*ii*) each holder of £1 shares with 87½p paid up to be repaid 37½p per share, and the shares then to rank as 50p shares fully paid, i.e. *extinguishing* the liability.

13. Possible reasons for reduction of capital.

(*a*) A company's paid up capital may not be adequately represented by available assets, owing, for example, to losses on fixed assets or on investments, and the assets concerned are to be written down.

(*b*) A company's capital may be in excess of requirements, in which case a return of capital might be advisable.

Thus, over capitalisation may be the result of closing down part of the business, and it is being found that capital invested outside the business at low rates of interest is resulting in an overall reduction of dividends.

(*c*) A company with a considerable adverse balance on profit and loss account, the result of an accumulation of previous losses, may wish to write off the balance.

14. Procedure.

(*a*) Preliminary discussion of an informal character will take place at a board meeting. Subsequently, the directors will probably consult the company's solicitors and accountants. Together they will plan a scheme of reduction.

(b) It is often advisable to do some preliminary research on the reaction of those who are most likely to be affected by the reduction.

(*i*) It might be well to ascertain the views of some of the largest shareholders, particularly those with voting power. If their support is not forthcoming there is a poor chance of passing a special resolution for reduction of capital.

(*ii*) It might also be advisable to invite some of the largest creditors (including debenture holders, if any) to a board meeting, with the object of explaining the scheme and how, if at all, it is likely to affect them and to solicit their support. This might forestall their later objections to the Court when the company petitions the Court for sanction.

(*c*) Convene a general meeting of the company, bearing in mind that the notice requires special attention:

(*i*) at least 21 days' notice is required;

(*ii*) it must set out the exact wording of the resolution to be passed, and state that it is to be a special resolution;

(*iii*) it is usually accompanied by a circular, setting out the reasons for the proposed reduction of capital.

NOTE: In the case of a company whose shares are listed, the stock exchange should also be supplied with a copy of this circular.

(d) At the meeting, the special resolution is passed authorising the reduction of capital; for example:

RESOLVED:That the capital of the company be reduced form £500,000 divided into 400,000 ordinary shares of £1 each and 100,000 6% preference shares of £1 each, all of which are issued and fully paid into £200,000 divided into 400,000 shares of 50p each fully paid up; the reduction to be effected:

(i) by repaying to the holders of the 400,000 £1 ordinary shares the sum of 50p per share, and by reducing the nominal amount of all the said 400,000 ordinary shares from £1 to 50p per share.

(ii) by cancellation of the 100,000 6% preference shares of £1 each, to be effected by repayment to the holders of the said 100,000 6% preference shares the sum of 105p per share, which sum includes a premium of 5p per share.

NOTE: If the Articles require alteration, i.e. where they do not already permit reduction of capital, this must also be done by special resolution, preferably at an earlier meeting. In this case, one special resolution will not serve the double purpose of both altering the Articles and authorising reduction of capital: *Re Patent Invert Sugar Co.* (1885).

(e) If a listed company, send four copies of the resolution to the stock exchange as soon as possible after the meeting.

(f) File a copy of the resolution with the Registrar of Companies, within 15 days of the passing of the resolution.

(g) Application can be made to the Court as soon as desired after the passing of the special resolution. It is presented in the form of a petition for confirmation of the reduction.

(h) The Court may then take such steps as it considers necessary to safeguard creditors (including debenture-holders) and to ensure that rights as between different classes of shareholders are maintained. Using its powers under s.67, it may:

(i) settle a list of creditors entitled to object to the reduction, and permit such creditors to submit their objections;

(ii) ascertain the wishes of the creditors;

(iii) decide that any class or classes of creditors are not entitled to object, where the circumstances justify that course;

(iv) dispense with the consent of any dissenting creditor, if the company secures payment of his debt in manner directed by the Court.

(*i*) The Court may then confirm the reduction of capital, but on such terms or conditions as it thinks fit. Thus the Court order may:

(*i*) direct the company that the words "and reduced" be added to its name for a specified period;

NOTE: The Act does not indicate any particular reason for making such an order, which is now rarely made.

(*ii*) direct the company to publish the reasons for the reduction of capital, and in some cases, the causes that led to the reduction: s.68.

NOTE: Under s.12 of the Companies Act 1980, if the court reduces the share capital of a public company to below £50,000 (the current authorised minimum capital) it must re-register as a private company. The court may authorise re-registration without the company having to follow the procedure specified under s.10 of the 1980 Act and the court order may specify and make the necessary changes in the company's constitution, e.g. in its name (*see* **16** *below*).

(*j*) Deliver to the Registrar of Companies, in accordance with the requirements of s.69:

(*i*) the Court order confirming the reduction of capital and a copy of the order;

(*ii*) copy of a minute in form approved by the Court, showing:
  (1) amount of the reduced share capital;
  (2) number of shares into which divided;
  (3) amount of each share, and
  (4) amount, if any, deemed to be paid up on each.

NOTE: This minute is deemed to be substituted for the corresponding part of the Memorandum.

(*k*) The Registrar having registered the Court order and copy of the minute, the resolution for reduction of capital becomes effective, and not before. His certificate as to the registration of the order and minute is conclusive evidence that all requirements of the Act have been complied with and that the share capital of the company is correctly stated in the minute: s.69(4).

(*l*) Publish notice of the registration of the order and minute, in manner directed by the Court; also, if applicable, add the words "and reduced" to the company's name on all stationery, and on the common seal.

(*m*) Ensure that all future copies of the Memorandum issued by the company include the minute, which now replaces the capital clause of the Memorandum: ss. 25 and 69. The Registrar must be forwarded an amended copy of the memorandum.

NOTE: It should also be borne in mind that every copy of the articles issued in future must have a copy of the special resolution for reduction embodied in or annexed to it: s.143.

(*n*) Where applicable, notify the stock exchange that the Court has confirmed the reduction of capital.

(*o*) Finally, deal with any or all of the following matters, according to the form of reduction.

(*i*) Submit application for a fresh listing to the stock exchange (if any new forms of security are to be issued) and submit a specimen (or printer's proof) of any new certificate(s), stating when the new certificate(s) will be ready.

(*ii*) Where capital is being returned to shareholders, issue cheques to them direct or instruct the company's bankers to handle the payment out of a special banking account opened for the purpose.

(*iii*) Call in the old share certificates, and issue new ones in return.

NOTE: In practice, companies often prefer *not* to call in the old share certificates, and either replace or endorse them if and when they are received for registration of transfer.

(*iv*) Make any alterations which may be necessary in the Register of Members and in the financial books.

15. Reduction and increase simultaneously.

(*a*) It will have been observed, from the examples given above (*see* 12), that reduction of capital may refer to reduction of *nominal* capital, reduction of *issued* capital or reduction of *paid up* capital.

(*b*) When a scheme involves a reduction in the *nominal* value of the share capital, a company usually takes the opportunity to make a simultaneous increase in the nominal value of the share capital.

(*c*) This enables the company to save loss of capital duty which it had already paid on the original authorised capital and, so long as the net effect of the simultaneous increase and reduction does not amount to an increase of capital, no further capital duty will be payable. If the amount of the increase exceeds the amount of the reduction, only the *net* increase will be subject to capital duty.

(*d*) In order to effect the alterations simultaneously, the following resolutions are necessary:

(*i*) a special resolution to reduce the capital; and

(*ii*) an ordinary resolution to increase the capital to its original figure, subject to the Court confirming the resolution for reduction of capital.

16. Reduction below public company's authorised minimum.

(*a*) Where the Court makes an order confirming a reduction of capital of a public company which would reduce the nominal value of its allotted share capital below the authorised minimum, the Registrar will not register the order unless the court directs otherwise, or the company is first re-registered as a *private* company.

(*b*) The Court making such an order may authorise the company to re-register as a private company without passing a special resolution and, if so, the Court order must also specify the alterations to be made in the company's Memorandum and Articles: Companies Act 1980, s.12.

PROGRESS TEST 11

1. You are secretary of a public company which has a Stock Exchange listing. An extraordinary general meeting of your company passes resolutions which:

(*a*) increase the authorised capital from £500,000 to £600,000 by the creation of 100,000 ordinary shares of £1 each which upon issue and becoming fully paid, will rank *pari passu* with the existing ordinary shares; and

(*b*) authorise the directors to offer these shares, at par, to the present holders of ordinary shares in proportion to their holdings.

You are required to prepare a programme, in numbered paragraphs, which will give effect to these decisions. *ICSA* (III, **35**; IX, **5**)

2. The former £1 shares of a public company have been reduced to shares of 75p each, fully paid, by paying off capital in excess of the wants of the company. The shares are listed on a stock exchange and do not bear distinguishing numbers. The directors are of opinion that it would be advantageous for the share capital now represented by the 75p shares to be consolidated and divided into shares of £1 each, fully paid. In numbered paragraphs, give details of the complete office procedure necessary to effect a consolidation and division. (**6**)

3. The directors of a company, the shares of which are listed on a stock exchange, are of opinion that the shares should be converted into stock. In numbered paragraphs, give details of the procedure necessary to effect the conversion. What are the practical advantages to be gained by converting shares into stock? **(7)**

4. In what ways may a company alter its share capital by ordinary resolution, if so authorised by its articles? State in every case the circumstances in which a company might desire to effect such alterations, and draft the resolutions necessary to carry out any TWO of the alterations you mention. **(1, 5–9)**

5. In what ways may a company alter its share capital by ordinary resolution? State in each case the circumstances in which a company might wish to effect such alterations. **(1, 5, 6–9)**

6. In what circumstances, and by what means, may a company reduce its capital? Are the debenture holders entitled to object to the reduction? In what circumstances, if any, is a company entitled to pay off shares without recourse to the Court? **(11, 12)**

7. Set out in numbered paragraphs the procedure necessary to effect a reduction of capital. *ICSA*   **(14)**

8. Only $32\frac{1}{2}$p has been called up on each of the £1 ordinary shares of A.B.C. Ltd. It is proposed to pay up a further $12\frac{1}{2}$p per share by transfer from reserve, and to cancel the liability for the balance. Outline the procedure to be followed, enumerating any resolutions required, and indicating any steps you would take to meet objections. **(14)**

9. Outline the procedure required to effect:
   (*a*) a reduction of capital;
   (*b*) a capital distribution or "bonus".
(III, **35**, XI, **14**)

10. "A company cannot legally reduce its capital without Court sanction." Discuss, and qualify the statement if you think it is necessary to do so. **(15)**

11. Write brief notes on the procedure relating to—(*a*) reduction of capital, (*b*) return of capital. **(11–15)**

CHAPTER XII

Reconstruction; Amalgamation; Schemes of Arrangement; The City Code; Register of Interests in Shares

SURVEY OF SCHEMES AVAILABLE

1. Circumstances that justify reorganisation of capital.

(*a*) Various forms of reorganisation of capital have already been dealt with in the previous chapter, where the comparatively straightforward procedures under ss.61 and 66 for altering and reducing capital, respectively, were explained.

(*b*) In this chapter, it is intended to deal with schemes of reconstruction, amalgamation and arrangement, which are usually more complicated than a mere alteration or reduction of capital, although many such schemes include alteration, reduction, or both.

(*c*) Schemes involving reconstruction, amalgamation, arrangements with creditors, and other forms of reorganisation are carried out for a variety of reasons, for example:

(*i*) to overcome the company's financial difficulties;

(*ii*) to make compromise or other arrangements with creditors;

(*iii*) to reorganise the company's capital structure and, at the same time, rid it of shares with exceptionally heaving voting power; or

(*iv*) to extend the company's objects, where its Memorandum states that the objects are unalterable.

2. Methods. The following methods are available, according to the purpose and circumstances.

(*a*) *Scheme of arrangement under s.206*, probably with the assistance of s.208. The principal features are that:

(*i*) it requires the approval of a specified majority of creditors and/or members;

(*ii*) the sanction of the Court must be obtained;

(*iii*) winding up is not required.

(*b*) *Reconstruction under s.287*. The principal features are that:

(*i*) it involves the winding up of the company;

(*ii*) Court sanction is not necessary.

(*c*) *Scheme of arrangement with creditors only, under s.306.* The principal features are that it:

(*i*) is available only for a company about to be, or in process of being, wound up;

(*ii*) must be sanctioned by extraordinary resolution;

(*iii*) requires the consent of three-fourths in number and value of all creditors.

(*d*) *Company's sale of its undertaking to a new company*, the sale being effected under powers contained in the vendor company's Memorandum. As will be explained later in this chapter, such a scheme has many legal complications.

(*e*) *Acquisition of, or amalgamation with, another company*, which may entail compulsory acquisition of shares under s.209.

(*f*) *Reconstruction by special Act of Parliament*, a method which is likely to be too slow and costly to be undertaken except in the most unusual circumstances.

SCHEMES OF ARRANGEMENT UNDER s.206

3. Form of arrangement. An arrangement or reconstruction under this section may take *any* form, provided it is:

(*a*) approved by a majority in number, representing at least three-fourths in value of the creditors (or class of creditors) or members (or class of members), as the case may be, who are present and voting in person or by proxy; and

(*b*) sanctioned by the Court.

4. Principal uses. The procedure for carrying out schemes under s.206 is usually complicated, and it is advisable to take legal advice at the outset; nevertheless, it is more widely used than other forms of reconstruction. Companies experiencing financial difficulties frequently make use of s.206 schemes for the following purposes.

(*a*) To make a compromise or arrangement with its creditors, or any class of creditors, for example:

(*i*) agreement by secured creditors to relinquish their security, or to permit the creation of a prior charge;

(*ii*) agreement by debenture-holders and/or trade creditors to take shares, or part shares and part cash, in satisfaction of their debts.

(*b*) To vary the rights of its members, or any class of members, usually by way of restricting their rights, for example:

(*i*) agreement by ordinary shareholders to surrender part of their holding to the preference shareholders, who have agreed to accept ordinary shares in lieu of dividend arrears;

(*ii*) agreement by preference shareholders to cancellation of dividend arrears and reduction of the fixed rate of dividend.

5. Schemes sanctioned. The Court has, however, sanctioned a wide variety of schemes under s.206, in addition to those which are mainly concerned with compromise and arrangement. The following are only examples.

(*a*) Reorganisation of capital structure, involving:

(*i*) reduction of share capital, perhaps with modification of shareholders' rights;

(*ii*) cancellation of (say) deferred shares with exceptionally burdensome dividend and/or voting rights;

(*iii*) alteration of share capital by subdivision of partly paid shares.

(*b*) Amalgamation with another company, including reorganisation of the capital structure of one or both companies.

(*c*) Formation of a new company for the purpose of replacing another company whose objects are wider. The Court may facilitate such a scheme by using powers under s.208 to dissolve the "transferor" company without the usual winding-up procedure.

6. Advantages of conducting schemes under s.206 are as follows.

(*a*) The company need not be wound up in order to carry out any scheme under this section; in that respect it differs from schemes under s.287.

(*b*) The facilities available under s.208 for schemes of reconstruction and amalgamation are applicable only to schemes under s.206. Section 208 enables the Court to make provision for all or any of the following:

(*i*) the transfer to the transferee company of the whole or any part of the undertaking and of the property or liabilities of any transferor company;

(*ii*) the allotting or appropriation by the transferee company of any shares, debentures, policies or other like interests in that company which under the compromise or arrangement are to be allotted or appropriated by that company to or for any person;

(*iii*) the continuation by or against the transferee company of any legal proceedings pending by or against any transferor company;

(*iv*) the dissolution, without winding up, of any transferor company;

(*v*) the provision to be made for any persons, who within such time and in such manner as the Court directs, dissent from the compromise or arrangement;

(*vi*) such incidental, consequential and supplemental matters as are necessary to secure that the reconstruction or amalgamation shall be fully and effectively carried out.

(*c*) The decision of the specified majority will overrule the minority in any scheme of arrangement, unless the Court directs otherwise. Thus, it will be unnecessary to purchase the interests of dissenting members and/or creditors. In this respect it has the advantage over schemes under s.287.

(*d*) It may prove less costly than a form of reconstruction under s.287, i.e. subject to certain conditions being fulfilled so as to take advantage of s.55 of the Finance Act 1927, the expenses of registration and stamp duty on transfer of assets can be avoided.

(*e*) Section 206 schemes can be applied in many cases where s.287 procedure is not available; that is, where more is involved than in a typical s.287 procedure.

7. Procedure.

(*a*) *Draft scheme.* The directors prepare a draft scheme, usually in consultation with legal and financial experts.

(*b*) *Canvass support.* Test the attitudes of the various parties affected, e.g. by inviting some of the largest debenture holders (or their trustees), creditors, and shareholders to separate board meetings, and soliciting their support.

(*c*) *Final form of scheme.* After these consultations, the final form of the proposed scheme is settled by the directors.

(*d*) *An explanatory statement* is then prepared, to explain to all interested parties the proposed scheme, and to recommend its acceptance. If the company's shares are "listed", a copy of the statement should be supplied to the stock exchange.

NOTE: At this stage, a draft of the scheme should be submitted to the Controller of Stamps, Inland Revenue, to decide what capital duty (if any) is payable. Where under a scheme or arrangement a company allots shares to the holders of shares in another company in consideration of the surrender or cancellation of their shares in that company, the surrendered or cancelled shares are treated as assets contributed to them to the first company. Accordingly, capital duty becomes chargeable, unless the transaction qualifies as an exempt transaction.

(*e*) *Accompanying documents.* According to the requirements of the scheme to be undertaken, some or all of the following documents are drawn up to accompany the explanatory statement, these being settled as regards form by counsel and finally approved by the board.

(*i*) *Scheme of Arrangement:* the form in which are set out details of the proposed scheme, and how it will affect creditors and shareholders.

(*ii*) *Notice convening the scheme meetings:* the same notice usually serves for all classes of creditor and shareholder, but the respective dates and times are stated for each meeting.

(*iii*) *Voting slips for use at scheme meetings:* usually on paper of a different colour for each class of creditor and/or shareholder. In some cases they are also made to serve as admission tickets.

(*iv*) *Form of proxy for use at scheme meetings:* in standard form approved by the Court, with space provided for voting "for" or "against"; usually printed on paper of different colours to make them readily distinguishable.

(*v*) *Notice convening an extraordinary general meeting:* where applicable, i.e. if the scheme involves *reduction* of capital a special resolution is necessary under s.66, and this cannot be passed at the scheme meeting.

(*vi*) *Voting slips for use at the extraordinary general meeting:* no special form is required, but columns are usually provided so that holdings of different classes of shares can be stated.

(*vii*) *Form of proxy for use at the extraordinary general meeting:* this must be in the form demanded by the company's Articles. It must be made clear in a footnote that the person appointed as proxy need not be a member: s.136.

(*f*) *Application to the Court.* The company's solicitors usually apply to the Court on the company's behalf. The application is by way of an originating summons in the Chancery Division of the High Court. It is supported by affidavit, giving a brief history of the company, the events which led up to the proposed scheme, and any other matters of which the Court may require notice.

NOTE: Application may be made to the Court by any creditor or member of the company or, in the case of a company being wound up, by the liquidator: s.206(1).

(*g*) *Documents to be produced to the Court.* When the application is made, certain documents will be exhibited to the Court, namely:

(*i*) Certificate of Incorporation;

(*ii*) Memorandum of Association;

(*iii*) Articles of Association;

(*iv*) copy of the company's last balance sheet;

(*v*) copy of the Scheme of Arrangement;

(*vi*) draft notice convening scheme meetings;

(*vii*) form of proxy for use at scheme meetings;

(*viii*) names of proposed chairmen for the scheme meetings.

NOTE: Documents (*vi*) and (*vii*) are submitted for the Court's approval.

(*h*) *At the hearing,* company's counsel asks the Court to make an order directing the holding of the scheme meetings.

(*i*) *Court orders the convening of scheme meetings,* i.e.

(*i*) a meeting of the creditors, or class of creditor;

(*ii*) a meeting of members, or class of member,

and gives any other directions it may consider necessary.

NOTE: The extraordinary general meeting (if required in order to pass a special resolution for reduction of capital) will *not* be subject to the directions of the Court.

(*j*) *Board meeting.* In order to carry out the Court's directions, a board meeting is held and a resolution passed, authorising the Secretary to convene scheme and, where applicable, extraordinary general meetings, and to send the various documents (already referred to) with the notices.

(*k*) *Secretary's procedure.* Before sending out notices and documents, the Secretary should take the following steps.

(*i*) Ensure that scheme documents are in the exact form approved by the Court.

(*ii*) If practicable, arrange to have proxy forms and voting slips completed as to name, address, holding, etc., in order to simplify and expedite the meeting procedure.

(*iii*) In a very large company, where this may not be practicable, the holders of proxies and voting slips should be instructed to fill in their names in block capitals.

(*iv*) Obtain a certificate of posting from the post office at the time of posting notices and documents.

(*l*) *Prepare a list of persons entitled to attend the meetings.* After posting the notices, but before the holding of the various meetings, it is advisable to prepare lists of persons entitled to attend the respective meetings, showing against each person's name his shareholding, debenture-holding or, in the case of a creditor, the extent of the debt to him.

(*m*) *At the scheme meeting* the following points ought to be borne in mind.

(*i*) The quorum will be that fixed by the Court, and *not* that specified in the company's Articles.

(*ii*) Voting by show of hands is pointless, and the result will finally depend on the results shown on completed voting slips and proxy forms.

(*iii*) Great care must be taken to ensure that the resolution is properly carried, i.e. by a majority in number, representing three-fourths in value of those of the class who are present and voting, either in person or by proxy.

(*iv*) At each scheme meeting, the chairman should be provided with an audited statement of the number and value of votes cast "for" and "against" the scheme on valid proxy forms, and the completed proxy forms should be available for reference.

(*n*) *At the extraordinary general meeting*, if required:

(*i*) the quorum must be in accordance with the company's Articles;

(*ii*) the majority required to pass a special resolution for reduction of capital (where applicable) will be that required by s.141, namely a three-fourths majority, and not that required for the scheme meetings.

(*o*) *Petition is presented to the Court.* Assuming that the scheme is approved by all parties at their respective meetings, a petition is presented to the Court for approval of the scheme and, where applicable, to sanction reduction of capital.

The petition sets out the terms of the scheme, a brief history of the company and circumstances which have made the scheme necessary. It must be accompanied by affidavits to prove that the necessary meetings have been held; that notices in proper form were sent out, and that the resolutions were passed by the requisite majorities.

(*p*) *Date for the hearing.* A date is fixed by the Court for hearing the petition. If the Court so directs, the presentation of the petition and the date for the hearing are advertised in the press to enable any dissenters to state their views.

(*q*) *The Court's powers.* At the hearing, the Court has power to sanction the scheme, to modify it or reject it, provided that:

(*i*) the scheme is reasonable;

(*ii*) it complies with the Act;

(*iii*) it has the approval of the necessary majorities, acting in good faith; and

(*iv*) it imposes no injustice on any of the parties concerned.

(*r*) *Court order*. Assuming that the scheme is approved, the Court makes an order sanctioning it. If the scheme involves the transfer of the whole or part of the company's undertaking to another company, the Court may, under s.208 (*see* **6**(*b*) *above*), order the transfer of property and otherwise facilitate the scheme, without a winding-up and without making any provision for dissentients.

(*s*) *Registration of the Court order*. As soon as possible after receipt of it, the Court's order sanctioning the scheme must be produced to the Registrar of Companies. At the same time an office copy of the order must be filed with him for registration.

NOTE: If the Court has also made an order under s.208, an office copy of it must also be filed within seven days.

(*t*) *Putting the scheme into effect*. Once the office copy of the Court order sanctioning the scheme has been filed, the scheme can be put into effect, but not before.

(*u*) *All subsequent issues of the Memorandum and Articles* must include, or have annexed, a copy of the Court's order. If the scheme has effected any alteration in the company's incorporating documents, amended copies of such must be delivered to the Registrar.

(*v*) *Within 15 days* of its being passed, file with the Registrar a copy of any special or extraordinary resolution passed in regard to the scheme.

(*w*) *Comply with stock exchange requirements*, where applicable:

(*i*) send four copies to the stock exchange of any resolution passed at the company's extraordinary general meeting;

(*ii*) notify the stock exchange of the Court's confirmation of the scheme;

(*iii*) apply for a listing, where any new securities are to be issued;

(*iv*) submit a specimen (or printers' proof) of any new share certificate(s), stating when they will be ready.

(*x*) *Subsequent procedure* to put the scheme into effect will, of course, vary according to the nature and aims of the scheme, but will almost certainly involve a great deal of work for the Secretary of the company; in particular:

(*i*) convening and attending board meetings for the purpose of passing resolutions to authorise the calling in of old share certificates, stock certificates, debenture and/or debenture stock certificates;

(*ii*) endorsement of old certificates, or preparation of new certificates;

(*iii*) preparation of Allotment Sheets, and convening and attending board meeting(s) to authorise the various allotments;

(*iv*) filing a Return of Allotments with the Registrar;

(*v*) handling correspondence, e.g. relating to lost certificates, and obtaining letters of indemnity in such cases;

(*vi*) answering queries from shareholders and debenture-holders;

(*vii*) issuing new share and/or debenture certificates, or returning the old certificates after suitable endorsement;

(*viii*) writing up the Register of Members and/or Register of Debenture Holders;

(*ix*) preparation of cheques and issuing them to shareholders, if the reorganisation involves a return of capital;

(*x*) writing up the minute books and, where applicable, the Register of Sealed Documents.

RECONSTRUCTION UNDER s.287

8. Purposes.

(*a*) *Working capital.* This form of reconstruction is often used when additional working capital is needed and other means of raising it are not available.

(*b*) *Other purposes.* It has, however, also been used for a variety of other purposes, including:

(*i*) alteration of the company's objects; if, for example, an attempt to alter them under s.5 has been ruled out by the Court's upholding objections of the requisite proportion of shareholders or debenture holders;

(*ii*) variation of shareholders' rights, where these are set out in the Memorandum and stated to be unalterable;

(*iii*) effecting a compromise with creditors, or with any class of creditor, e.g. debenture-holders.

9. Method. The method generally adopted is broadly as follows.

(*a*) A new company is formed (i.e. the "transferee" company), to acquire the undertaking of an existing company.

(*b*) The existing company (i.e. the "transferor" company) is wound up voluntarily.

(*c*) The assets of the old company are sold to the new company.

(*d*) The consideration given by the new company usually consists of shares in its undertaking, and the taking over of the old company's debts.

(*e*) The shares in the new company are distributed to shareholders of the old company either directly or through the liquidator.

10. Advantages. The advantages of reconstruction under s.287 are that:

(*a*) procedure is comparatively simple;

(*b*) sanction of the Court is not necessary, unless it is desired to make the scheme immediately binding on the creditors;

NOTE: If sanction to bind creditors is applied for but refused:

(*i*) shareholders will be bound at once; but

(*ii*) creditors will not be bound until one year has elapsed after date of execution of the scheme;

(*c*) relief from capital duty and transfer duty is granted where conditions of the Finance Act 1927 are complied with, but the scheme should be submitted at the draft stage to the Controller of Stamps, Inland Revenue, to ascertain the stamp duty position.

11. Procedure.

(*a*) *Agreement for sale.* Prepare, or instruct the company's solicitors to prepare, an agreement for sale to the transferee company of the assets and undertaking of the transferor company containing details of the proposed scheme.

(*b*) *Board meeting.* A board meeting is held to prepare a statutory declaration of solvency under s.283 and, after it has been prepared, to authorise its subsequent filing with the Registrar.

NOTE: For the purpose of the Act, such a declaration is of no effect unless made not more than five weeks before the date of the resolution to wind up, or on that date but before the passing of that resolution and shall be delivered to the Registrar before the expiry of the period of fifteen days immediately following the date on which the resolution for winding up is made. If a declaration of solvency cannot be made, it will be necessary to wind up the company in a creditors' voluntary winding up and *not* as a members' voluntary winding up.

(*c*) *Creditors*. To obviate opposition from creditors at a later date, suitable arrangements should be made with the old company's creditors, for example:

(*i*) debenture holders may be persuaded to take debentures in the new company in exchange for their existing debentures;

(*ii*) unsecured creditors will be asked to accept the new company as their debtor;

(*iii*) unsecured creditors who do not agree to accept the new company as their debtor must either be paid off or secured, e.g. they may be prepared to accept debentures in full or part settlement of their debts.

(*d*) *Extraordinary general meeting*. It will be necessary to convene an extraordinary general meeting (the notice being accompanied by a circular describing the scheme) for a date within five weeks of making the Declaration of Solvency.

NOTE: In preparing the circular, no doubt the scheme will be made as attractive as possible; nevertheless, care must be taken to avoid misrepresentation.

(*e*) *Resolutions*. At the extraordinary general meeting, *two* special resolutions are passed:

(*i*) winding up the company and appointing a liquidator;

(*ii*) authorising the liquidator to enter into an agreement for sale with the new company, when formed.

(*f*) *Send four copies of the resolutions to the stock exchange*, as soon as possible after the meeting.

(*g*) *Publication*. Notice of the resolution for winding up (and of the liquidator's appointment) must be inserted in the *London Gazette* within 14 days: s.279.

(*h*) *File a copy of each resolution* with the Registrar within 15 days of the passing of the resolutions: s.143, such to be accompanied by the Declaration of Solvency which must at the latest be filed within fifteen days of the passing of the resolution for winding up.

(*i*) *Incorporation of the new company*. Steps can now be taken to incorporate the new company and, when this has been done, to put into effect the agreement for sale.

(*j*) *Shares in the new company are distributed* to the old company's shareholders, either directly or through the liquidator.

NOTE: If the shares are allotted directly, transfer fees and stamp duties are avoided and, if partly paid shares are involved, it also saves the liquidator from incurring personal liability.

(*k*) *File a Return of Allotments* with the Registrar within one month of allotment: s.52.

(*l*) *Completion of winding up.* Finally, the winding up of the old company is completed; that is, either:

(*i*) as a *members'* voluntary winding up, if a Declaration of Solvency was filed; or

(*ii*) as a *creditors'* voluntary winding up, if no Declaration was filed.

(*m*) *Final general meeting of the company.* In either case, as soon as the old company's affairs are fully wound up, the liquidator prepares his accounts, calls the final general meeting, by advertisement in the *London Gazette* at least one month before the meeting, and lays his accounts before the meeting.

(*n*) *Liquidator's return to the Registrar.* Within one week after the final general meeting, the liquidator must send to the Registrar:

(*i*) a return of the meeting and of its date; and

(*ii*) a copy of his account of the winding up.

(*o*) *Dissolution.* On the expiration of three months from the registration of the return, the company is deemed to be dissolved: s.290.

12. Important points to be noted in schemes under s.287.

(*a*) *Treatment of dissentient shareholders.*

(*i*) As they have important rights, the utmost care is necessary in dealing with dissentient shareholders.

(*ii*) If considerable opposition is expected, they should be circularised before the meeting, to ascertain their views beforehand.

(*iii*) The passing of a special resolution to approve the scheme is not in itself an indication that there will necessarily be few dissentients, as the meeting might not have been truly representative.

(*iv*) If there are many dissentients, the scheme may have to be revised or abandoned altogether.

(*v*) If, on the other hand, the amount of dissent is unlikely to prevent the scheme going through, provisions must be made for dealing with dissentients.

(*b*) *Dissentients.*

(*i*) A dissentient is any shareholder who did *not* vote in favour of the scheme.

(*ii*) Within seven days of the passing of the resolution, a dissentient may serve written notice at the company's registered office, stating that he dissents and requires the liquidator either to refrain from proceeding with the scheme, or to acquire his shares.

(*iii*) The fact that such a notice is deposited out of time, or at some place other than the registered office, may not invalidate the notice, if accepted by the liquidator: *Brailey* v. *Rhodesia Consolidated* (1910).

(*iv*) The notice may, however, be invalidated if it fails to specify the alternative courses which are open to the liquidator: *Re Demerara Rubber Co.* (1913).

(*c*) *Fund for purchase of dissentients' interests.* The scheme ought to provide for creating a separate fund out of which to purchase the interests of any dissentient shareholders. In order to create such a fund, certain of the old company's assets may be excluded from the agreement for sale; alternatively, the agreement may provide that the new company is to set up the necessary fund.

(*d*) *Distribution of the new company's shares* to shareholders of the old company.

(*i*) Distribution is usually in accordance with powers given in the old company's Memorandum or Articles.

(*ii*) If, however, distribution rights are fixed by the Articles, they may be altered by special resolution if the rights fixed are not in keeping with the requirements of the scheme.

(*e*) *Failure to claim new shares.* Arrangements for shareholders who fail to claim their new shares are as follows.

(*i*) Although legally such shareholders lose their rights in the new company, in practice provision is usually made for them in the agreement for sale; for example, a shareholder may be entitled to the proceeds of the sale of the shares to which he would have been entitled.

(*ii*) In such cases, the liquidator may have authority to sell any unclaimed shares in the new company by tender, and to distribute the proceeds of the sale (less advertising and other expenses) to shareholders so entitled, in accordance with the provisions of the agreement for sale.

13. Example of a scheme of reconstruction carried out under s.287. A company trading under the name of Old Hat Ltd. is short of working capital, its fixed assets are grossly overvalued, and an accumulated loss needs to be written off. Because of the company's poor dividend record and the unsound financial position in which it stands, efforts to raise new capital have so far proved unsuccessful. At this point the company's balance sheet appeared as overleaf.

BALANCE SHEET AS AT ....19......

Authorised and issued capital:		Fixed assets:	
80,000 ordinary		Plant and machinery	£46,000
shares of £1 each,		Patent rights	21,000
fully paid	£80,000	Goodwill	10,000
20,000 6% preference			
shares of £1 each,			77,000
fully paid	20,000	Current assets:	
		Stock	10,000
	100,000	Debtors	16,890
Creditors	30,000	Cash at bank	110
		Profit and loss	
		account (Dr)	26,000
	£130,000		£130,000

The following scheme was carried out under s.287, after obtaining the approval of the shareholders and creditors.

(a) A new company under the name of New Hat Ltd. is to be formed with authorised capital of £100,000.

(b) The new company is to take over the assets and liabilities of Old Hat Ltd., which is to be wound up.

(c) The assets to be taken over are to be dealt with as follows:

(i) plant and machinery and patent rights are to be written down to £40,000 and £18,000 respectively;

(ii) goodwill and the profit and loss account (Dr.) balance are to be written off completely;

(iii) the current assets are to remain at book value.

(d) The old company's creditors are to be discharged by the new company as to 50p in the £ in cash and the balance in 6% debentures.

(e) The preference shareholders agree to accept an equivalent number of ordinary shares in the new company, credited with 75p per share paid up, in return for which they agree to surrender their preference shares and forgo their arrears of dividend. The 25p per share balance is to be paid up as to $12\frac{1}{2}$p per share on application and the $12\frac{1}{2}$p per share balance on allotment.

(f) The ordinary shareholders agree to accept an equivalent number of ordinary shares in the new company, credited with 50p per share paid up, the 50p per share balance to be paid up as to 25p per share on application and the remaining 25p per share on allotment.

BALANCE SHEET AS AT .... 19......

Authorised and issued capital:		Fixed assets:	
100,000 shares of £1 each, fully paid	£100,000	Plant and machinery	£40,000
6% debentures	15,000	Patent rights	18,000
			58,000
		Current assets:	
		Stock	10,000
		Debtors	16,890
		Cash at bank	30,110
	£115,000		£115,000

After the scheme had been carried out, and all moneys received from preference and ordinary shareholders on application and allotment, the balance sheet of New Hat Ltd. appeared as above.

OTHER SCHEMES OF RECONSTRUCTION

14. Scheme of arrangement with creditors under s.306

(a) A scheme of arrangement under this section must be carried through between a company about to be, or actually in the course of being wound up, and its creditors alone.

(b) Such a scheme becomes binding:

(i) on the *company*, when sanctioned by an extraordinary resolution;

(ii) on the *creditors*, when acceded to by three-fourths in number and value of the creditors.

NOTE: Any creditor may, however, within three weeks from completion of the arrangement, appeal against it to the Court, which has power to amend, vary or confirm the arrangement: s.306(2).

(c) This method is rarely used, principally because it is usually difficult to obtain a three-fourths majority in number and value of *all* creditors; even one large creditor might upset the scheme.

(d) An arrangement under s.206 is usually preferred, and for a number of reasons, for example:

(i) it requires only a simple majority in number representing three-fourths in value of the creditors actually present and voting;

(*ii*) it may be used to bind a class of creditors, and creditors have no right of appeal.

NOTE: A scheme under s.206 must, however, receive Court sanction, and the expense and delay involved in applying to the Court must be set off against the above advantages.

15. Sale by a company of its undertaking to a new company under powers in its Memorandum.

(*a*) It has been held that a sale under powers given in a company's Memorandum is legal if liquidation is neither contemplated nor in progress: *Bisgood* v. *Henderson's Transvaal Estate* (1908), i.e. if it genuinely intended to retain the proceeds of the sale in the business without winding up, then the power given by the Memorandum may be used.

(*b*) It is, however, doubtful whether such a scheme is now practicable, for the following reasons.

(*i*) To put it into effect does usually involve liquidation and the Court's power to transfer a company's assets without a winding up, under s.208, is intended only for schemes under s.206.

(*ii*) Provision must be made for dissentients, otherwise the scheme might justifiably be regarded as an evasion of s.287.

(*c*) Therefore, unless there is complete unanimity among the shareholders, so that there is no likelihood of a dissentient shareholder taking the matter to the Courts, it is usually considered to be safer to carry out such a scheme under s.287 in which adequate provision is made for dissentients.

16. Acquisition of another company, or of controlling interest in another company.

(*a*) This method amounts to an amalgamation and can be effected either:

(*i*) by purchasing *all* the shares of another company; or

(*ii*) by purchasing sufficient shares of another company to acquire a majority of the voting power.

(*b*) In some cases, it may be possible to purchase sufficient shares on the open market to acquire a controlling interest—but this may prove to be a costly method unless the buying is spread over a long period, as the demand created might well cause the price of the shares to rise excessively.

(*c*) Nowadays, the "takeover bid" technique, which amounts to amalgamation or acquisition by share purchase, is usually effected in the following stages.

(*i*) An agreement may be reached between the directors of the "transferor" and "transferee" companies respectively, the agreement, of course, being subject to ratification by a sufficient majority of the "transferor" company's shareholders (or class of shareholders) affected, within a fixed period.

(*ii*) The "transferor" company's directors then circularise their shareholders, explaining the scheme, setting out its advantages and recommending acceptance.

NOTE: If the directors of the "transferor" company are not in agreement with the "transferee" company's offer, they will no doubt consider it is their duty to circularise their shareholders, explaining the scheme, pointing out its disadvantages and recommending rejection of the offer.

(*iii*) If the scheme is ratified within the time specified and by the requisite majority, it then becomes effective, though still subject to the right of dissenting shareholders to appeal to the Court.

(*d*) Thus, a "transferee" company which has already acquired 90 per cent of the "transferor" company's shares in a scheme of the sort described above is given power under s.209 to acquire the remaining 10 per cent if the following conditions are fulfilled.

(*i*) The scheme has been approved within four months of the offer being made, i.e. by the holders of not less than nine-tenths in value of the shares concerned.

(*ii*) Notice has been given by the "transferee" company to any dissenting shareholder within two months (after expiration of the four-month period referred to above) that it desires to acquire his shares.

(*e*) The "transferee" company is then entitled and bound to acquire the shares of a dissenting shareholder on the same terms as those offered to the approving shareholders, unless the Court on application of the dissenting shareholder within one month of the date of the notice, thinks fit to order otherwise.

NOTE: Even if the transferee company was already the holder of more than one-tenth of the shares affected at the time of the offer, compulsory acquisition under s.209 is still available, provided the transferee company offers the same terms to all shareholders of the class affected, and the terms are approved by not less than nine-tenths in value of the remaining shares and not less than three-fourths in number of their holders: s.209(1).

(*f*) An alternative is provided by s.209(2) which provides that, where the transferee company holds nine-tenths in value of the shares affected:

(*i*) the transferee company must, within one month, give notice to that effect to holders of the remaining shares who have not assented to the scheme;

(*ii*) any such holder may within three months of the notice serve counter notice on the transferee company, requiring it to acquire his shares; and

(*iii*) the transferee company is then entitled and bound to acquire the shares on the same terms as were offered to the approving shareholders, or on such other terms as may be agreed, or as the Court thinks fit to order.

(*g*) This method of amalgamation or acquisition by purchase of shares is now frequently used, because it has advantages over other forms of reconstruction; in particular

(*i*) it can be used to acquire control of one or a number of companies;

(*ii*) the company (or companies) acquired may be allowed to retain their separate identities, continue to trade under their own names and preserve any goodwill they have built up; and

(*iii*) it may prove less costly than other forms of reconstruction, as a controlling interest may be acquired without purchasing the whole of the undertaking.

THE CITY CODE

17. The background to the Code. The Code arose as a result of adverse criticism concerning the methods used in some takeovers and mergers in the 1950s and 1960s. In particular, there was concern regarding:

(*a*) the inequality of terms offered to investors;

(*b*) the manoeuvres adopted by the boards of companies in order to force through or fight off a bid;

(*c*) the quality of disclosure made to the market in respect of takeover deals;

(*d*) the secrecy surrounding the purchase of shares in bid for companies during the course of bids, either by the bidding company itself, or by its associates.

The City Code on Takeovers and Mergers, to give it its full title, first appeared in its present form in March 1968. It was prepared and issued by the City Working Party, a body originally set up in 1959, and reconvened by the Governor of the Bank of England in 1967 for that purpose. The Code was revised in the light of experience after it had been in operation for less than a year and a second edition was published in February 1972; certain amendments were made to it in June 1974. A fourth edition was published in 1976 and a fifth edition in February 1981 on the authority of the Council for the Securities Industry whose Markets Committee had succeeded the *ad hoc* City Working Party as the body responsible for carrying out periodical revision of the Code.

18. The nature of the Code. The Code represents the collective opinion of those professionally concerned in the field of takeovers and mergers on a range of business standards. It is not concerned with the evaluation of the financial or commercial advantages or disadvantages of a takeover or merger. These are considered to be the concern of the company and its shareholders and in certain circumstances of the Government, advised by the Monopolies and Mergers Commission.

The Code has not, and does not seek to have, the force of the law, though it operates within the legal framework of, and is complementary to, the existing statute and case law on takeovers and mergers. Its observance is purely voluntary though backed by the disciplinary sanctions administered by the City institutions over their members.

19. The scope of the Code. The Code has been drafted with listed public companies particularly in mind. It also applies, nevertheless, to takeovers of unlisted companies but not to private companies.

20. Operation and enforcement of the Code. The Code is administered and enforced by the Panel on Takeovers and Mergers (the Panel), a body representative of those using the securities markets and concerned with the observance of good business practice, not the enforcement of the law.

The Panel works on a day-to-day basis through its executive, headed by the Director General, but there is a right of appeal against his rulings as to the interpretation and enforcement of the Code to the Panel. Further, he may refer such questions to the Panel as are all allegations that the provisions of the Code have been broken.

If the Panel finds that there has been a breach of the Code it may administer a private reprimand or a public censure, or in more serious cases take steps to ensure that the offender is prevented from availing himself of the facilities of the securities market.

Appeal lies to the Appeal Committee of the Panel.

21. Structure of the Code. In addition to an introductory section, the Code, as published in its fifth edition, consists of four sections:

(*a*) *Definitions.* The Code commences by defining a number of terms used in the main body of the Code.

(*b*) *General Principles.* The General Principles, of which there are fourteen in number, are a codification of good standards of commercial behaviour as such relates to takeover and merger situations.

(*c*) *Rules.* These lay down certain precise procedures and requirements which must be observed in takeover and merger situations. Some are examples of the application of the general principles whilst others are rules of procedure designed to govern specific forms of takeover and merger transactions practised in the United Kingdom. There are thirty-nine such rules.

(*d*) *Practice Notes.* These notes, of which there are now seventeen, are to be read in conjunction with the particular section of the Code to which they refer. They are intended to serve as a guide only and are subject to amendment in the light of experience.

22. General Principles of the Code.

(*a*) Such constitute the legal framework within which the Code operates. But as recognised in the first of the Principles it is impracticable to devise rules in such detail as to cover all the various circumstances which arise in takeover or merger transactions. Accordingly, persons engaged in such transactions should be aware that the spirit as well as the precise wording of the General Principles and of the Rules must be observed. Moreover, it must be accepted that the General Principles and the spirit of the Code will apply in areas or circumstances not explicitly covered by any Rule.

(*b*) The General Principles specifically provide that the boards of companies involved in takeover and merger situations act in the best interests of their respective shareholders; that shareholders shall be provided with sufficient information and time to assess the situation concerned; that no *bona fide* offer should be frustrated; that the creation of a false market should be avoided; that an offeree board should seek competent independent advice; that rights of control should be exercised in good faith and there should be no oppression of minority shareholders; that all shareholders should receive equality of information; that directors involved should ignore personal interests and act in the interests of shareholders, employees and creditors; that offer documents should be drafted with the same care as a prospectus; and that an offer should only be made after the most careful and responsible consideration and in the knowledge that the financial obligations undertaken can be fulfilled.

23. Rules of the Code.

(*a*) The Rules of the Code give more precise content to its General Principles but in no way restrict the latter's applications to situations which are analogous to, or slightly different from, those covered specifically by the Rules.

(*b*) The Rules are concerned with:

    (*i*) the approach;

    (*ii*) consideration of an offer;

    (*iii*) documentation;

    (*iv*) mechanics of the formal offer;

    (*v*) restrictions on dealings; and

    (*vi*) registration of transfers.

REGISTER OF INTERESTS IN SHARES

24. Register of interests in shares.

(*a*) Section 93 of the Companies Act 1981 requires every public company to keep a register and to enter into it against the name of the person concerned any information it receives from a person in consequence of the fulfilment of an obligation imposed on him by ss.63–65 of the 1981 Act. The date of the entry must also be recorded in the register.

(*b*) Entries in the register must be in chronological order and have to be made within three days of receipt of the information.

(*c*) The register has to be kept at the same place as the register of members and is open to public inspection.

25. Obligation of disclosure for the purpose of the register.

(*a*) Section 63 of the 1981 Act requires a person who knows or becomes aware that he has acquired or ceased to have an interest in 5 per cent of a public company's issued capital carrying unrestricted voting rights or, if already interested in 5 per cent or more of such share capital of a public company, he increases or reduces the extent of his interest, to notify the company thereof in writing within five days.

(b) Such notice must specify the share capital to which it relates and either the number of shares in which the person concerned has or still has an interest if he has or retains more than 5 per cent of the company's relevant share capital or that he has ceased to hold more than 5 per cent where such is the case. Further, by s.65 of the 1981 Act, except in the case of a notification as regards cessation of a notifiable holding, the notification must state the identity of each registered shareholder to which it relates and the number of shares held by that holder so far as known to the person making the notification.

(c) Sections 66 and 67 of the 1981 Act specify what constitutes an interest for the purposes of ss.63–65 of that Act and s.67 specifically extends the provisions to accommodate the concert party arrangement and the consequential dawn raid.

(d) Section 70 of the 1981 Act lays down rules for determining whether a person has a notifiable interest for the purposes of ss.63–65 of that Act; and s.71 of the Act establishes those interests that might be disregarded for those purposes.

26. Investigation by a company of interests in shares.

(a) Section 74 of the Companies Act 1981 enables any public company by notice in writing to require any person whom the company knows or has reasonable cause to believe to be, or, at any time during the three years immediately preceding the date on which the notice is issued, to have been interested in shares forming part of the company's issued capital carrying unrestricted voting rights, to confirm that fact or (as the case may be) to indicate whether or not it is the case, and, whether he holds, or has during that time held, any interest in shares so compromised.

(b) Where information is received under s.74 of the 1981 Act the company must enter against the name of the registered holder of those shares in a separate part of the company's register of interests in shares:

(i) the fact that the requirement was imposed and the date on which it was imposed; and

(ii) any information received in response to such a request.

(c) The powers made available to a company by s.74 of the 1981 Act (see (a) above) may under s.76 of that Act be required to be exercised on the requisition of the holders of not less than one-tenth of the company's share capital carrying the right to vote.

(*d*) In order to obtain information from a person on whom a notice is served under s.74 of the 1981 Act, s.77 thereof gives the company rights to apply to the court for an order directing that the shares in question shall be subject to the restrictions imposed by s.174 of the 1948 Act relating to the transfer, voting or dividend rights in respect of such shares (*see* X, **9**).

PROGRESS TEST 12

1. In what circumstances would a "reorganisation of capital" be recommended by you to your board, and what statutory duties would follow the adoption of such a scheme? (**1, 2**)

2. You are asked to prepare a scheme for the amalgamation of two companies known as A Ltd. and B Ltd. Both have share capitals which consist entirely of ordinary shares of £1 each fully paid. The capital of A Ltd. is £1,200,000 and of B Ltd. £800,000. Agreement has been reached on the valuation of the shares: A Ltd. at £3 and B Ltd. at £1.50 per share. Outline in numbered paragraphs the procedure you consider should be followed to effect the amalgamation. *ICSA* (**5, 7**)

3. You are secretary of a company which has just adopted a reconstruction scheme. The holders of the company's debenture stock have agreed to surrender it in return for £60 of a new debenture stock plus 40 ordinary shares of £1, fully paid, in exchange for each £100 of the old debenture stock. All the necessary resolutions have been passed and you are required to prepare, in numbered paragraphs, a programme showing in detail the procedure required to make this conversion. *ICSA* (**7**)

4. PQR Plc. has made trading losses for many years. Today its assets comprise office furniture valued at £4500, a bank balance of £5000 and a patent which it is unable to work itself, but which, in conjunction with the goodwill associated with the name of the company, earns about £30,000 per annum in licence fees. It has issued to the public £20,000 5 per cent debentures secured by a floating charge, £5000 6% preference stock and £60,000 ordinary stock. Draft a report suggesting how the company may be reconstructed, making such assumptions as you may feel necessary (income tax aspects may be ignored). (**8–11**)

5. Your company is solvent but has accumulated losses. Set out in

the form of a memorandum to your board your suggestions as to how a reconstruction may be effected. *ICSA* (**11**)

6. What are the rights of a shareholder who objects to the transfer, during a winding up, of the company's property to another company, and how does he exercise them? (**12**)

7. How can the amalgamation of companies be effected where it is desired to preserve the goodwill of the separate companies concerned? Can shareholders validly object? (**16**)

8. Your company is considering making an offer to acquire the shares of another company. Summarise the procedure from the aspects of both companies, and explain how complete control may be achieved should not all shareholders in the offeree company accept. *ICSA* (**16**)

9. Examine fully the functions served by the City Code on Takeovers and Mergers and the role of the Panel on Takeovers and Mergers in relation to the Code. (**17–23**)

10. Explain how a public company may ascertain who is interested in its voting share capital. (**24–26**).

CHAPTER XIII

Winding Up

INTRODUCTION

1. Definition. The winding up or liquidation of a company is a legal process whereby it is dissolved and its property administered for the benefit of its creditors and members.

NOTE: A company cannot be made bankrupt.

2. Methods of winding up. According to s.211, a company may be wound up:

(*a*) by the court; that is a compulsory winding up;

(*b*) voluntarily, either as (*i*) a *members'* voluntary winding up; or (*ii*) a *creditors'* voluntary winding up;

(*c*) subject to the supervision of the Court.

WINDING UP BY THE COURT

3. A company may be wound up by the Court (under s.222) in the following circumstances.

(*a*) *Special resolution.* Where the company has, by special resolution, resolved that the company be wound up by the Court.

(*b*) In the case of a public company which was registered as such on its original incorporation, the company has not been issued with a certificate under s.4 of the Companies Act 1980 and more than a year has elapsed since it was so registered: Companies Act 1980, Schedule 3, 27.

(*c*) *Failure to commence business.* Where the company does not commence business within a year of its incorporation, or suspends its business for a year.

NOTE: The court will not, as a rule, wind up a company under these circumstances unless it appears that the company has no intention of commencing business or of continuing its business.

(*d*) *Number of members.* Where the number of members of the company is reduced below two: s.222 as amended by the Companies Act 1980.

(e) *Inability to pay its debts.* Where the company is unable to pay its debts, as described in s.223:

(*i*) if a creditor whose debt exceeds £200 serves notice requiring payment and is not paid within three weeks; or

(*ii*) if execution in favour of a creditor of the company is returned unsatisfied, in whole or in part; or

(*iii*) if the Court is satisfied that the company cannot pay its debts.

NOTE: In practice the court applies the same minimum of £200 in cases (*ii*) and (*iii*) as is prescribed by (*i*).

(f) *The just and equitable ground.* Where the Court is of the opinion that it is just and equitable that the company should be wound up, for example:

(*i*) where the substratum (main object) of the company has ceased to exist: *Re German Date Coffee Co.* (1882);

(*ii*) where the company is in substitute a partnership between the persons owning its share capital and there are grounds for dissolving a partnership: *Re Yenidje Tobacco Co. Ltd.* (1916);

(*iii*) where the company never had a business to carry on; that is, it was merely a "bubble" company: *Re London County Coal Co.* (1866);

(*iv*) where in the case of a domestic and family company there has been mismanagement by the directors who hold a majority of the voting shares: *Loch* v. *John Blackwood Ltd.* (1924);

(*v*) where the company has been formed to carry out a fraud or to carry on an illegal business: *Re International Securities Corporation* (1908).

NOTE: In the case of a petition on the just and equitable ground by a contributory, if the court considers that the petitioner has some other remedy, but that otherwise it would be just and equitable to order a winding up, the court is bound to make the order, unless it considers the petitioner is acting unreasonably in asking for a winding up instead of pursuing his other remedy: s.225(2).

(g) *Failure to re-register.* Where an "old public company" has failed to re-register under the classification introduced by the Companies Act 1980 within the transitional period specified by that Act.

4. The winding-up petition.

(a) *Appropriate Court.* Under s.218 a winding-up petition must be presented to the Court having the necessary jurisdiction:

(*i*) the *High Court*, which has jurisdiction to wind up *any* company registered in England;

(*ii*) the *county court of the district* in which the company's registered office is situated, if the paid-up capital does not exceed £120,000;

(*iii*) the *court exercising the Stannaries* jurisdiction (now the County Court of Cornwall), where the company was formed for working mines within the Stannaries, whatever its capital.

(*b*) *The petition.* The petition must be supported by affidavit, setting out:

(*i*) date of incorporation of the company;

(*ii*) address of its registered office;

(*iii*) capital;

(*iv*) objects;

(*v*) grounds for presenting the petition.

(*c*) *Time and place for hearing.* After the presentation of the petition, the Registrar will fix the time and place for the hearing of the petition.

(*d*) *Hearing advertised.* Seven days prior to the hearing, it must be advertised, as an invitation to creditors and contributories to support or oppose the petition:

(*i*) in the *London Gazette*; and

(*ii*) in a newspaper circulating in the district in which the company's registered office is situated.

(*e*) *The petitioner (or his solicitor) attends before the Registrar.* It is one of the formalities of the Winding-up Rules (1949) that the petitioner, or his solicitor, attends before the Registrar (after the presentation of the petition) to satisfy him that all requirements of the Rules have been complied with. A winding-up order will not be made unless this formality is observed.

(*f*) *Provisional liquidator.* After a petition has been presented, the Court has power, under s.238, even before the hearing of the petition, to appoint the official receiver, or any other person, to be provisional liquidator (usually because the assets are in jeopardy) with the following effects.

(*i*) He takes into custody, or under his control, all the company's property.

(*ii*) Legal proceedings cannot be commenced or continued against the company, without leave of the Court.

(*g*) *Court power to stay proceedings.* At any time after the presentation of the petition, and before making the winding-up order, the

Court (on application of the company or any creditor or contributory) may also stay or restrain any legal proceedings against the company: s.226.

5. Hearing of the petition.

(*a*) *Entitlement to attend the hearing.* On the date fixed for the hearing, the company, creditor and any contributory may attend, provided that:

(*i*) any creditor or contributory gives notice to the petitioner that he intends to appeal and states whether he will support or oppose the petition;

NOTE: A "contributory" is defined as every person liable to contribute to the assets of a company in the event of its being wound up and, in the course of winding-up proceedings, includes any person alleged to be a contributory: s.213.

(*ii*) if he is opposing the petition, his opposition must be supported by affidavit, and this must be filed within seven days of the date on which the affidavit supporting the petition was filed;

(*iii*) the petitioner can file affidavit in reply to the opposition within three days, and the deponent is liable to be called for cross-examination on his affidavit.

(*b*) *Result of the hearing.* When the hearing takes place, the Court has power to:

(*i*) dismiss the petition, with or without costs;

(*ii*) adjourn the hearing, conditionally or unconditionally;

(*iii*) make an interim order, or any other order that it thinks fit;

(*iv*) order the petition to stand over for a time, as in *Re Brighton Hotel Co.* (1868);

(*v*) make an order for winding up under supervision of the Court;

(*vi*) make a compulsory order for winding up of the company.

(*c*) *If the petition is successful,* i.e., where the Court makes a compulsory order for winding up the company:

(*i*) an appeal can be made against the winding-up order, if brought within 14 days;

(*ii*) *petitioner's costs*: the Court will usually order that the petitioner's costs shall be a first charge on the assets of the company available for ordinary creditors, but not on property securing debentures.

6. Commencement of the winding up.

(*a*) It is important to fix the date on which the winding up commenced.

(*b*) In a winding up by the Court, i.e. a compulsory liquidation, the commencement of winding up is:

　　(*i*) the time of presentation of the petition for winding up; or

　　(*ii*) the date of the resolution for winding up, i.e. if the company is already in *voluntary* liquidation, the effect is to make the order retrospective to the date of the resolution for voluntary winding up: s.229.

7. Consequences of the winding up.

(*a*) A copy of the winding-up order must be filed with the Registrar of Companies: s.230.

(*b*) Any disposition of the company's property, any transfer of its shares, or alteration in status of its members, made after commencement of the winding up are, unless the Court orders otherwise, void: s.227.

> NOTE: This prevents the dissipation of the company's assets and the shedding of liability, which might otherwise take place between presentation and hearing of the petition.

(*c*) No actions can be commenced or proceeded with against the company, without leave of the Court: s.231.

(*d*) The official receiver becomes provisional liquidator under s.239 and continues to act until another liquidator is appointed.

(*e*) If the business is to be carried on, the Court may, on the application of the official receiver, appoint a special manager until a liquidator is appointed or for such time as the Court may decide.

(*f*) Servants of the company may be dismissed: *Chapman's Case* (1866), but this will depend upon the circumstances of each case.

(*g*) The official receiver takes control of all books and papers of the company immediately the winding-up order is made.

(*h*) A statement of affairs must be submitted to the official receiver. The official receiver serves notice on the directors and secretary who were in office at the date of the winding up, ordering them to submit to him a statement of the company's affairs.

8. The Statement of Affairs in s.235.

(*a*) *When required.* This must be submitted in duplicate to the official receiver within 14 days of the appointment of a provisional liquidator, or of the date of the winding-up order.

(b) *Form of the statement.* The statement must be in the form prescribed and verified by affidavit by one or more of the company's directors and the Secretary, or by persons required to do so by the official receiver, e.g. by a person who has been a director, promoter or officer of the company.

(c) *Contents.* It must contain (*inter alia*) particulars of the company's assets, debts and liabilities; the names, residences and occupations of its creditors and the securities held by them; dates on which the securities were given; and any further information the official receiver requires.

9. Report of the official receiver in s.236.

(a) This is a preliminary report sent to the Court as soon as practicable after the official receiver receives the statement of affairs.

(b) If he receives no statement of affairs—the Court having ordered otherwise—he must submit his report as soon as possible after the date of the winding-up order.

(c) The official receiver's report must set out the following particulars:

    (i) the amount of capital issued, subscribed and paid up;

    (ii) the estimated amount of assets and liabilities;

    (iii) if the company has failed, the causes of failure;

    (iv) whether further enquiry is desirable, as regards promotion, formation, failure of the company or conduct of the business.

(d) The official receiver may send a further report to the Court if, in his opinion, fraud has been committed in the promotion or formation of the company—in which case the person or officer responsible may be directed to attend the Court for public examination under s.270(1).

NOTE: The official receiver's report is given absolute privilege, which means that no action can be taken by a director, officer of the company or other person concerned, if the report contains statements which they consider to be defamatory.

If a public examination is made, the official receiver will take part.

10. The first meeting of creditors and contributories in s.239.

(a) *Convening the meetings.* Separate meetings, of creditors and contributories respectively, are summoned by the official receiver within one month after the making of the winding-up order, or within six weeks if a special manager has been appointed.

(b) *Notice required.* The first meetings of creditors and contributories are called by seven days' notice in the *London Gazette* and in a local newspaper, also by post to every creditor and contributory, accompanied, or followed as soon as practicable, by a summary of the company's statement of affairs and a statement of the causes of failure, where applicable.

(*c*) *The purposes of the meetings* are:

(*i*) to enable those attending to hear the official receiver's statement and to ask any questions relating to it;

(*ii*) to decide whether to apply to the Court to appoint a liquidator, in place of the official receiver: s.239;

(*iii*) to determine whether to apply to the Court to appoint a committee of inspection to act with the liquidator;

(*iv*) to decide who are to be members of the committee of inspection, if one is to be appointed.

(*d*) *Receiver's powers.* The official receiver may summon any director or officer of the company to attend the meetings.

(*e*) *The chair* is taken by the official receiver himself.

(*f*) *The Winding-up Rules* govern these and all other meetings of the kind as to notice and procedure.

11. Appointment of liquidator(s).

(*a*) Following the first meetings of creditors and contributories, the Court may:

(*i*) appoint a liquidator, and so give effect to the determination of the meetings; or

(*ii*) if the meetings do not agree, decide the difference, and act as it thinks fit;

(*iii*) decide not to appoint a liquidator, in which case the official receiver shall be the liquidator of the company: s.239.

(*b*) Assuming that the Court appoints a liquidator, that is, other than the official receiver:

(*i*) he cannot act until he has notified his appointment to the Registrar of Companies and has given security to the satisfaction of the Department of Trade and Industry;

NOTE: The bond of an approved guarantee society is usually acceptable.

(*ii*) he must given the official receiver any information he requires and afford him access to the books and documents of the company: s.240;

(*iii*) his appointment must be gazetted by the Department of Trade and Industry and advertised by the liquidator himself in the manner directed by the Court, after he has given the necessary security.

(c) A corporate body may not act as a liquidator (s.335), nor may an undischarged bankrupt (s.187, as amended) or a person against whom a disqualification order has been made under s.188 (as amended) or s.9 of the Insolvency Act 1976 (as amended).

12. The committee of inspection in s.252.

(a) If it is decided, at the first meetings of creditors and contributories, to apply to the Court to appoint a committee of inspection to act with the liquidator, the Court may make the appointment.

(b) If the meetings do not agree, the matter may be determined by the Court.

(c) If a committee of inspection is appointed:

(i) it will consist of creditors and contributories, or their attorneys;

(ii) no statutory number is fixed for the committee, but the respective numbers of creditors and contributories respectively may be determined at the meetings—or by the Court, if the meetings fail to agree;

(iii) the committee must meet at least once a month, but the liquidator, or any member of the committee, may call a meeting as and when necessary;

(iv) at such meetings, a majority of the committee constitutes a quorum;

(v) resolutions are passed by a majority of members present.

(d) The function of the committee is to assist and, to some extent, control the liquidator; but the directions of creditors and contributories prevail over those of the committee: s.246;

(e) If no committee of inspection is appointed, its place may be taken (on the application of the liquidator) by the Department of Trade and Industry, whose powers may be exercised by the official receiver.

(f) A member of the committee holds a position of trust; he must not, therefore, make a profit out of it for himself.

(g) Membership of the committee may cease:

(i) by the member giving his resignation in writing to the liquidator; or

(ii) if he becomes bankrupt or compounds with his creditors; or

(iii) by his absence without leave from five consecutive meetings of the committee; or

(iv) if he is removed by ordinary resolution, passed at a meeting of either creditors or contributories, according to which he represents.

(*h*) When a vacancy does occur on the committee the liquidator may call a meeting of creditors and/or contributories to fill the vacancy; or, if he thinks it unnecessary to fill the vacancy, he may apply to the Court to order that the vacancy shall *not* be filled. In that case, the continuing members, if not fewer than two, may continue to act.

13. Duties of the liquidator.

(*a*) To take into his custody, or bring under his control, all the company's property: s.243.

(*b*) To collect and realise the company's assets.

(*c*) To settle the lists of creditors and contributories, unless the Court decides this may be dispensed with: s.257.

(*d*) To pay the company's creditors.

(*e*) To adjust the rights of the contributories and distribute any surplus among them.

(*f*) To summon meetings of creditors and contributories, if requested in writing by one-tenth (in value) of the creditors or contributories respectively.

(*g*) To have due regard for the directions, given by resolution, of the creditors, contributories or committee of inspection, at their respective meetings.

(*h*) To keep the prescribed books: s.247.

(*i*) To pay all money received into the Insolvency Services Account kept by the Secretary of State with the Bank of England: Insolvency Act 1976, s.3.

(*j*) To send his accounts to the Department of Trade and Industry for audit twice a year: s.249.

(*k*) To apply to the Department of Trade and Industry for his release on completion of the winding up: s.251.

VOLUNTARY WINDING UP

14. A voluntary winding up enables the company concerned and its creditors to settle their affairs without many of the formalities already described in a winding up by the Court. It is the method most commonly adopted.

15. When appropriate. A company may be wound up voluntarily in the following circumstances, as provided in s.278.

(*a*) When the period (if any) fixed for the duration of the company by the Articles expires, or the event (if any) occurs on the occurrence of which the Articles provide that the company shall be dissolved, and the company in general meeting has passed a resolution requiring the company to be wound up voluntarily.

NOTE: An *ordinary* resolution is sufficient, unless another form of resolution is required by the Articles.

(*b*) If the company resolves by *special* resolution to be wound up voluntarily.

(*c*) If the company resolves by *extraordinary* resolution that it cannot, by reason of its liabilities, continue its business and that it is advisable to wind up.

NOTE: A minimum of seven days' notice is required of the meeting at which any resolution for the initiation of a voluntary winding up is to be proposed: s.293 as amended by s.106 of the Companies Act 1980.

16. Notice of the resolution to wind up voluntarily must be advertised in the *London Gazette* within 14 days after the passing of the resolution: s.279.

NOTE: Failure to give such notice renders the company and every officer in default liable to fines: s.279(2).

17. Commencement of the winding up: s.280.

A voluntary winding up dates from the passing of the resolution which authorised it.

18. Consequences of the winding up.

(*a*) *Business.* As from the commencement of the winding up, the company ceases to carry on its business, except for the purpose of its beneficial winding up.

(*b*) *Status.* The corporate state and powers of the company continue until it is dissolved: s.281.

(*c*) *Transfer of shares* after the commencement of the winding up are void, unless made to, or with the sanction of, the liquidator.

(*d*) *Status of members.* Any alteration in the status of the members made after commencement of the winding up shall be void: s.282.

(*e*) *A statement* that the company is being wound up must be made on every invoice, order for goods or business letter issued by or on behalf of the company or the liquidator on which the company's name appears: s.338.

NOTE: This section applies in *all* forms of winding up, and the company and any person wilfully authorising or permitting the default are liable to a fine.

(*f*) *Company's servants.* The winding up may operate as a dismissal of the company's servants; if, for example, the company is insolvent, it will probably act as a dismissal, but if for the purpose of amalgamation, it will not necessarily operate as a discharge: *Midland Counties Bank* v. *Attwood* (1905). In any case, the liquidator may continue to employ the company's servants to wind up the company under a new contract of employment.

(*g*) *Stay of proceedings.* The Act makes *no* provision for the stay of proceedings (such as applies in a winding up by the Court), but the Court may stay proceedings if the liquidator can show the need to do so.

19. Forms of voluntary winding up. There are two forms of voluntary winding up:

(*a*) a *member's* voluntary winding up; that is, a "solvent" winding up; and

(*b*) a *creditors'* voluntary winding up; that is an "insolvent" winding up.

PROCEEDINGS IN A MEMBERS' VOLUNTARY WINDING UP

20. Statutory Declaration of Solvency. The directors of the company (or, if there are more than two, a majority of them) may, at a board meeting, make a statutory declaration of solvency which under s.283:

(*a*) must contain a declaration by the directors that, having made full enquiry into the company's affairs, they are of the opinion that the company will be able to pay its debts in full within twelve months of the commencement of the winding up;

(*b*) must be made not more than five weeks before the date of the resolution to wind up or on that date, but before the passing of that resolution;

(*c*) must be filed with the Registrar of Companies before the expiry of the period of fifteen days immediately following the date on which the resolution for winding up is made;

(*d*) must contain a statement of the company's assets and liabilities as at the last practicable date before making the declaration of solvency.

NOTE: Unless the above provisions are complied with, the declaration is of no effect, and there are heavy penalties for making the declaration without sufficient grounds, the onus being upon the directors to show they had reasonable grounds for their opinion: s.283(3).

21. Resolution for winding up. Assuming that a declaration of solvency can be made and will subsequently be filed in accordance with the above provisions:

(*a*) the company in general meeting passes the appropriate resolution for winding up, i.e.

(*i*) an ordinary resolution, if the duration of the company fixed by the Articles has expired; or

(*ii*) a special resolution, if no reason is stated;

(*b*) one or more liquidators are appointed to wind up the company's affairs and distribute its assets: s.285;

(*c*) the remuneration of the liquidator(s) may be fixed.

NOTE: Although the Secretary of the company might legally be appointed liquidator in *any* form of winding up, such an appointment is more likely in a *members'* voluntary winding up; in other forms of winding up, the creditors usually wish to appoint someone of their choice.

22. Effect and notice of liquidator's appointment.

(*a*) *Effect of liquidator's appointment.* On appointment of the liquidator(s) all powers of the directors cease, unless the company in general meeting, or the liquidator himself, sanctions their continuance: s.285(2).

(*b*) *Notice of liquidator's appointment.* Within 14 days after his appointment, the liquidator must publish in the *London Gazette* and deliver to the Registrar a notice of his appointment. Failure to do so renders him liable to a fine during the continuance of the default.

23. Liquidator's duty in case of insolvency: s.288. If the liquidator is of the opinion that the company will not be able to pay its debts in full within the period stated in the statutory declaration of solvency, he must:

(*a*) summon a meeting of the creditors;

(*b*) lay before the meeting a statement of the assets and liabilities of the company.

NOTE: If this occurs, the winding up becomes, in effect, a creditors' voluntary winding up.

24. Liquidator's normal duties. Assuming that the winding up continues as a *members'* voluntary winding up, these are:

(*a*) to wind up the company's affairs and distribute its assets;

(*b*) to obtain the sanction of an extraordinary resolution of the company when he wishes to pay any class of creditors in full; to make a compromise or arrangement with creditors; to compromise calls, debts and other liabilities between the company and its members, or to take any security for the discharge of such debts and to give a complete discharge for them: s.303;

NOTE: For similar purposes in a creditors' voluntary winding up, he must obtain the sanction of the Court or of the committee of inspection, or, if there is no such committee, of the creditors at a meeting of the creditors.

(*c*) to summon a general meeting of the company at the end of the first and each succeeding year of the liquidation, or within three months after the end of the year, or any longer period permitted by the Department of Trade and Industry: s.289;

(*d*) to lay before the meeting an account of his acts and dealings, and of the conduct of the winding up.

25. The conclusion of the winding up. The liquidator must, according to s.290:

(*a*) summon a general meeting of the company, by notice in the *London Gazette*, the notice to be given at least one month before the meeting, specifying the time, place and object of the meeting;

(*b*) prepare an account of the winding up, lay it before the meeting and give any explanations required;

NOTE: At this meeting, if the accounts are approved, an extraordinary resolution may be passed by the members as to the disposal of the company's books and papers: s.341.

(*c*) send to the Registrar, within one week after the meeting, a copy of his account and a return of the holding of the meeting.

NOTE: If there was less than a quorum present at the final meeting (i.e. the quorum required by the company's Articles or, failing that, the Act), his return to the Registrar must state that the meeting had been called and that no quorum was present. This is then deemed to comply with the Act as to the making of the return.

Failure to summon the meeting renders the liquidator liable to a fine.

26. Dissolution of the company. On receipt of the relevant return as to the holding of the final meeting, it is then the duty of the Registrar to enter it in his register; on the expiration of three months from the date of registration of the return, the company is deemed to be dissolved and its name is struck off the Register: s.290(4).

NOTE: It is provided, however, that the Court has power to defer the date of dissolution, on the application of the liquidator or any interested persons under s.290(4), and to set aside a dissolution within two years of its being made: s.352.

27. Disposal of company's books and papers: s.341.

(*a*) The books and papers of the company and of the liquidator(s) may be disposed of as directed by extraordinary resolution of the company.

(*b*) After five years from date of dissolution, neither the liquidator nor any other person who has had custody of the company's books and papers will be held responsible if the books and papers cannot be produced to any person who claims to be interested.

PROCEEDINGS IN A CREDITORS' VOLUNTARY WINDING UP

In any case where a Declaration of Solvency is not filed with the Registrar, the winding up is a creditors' voluntary winding up to which the following provisions apply.

28. The company must summon two meetings.

(*a*) *A general meeting of the company*, for the purpose of passing a resolution for winding up, under s.278. An extraordinary resolution will be required in this case, as the company is to be wound up because it cannot continue its business by reason of its liabilities.

(*b*) *A creditors' meeting*, to be held on the same day as the general meeting of the company, or on the following day.

NOTE: Resolutions passed at the creditors' meeting require a majority in number and value of the creditors present personally or by proxy and actually voting (Rule 134, Winding-up Rules).

29. Creditors' meetings.

(*a*) The notice to the creditors must be posted simultaneously with the notices sent to members and, in addition, must be advertised in the *London Gazette* and two local newspapers circulating in the district where the registered office of the company is situated.

(*b*) At the meeting of creditors:

(*i*) a director of the company, appointed by the other directors, must preside: s.293;

(*ii*) a full statement of the company's affairs, a list of creditors and their estimated claims, must be laid before the creditors by the directors of the company;

(*iii*) a liquidator may be nominated (*see* **30** *below*);

(*iv*) a committee of inspection may be appointed, consisting of not more than five persons: s.295.

30. Appointment of liquidator.

(*a*) Both the creditors and the company, at their respective meetings, have power to nominate a liquidator: s.294.

(*b*) If different persons are nominated by creditors and company respectively, the person nominated by the creditors shall be liquidator; but,

(*i*) if the creditors make no nomination, the person nominated by the company shall be liquidator; or

(*ii*) any director, member or creditor may apply to the Court, within seven days of the nomination, to uphold the company's nomination or to appoint some other person: s.294.

(*c*) The liquidator's remuneration is fixed by the committee of inspection or, if there is no such committee, by the creditors: s.296.

(*d*) After his appointment, all powers of the directors cease, unless the committee of inspection (or the creditors, if there is no committee) sanction otherwise: s.296(2).

(*e*) Any vacancy in the office of liquidator caused by his death, resignation or otherwise, may be filled by the creditors, unless he was a liquidator appointed by the Court: s.297.

31. Liquidator's powers and duties.

(*a*) With the sanction of the Court, or committee of inspection or (if no committee is appointed) a meeting of the creditors, he may exercise the powers indicated in s.303; namely to:

(*i*) pay any classes of creditors in full;

(*ii*) make compromises or arrangements with creditors; or

(*iii*) compromise all calls and liabilities to calls, debts and liabilities capable of resulting in debts.

(*b*) Without sanction, he may exercise any of the other powers given by the Act to the liquidator in winding up by the Court.

(*c*) He may exercise the power of the Court, under the Act, of settling a list of contributories, and the list of contributories shall be *prima facie* evidence of the liability of the persons named therein to be contributories.

(*d*) He may exercise the power of the Court to make calls.

(*e*) He has power to summon general meetings of the company for the purpose of obtaining sanction by special or extraordinary resolution, or for any other purpose the liquidator may think fit.

(*f*) He must pay the debts of the company and adjust the rights of the contributories among themselves.

NOTE: When several liquidators are appointed, any power given by the Act may be exercised by "such one or more of them as may be determined at the time of their appointment or, in default of such determination, by any number not less than two."

32. Appointment of a committee of inspection: s.295.

(*a*) The creditors have power to appoint not more than five persons as members of a committee of inspection. This appointment may be made either at the first or subsequent meeting of the creditors.

(*b*) If the creditors make such an appointment, the company may also appoint not more than five persons to act as members of the committee, along with those appointed by the creditors. This appointment may be made either at the first or subsequent general meeting of the company.

(*c*) The creditors may, however, reject the company's nominees, unless the Court otherwise directs and (on receiving application) appoint other persons to act as members of the committee.

(*d*) The provisions relating to meetings etc. of the committee of inspection are the same as in the winding up by the Court, except that there is no limit to the number of members for the committee in a winding up by the Court.

33. If the winding up continues for more than one year, it is the duty of the liquidator:

(*a*) to summon a general meeting of the company and a meeting of creditors at the end of the first and each succeeding year of the winding up, or within three months after the end of the year, or such longer period as the Department of Trade and Industry may allow;

(*b*) to lay before the respective meetings an account of his acts and dealings, and of the conduct of the winding up during the preceding year: s.299.

34. On completion of the winding up, the liquidator must:

(*a*) prepare an account of the winding up: s.300;

(*b*) call a general meeting of the company and a meeting of creditors, by notice in the *London Gazette* at least one month before the meeting, specifying the time, place and object of the meeting;

(*c*) lay his account before the meetings and give any explanations required;

(*d*) send to the Registrar, within one week after the date of the meetings (or after the date of the later meeting, if not held on the same day), a copy of his account, and a return of the holding of the meetings;

(*e*) if there was less than a quorum present at either meeting, his return to the Registrar must state that the meeting was called but no quorum was present (a return made in this way is deemed to comply with the Act as to the making of the return): s.300(3).

35. Dissolution of the company. On the expiration of three months from the date of registration of the return, the company is deemed to be dissolved: s.300(4).

The Court may defer the date of dissolution, on the application of the liquidator or any other interested party under s.300, or set aside the dissolution within two years of its being made: s.352.

After five years from the date of dissolution, no responsibility will rest on the company, the liquidator(s) or any other person who had custody of the books and papers of the company if the books and papers cannot be produced to any person claiming to be interested: s.341(2).

WINDING UP SUBJECT TO SUPERVISION OF COURT

36. Court's power to make a supervision order: s.311. When a company has passed a resolution to wind up voluntarily, the Court may order that the voluntary winding up shall continue but:

(*a*) subject to the supervision of the Court;

(*b*) with such liberty for creditors, contributories and others *to apply to the Court*, and generally on such terms and conditions as the Court thinks just.

37. The petition for winding up subject to supervision.

(*a*) *Presentation*. The petition may be presented by one or more of the parties entitled to petition for a compulsory winding up of the company.

(*b*) *Effect*. The presentation of the petition gives the Court the same power to stay proceedings against the company as in a petition for winding up by the Court: s.312.

(*c*) *Form of petition*. The form of the petition and procedure are very similar to those adopted for a compulsory winding up.

NOTE: Petitions for winding up subject to supervision are comparatively rare, as s.307 now gives creditors and others wide powers to apply to the Court in a voluntary winding up, e.g. to have various questions determined or powers exercised. Thus the principal reason for the petition no longer exists.

38. Commencement of the winding up.
As a winding up under supervision is merely a continuation of a voluntary winding up, the date of passing the resolution for voluntary winding up continues to be the effective date of the winding up under supervision.

39. The supervision order and its effects.

(*a*) *Before granting a supervision order.*

(*i*) The Court may call upon the petitioner to prove that the existing voluntary liquidation cannot continue with fairness to all concerned; and

(*ii*) may exercise its powers under s.346, by directing that meetings of creditors and contributories be held, in order to ascertain their wishes.

(*b*) *Effect of the order.*

(*i*) Sections 227–8 of the Act apply as in a compulsory winding up, that is,

(1) dispositions of property, etc., after commencement of the winding up are void, unless the Court orders otherwise;

(2) attachments, executions, etc., put in force against the company after commencement of the winding up are void.

(*ii*) The order is deemed to be an order for winding up by the Court, but subject to the exceptions set out in the Eleventh Schedule to the Act, which render some sections inapplicable, for example:

(1) Section 235, requiring a Statement of Affairs to be submitted to the official receiver;

(2) Section 236, requiring a report by the official receiver;

(3) Section 237, giving the Court power to appoint liquidator(s);

(4) Section 238, giving the Court power to appoint a provisional liquidator and limit or restrict his powers;

(5) Section 239, whereby the official receiver becomes provisional liquidator;

(6) Section 240, containing provisions applicable where someone other than the official receiver is appointed liquidator.

40. Power of Court to appoint or remove liquidators. Generally, the liquidator appointed for the voluntary winding up continues in office, subject to his giving security; but s.314 gives the Court the following powers:

(*a*) to appoint an additional liquidator, who has the same power, is subject to the same obligations and is in the same position as if he had been appointed in a voluntary winding up;

(*b*) to remove any liquidator so appointed by the Court or any liquidator continued under the liquidation, and to fill any vacancy caused by his removal, death or resignation.

41. Liquidator's powers. Under s.315, when the supervision order is made, the liquidator may exercise all the powers of liquidator in a voluntary winding up, and without Court sanction, subject to certain exceptions; namely:

(*a*) where the Court imposes restrictions in the order; and

(*b*) where the liquidator wishes to make compromises or arrangements with creditors, or make compromises with contributories or debtors, in which case he must get Court sanction.

42. The committee of inspection. If appointed for the voluntary winding up, continues in office and continues to exercise its powers.

43. Dissolution.

(*a*) Liquidation proceeds as in a voluntary winding up and the affairs of the company having been wound up, the Court will make an order that the company is dissolved.

(*b*) The company is then deemed to have been dissolved as from the date of the order: s.274.

(*c*) Within 14 days from the date of the order, the liquidator must forward a copy of the order to the Registrar, who makes a minute in his books of the dissolution of the company.

(*d*) Finally, the liquidator may apply to the Department of Trade and Industry for his release.

44. Power of a company to provide for employees on cessation or transfer of business: Companies Act 1980, s.74.

(*a*) The powers of a company are now deemed to include (if they would not otherwise do so) the power to make provision for its own, or a subsidiary's employees or former employees, when the company itself, or that subsidiary:

(*i*) ceases to carry on the whole, or any part, of its undertaking or

(*ii*) transfers the whole, or any part, of its undertaking, notwithstanding that the exercise of such power is not in the best interests of the company: s.74(2).

NOTE: This reverses the effect of the decision in *Parke* v. *Daily News Ltd.* (1962), in which the Court held that the company had no power to make payments to its employees because they were not made for the benefit of the company.

(*b*) If the company has power to make provisions for employees by virtue only of s.74, it can only be exercised by the company if sanctioned:

(*i*) by an ordinary resolution of the company, or,

(*ii*) if so authorised by the Memorandum or Articles, by a resolution of the directors, or,

(*iii*) if the Memorandum or Articles require the power to be sanctioned by resolution of the company which requires more than a simple majority of the members voting, with a sanction of that description.

In addition to such sanction, any other requirements of the Memorandum or Articles must be complied with.

(*c*) On the winding up of a company.

(*i*) In a winding up (whether by the Court or as a voluntary winding up) the liquidator may make any payment which the company had, before the commencement of the winding up, decided to make.

(*ii*) The power acquired by the company in compliance with

s.74(1) to provide for employees may be exercised by the liquidator after the winding up of the company has commenced if:

(1) the company's liabilities have been satisfied,

(2) provision has been made for the costs of the winding up, and

(3) the exercise of that power has been sanctioned by such resolution of the company in general meeting as the Memorandum or Articles require or, otherwise, by ordinary resolution: s.74(5).

NOTE: In exercising either of the powers in (*i*) and (*ii*) above, the liquidator in a winding up by the Court is subject to the control of the Court under s.245(3) of the 1948 Act.

(*iii*) Any payment made by a company under s.74:

(1) before the commencement of a winding up, may be made out of *profits* which are available for dividend, and

(2) in the case of any other payment, out of the *assets* of the company which are available to the members on its winding up.

PROGRESS TEST 13

1. Upon what grounds might a company be wound up compulsorily? When is a company deemed to be unable to pay its debts? (**3**)

2. (*a*) Describe the various ways in which a company may be liquidated, indicating how each method is initiated.

(*b*) How is a committee of inspection formed and what are its functions?

(*c*) Who are the contributories in the liquidation of a company and what are their liabilities?
ICSA (**2, 3, 12**)

3. What is the meaning of each of the following terms used in connection with the winding up of companies:

(*a*) committee of inspection;

(*b*) lists of contributories;

(*c*) proof of claims;

(*d*) final return.
ICSA (**12, 13**)

4. When does a voluntary winding up commence, and what are the immediate effects of such commencement? *ICSA* (**17, 18**)

5. You have been appointed liquidator in a voluntary winding up. Explain how your appointment affects:

(*a*) the continuance of the company's trade;
(*b*) the transfer of its shares;
(*c*) the employment of its servants;
(*d*) the company's existence.
ICSA   (**18**)

6. The reason for which your company was originally formed having ceased to exist, it has been decided to wind up the company and distribute the considerable surplus to the shareholders. The necessary meetings have been held and you have been appointed liquidator. Detail all the steps you would take from the time of your appointment until the winding up is complete, assuming that this takes more than a year. *Corporation of Secretaries*   (**20–25, 33**)

7. Describe how a members' voluntary winding up is initiated and the proceedings thereunder. *ICSA*   (**20–27**)

8. Set out the procedure for members' winding up. What would you do as a liquidator if it became apparent during the course of the liquidation that the company would not in fact be able to pay its debts in full? *ICSA*   (**20–27, 28**)

9. You have been appointed liquidator of a company whose shares are partly paid. It is expected that it will be necessary to call up the amounts unpaid. Set out the procedure you would adopt. *ICSA*   (**28–31**)

10. What meetings are required to be called by a liquidator? What are his duties when the affairs of the company are fully wound up? *ICSA*   (**10, 13, 24, 27, 29, 33–35**)

11. You are secretary of a small manufacturing company. There are only two shareholders who are also the only directors. They concern themselves with the manufacturing and sales aspects of the business and rely on you for guidance on accountancy and finance. The company has had a succession of adverse trading years and you reach the conclusion that the company is only just solvent but that it is unlikely that even this can be held for more than one or two months unless business improves. Prepare a memorandum on the situation, for consideration by your two directors, covering the following points:

(*a*) the present financial position, explaining what is meant by "solvent";

(*b*) the possible courses of action with an outline of the probable consequences of each;

(*c*) your recommended course of action, giving reasons.
ICSA   (**14, 28–35**)

12. Explain fully the meaning of each of the following terms used in connection with the winding up of a company:

(*a*) declaration of solvency;

(*b*) proof of claim;

(*c*) statement of affairs;

(*d*) dissolution.

ICSA   (**8, 20, 26, 35**)

CHAPTER XIV

Directors, Secretaries and Auditors; Directors' Report

DIRECTORS

1. Definition and status of directors.

(*a*) *Definition.* A director is defined in the Act (s.455) as "any person occupying the position of director by whatever name called".

(*b*) *As trustees.*

(*i*) A director *is*, to some extent, a trustee for the company; that is, of its money and property, and of the powers entrusted to him.

(*ii*) He is *not*, however, a trustee for the individual shareholder: *Percival* v. *Wright* (1902).

(*c*) *As agents.* He *is* an agent for the company, and contracts made by him will bind the company so long as he acts within the scope of his authority.

(*d*) *As managers.*

(*i*) *Functions.* It is the principal function of the directors, acting as a board, to manage the company, and this function may be divided roughly into three basic activities: forecasting, planning and control.

(*ii*) *Responsibilities.* In carrying out their function of management, the directors are in a fiduciary position in relation to the shareholders who appointed them to manage the company. They have a duty to, and are expected by, the shareholders to maximise profits and give them a reasonable return on their capital investment.

But they also have responsibilities to the company's employees and, in the performance of their managerial functions, they must have regard to the interests of employees as well as the interests of the company's members: Companies Act 1980, s.46.

(*e*) *As officers.* A director is an officer of the company, a term defined as including a director, manager or secretary.

(*f*) *As employees.*

(*i*) Directors are not, as such, employees of the company or employed by the company: *Hampson* v. *Prices Patent Candle Co.* (1876); nor are they servants of the company or members of its staff: *Hutton* v. *West Cork Railways* (1883).

(*ii*) A director may, however, hold a salaried employment or an office in addition to his directorship which may, for these purposes, make him an employee or servant and in such a case he would enjoy any rights given to employees as such.

(*iii*) Whether a director is an employee for the purposes of employment protection legislation is a question of fact in each case: *Parsons* v. *Parsons (Albert J.) & Sons Ltd.* (1979). On the other hand a director is generally regarded as an employee for tax purposes.

2. Appointment.

(*a*) *The first directors.*

(*i*) The Companies Act 1976, s.21, provides that a Memorandum delivered for registration must be accompanied by a statement in prescribed form, signed by the subscribers to the Memorandum, giving particulars of the first directors and containing a consent signed by each person named.

(*ii*) On incorporation, the persons named shall be deemed to have been appointed as first directors of the company.

(*iii*) Any Articles of Association delivered with the Memorandum shall be *void* unless they name, as first directors, the persons named in the statement.

(*b*) *Subsequent appointments.*

(*i*) These must be made in accordance with the Articles, but usually by the company in general meeting.

(*ii*) Casual vacancies, caused by resignation, death or dis-qualification, etc., are usually filled by the continuing directors—but this, too, is subject to the requirements of the Articles.

(*c*) *All appointments.*

(*i*) When directors of a public company are elected in general meeting the appointment of each director must be voted on separately unless the meeting previously agrees without dissent to waive the rule: s.183.

(*ii*) A procedural defect in the appointment of a director does not usually invalidate the acts of that director: s.180.

(*iii*) An undischarged bankrupt may not (except with leave of the Court by which he was adjudicated bankrupt) be a director of, or otherwise concerned in the management of, any company: s.187 (as amended).

3. Share qualifications.

(*a*) *When required.* A share qualification is not essential, unless the Articles so provide.

(b) *If a share qualification is required* it is only satisfied by the director being the registered holder of the required number of shares, hence the holding of share warrants to bearer is not sufficient (s.182). To hold shares as nominee of the owner or jointly with another will, however, suffice. If the articles require a holding in his own right this merely excludes a case where the company is aware that someone else is entitled to have the shares transferred out of his name, e.g. his trustee in bankruptcy.

(c) *Obtaining share qualification.* Where a share qualification *is* required by the company's Articles, each director must take up his qualification shares within two months after his appointment, or within any shorter period determined by the Articles: s.182. A director vacates office immediately if he ceases to hold the required qualification shares.

(d) *Table A* states that no share qualification is necessary, unless and until the company fixes one in general meeting: Article 77.

4. Age limit.

(a) The Act prohibits the appointment of a person who has attained the age of 70 as director of a company under s.185, but this is subject to the following exceptions.

(i) *Private companies.* The prohibition does not apply to a private company, unless it is a subsidiary of a public company.

(ii) *Where special notice is given.* There is no prohibition against the appointment of a director at any age (nor is he bound to retire on attaining the age of 70) if his appointment has been made or is made or approved at a general meeting, provided special notice is given of the resolution stating the age of the proposed director.

(iii) *Provisions of Articles.* Where the company has by its Articles excluded or modified the provisions of s.185, e.g. by fixing another age limit or stating that there shall be no age limit.

(b) Directors have a duty to disclose their age. Where s.185 applies, a director reaching the prescribed age limit must notify the company. Failure to do so exposes the director concerned to a fine: s.186.

(c) Also, where s.185 applies and is not excluded by the Articles:

(i) a person may not be appointed a director if he has attained the age of 70 (but see (d) below);

(ii) a director shall vacate office at the conclusion of the first annual general meeting held after he attains the age of 70.

NOTE: A director in office at the commencement of the Act was not compelled to terminate office until the conclusion of the *third* annual general meeting held after the commencement of the Act, unless he was in any case due to retire before the holding of the third annual general meeting.

(*d*) A director of any age may, however, be elected or re-elected by ordinary resolution at a general meeting of the company, provided that *special* notice is given.

(*i*) Notice of intention to put the motion must be given to the company not less than 28 days before the meeting: s.142.

(*ii*) The company must give its members notice of the motion at the same time and in the same manner as the notice of the meeting, i.e. at least 21 days' notice if it is to be moved at the annual general meeting, but 14 days' notice at least for an extraordinary general meeting.

(*iii*) If this is found to be impracticable, the notice to the members may be given by advertisement in the Press, or in any other way permitted by the company's Articles, not less than 21 days before the meeting.

5. Retirement.

(*a*) It is normal for directors to retire by rotation, a specified proportion retiring at each annual general meeting.

(*b*) Under Table A, for example, all directors retire at the first annual general meeting and one-third of them retire at each subsequent annual general meeting. A managing director (Article 107) and any director who was appointed to fill a casual vacancy is disregarded in arriving at the numbers to retire. Those longest in office since their last election shall retire first (Articles 89–91). The chairman, unless also a managing director, is subject to normal retirement by rotation.

6. Vacation of office.

(*a*) Article 88 of Table A states that the office of director shall be vacated if the director:

(*i*) ceases to be a director by virtue of s.182 (*see* **3**) or s.185 (*see* **4**) of the Act; or

(*ii*) becomes bankrupt or makes any arrangement or composition with his creditors generally; or

(*iii*) becomes prohibited from being a director by reason of any order made under s.188 of the Act; or

(*iv*) becomes of unsound mind; or

(*v*) resigns his office by notice in writing to the company; or (*vi*) shall for more than six months have been absent without permission of the directors from meetings of the directors held during that period.

(*b*) Section 188(1)(*a*) of the 1948 Act (as amended) provides that where:

(*i*) a person is convicted of an indictable offence (whether on indictment or summarily) in connection with the promotion, formation, management or liquidation of a company or with the receivership or management of the property of a company; or

(*ii*) it appears to the Court that a person has been persistently in default in relation to the relevant requirements; or

(*iii*) in the course of the winding up of a company it appears that a person:

(1) has been guilty of an offence for which he is liable (whether he has been convicted or not) under s.332 of the 1948 Act; or

(2) has otherwise been guilty, while an officer or liquidator of the company or receiver or manager of the property of the company, of any breach of his duty as such officer, liquidator, receiver or manager.

the court may make a disqualification order against such person.

(*c*) Section 188(1)(*b*) (as amended) provides that where a person is convicted of a relevant offence, and during the five years ending with the date of that conviction he has made against him or has been convicted of, in total, not less than three default orders, i.e. under ss. 337, 375 or 428 of the 1948 Act or under s.5(1) of the 1976 Act, and relevant offences the court by which he is convicted of that offence may make a disqualification order against that person. A relevant offence is an offence of which a person is convicted by virtue of any contravention of, or failure to comply with, any provision of the Companies Acts 1948–81 (which requires any return, account or other document to be filed with, delivered to or sent to the Registrar).

(*d*) A disqualification order for the purposes of (*b*) and (*c*) above is an order that the person against whom the order is made shall not without leave of the court be a liquidator or a director or a receiver or manager of the property of a company or in any way, directly or indirectly, be concerned or take part in the promotion, formation or management of a company for such period, not exceeding the relevant period (i.e. in the case of an order made by a court of summary jurisdiction or an order made in pursuance of s.188(1)(*a*) (as amended)) of five years and in relation to any other order, fifteen years.

(*e*) Section 9 of the Insolvency Act 1976 (as amended) provides where on an application it appears to the court:

(*i*) that a person:

(1) is or has been a director of a company which has at any time gone into liquidation (whether while he was a director or subsequently) and was insolvent at that time; and

(2) is or has been a director of another such company which has gone into liquidation within five years of the date on which the first-mentioned company went into liquidation; and

(*ii*) that his conduct as director of any of those companies makes him unfit to be concerned in the management of the company the court may make an order not exceeding fifteen years, that the person shall not without leave of the court be a director of or in any way, whether directly or indirectly, be concerned, take part in the promotion, formation or management of a company, or be a liquidator of a company, or be a receiver, or manager of the property of a company.

7. Removal of directors.

(*a*) The members have a statutory power of removal by passing an ordinary resolution in general meeting to remove any director from office, notwithstanding the provisions of the articles or any other agreement: s.184.

(*b*) If this statutory power is to be exercised, special notice (s.142) must be given of the resolution and the director has the right to make his defence both by written representations circulated to members and by addressing the meeting before a vote is taken.

(*c*) Removal under the provisions of s.184 does not deprive the director concerned of compensation or damages payable to him in respect of the termination of his appointment as director or of any appointment terminating with that as director.

(*d*) Section 184 does not derogate from any power to remove a director which may exist apart from the section.

(*e*) The articles may give a director's shares special voting rights on a resolution to remove him: *Bushell* v. *Faith* (1970) (though the ratio of the case seems to limit the application of such articles to private companies).

NOTE: Section 184 does not apply to a director of a private company who held office for life on 18th July 1945.

8. Assignment of office.

(*a*) A director may only assign his office provided such is either authorised by the articles, or there is an agreement to that effect between the company and the director concerned and in either case is approved by a special resolution of the company: s.204.

(b) Assignment of office is absolute, i.e. the assignor no longer holds the office and, in this respect, should be contrasted with the appointment of an alternate director (see 9 below).

9. Alternate (or substitute) directors.

(a) A director has no power to delegate his authority to an alternate (or substitute) director, e.g. during his temporary incapacity or absence abroad, unless:

(i) this is sanctioned by the *Articles*; or

(ii) power to do so is included in the terms of his appointment.

(b) If a director has power to appoint an alternate, the appointment is usually required to be in writing, and subject to the approval of the board. The Articles, or other authority giving him the necessary power, usually set out:

(i) the extent of the alternate director's powers and liabilities;

(ii) his remuneration (if any) and by whom it is payable— usually the director by whom he is appointed;

(iii) what share qualification (if any) he must hold.

(c) Particulars of the appointment of an alternate director must be filed with the Registrar within 14 days of the appointment.

(d) The appointment will also entail alterations in:

(i) the Register of Directors and Secretaries: s.200;

(ii) The Register of Directors' Interests: Companies Act 1967, s.29; and

(iii) where applicable, letter heads, trade circulars, etc.: s.201.

(e) Further provisions of the Act which apply equally to alternate directors are as follows:

(i) s.185 relating to the director's age limit;

(ii) section 199, requiring disclosure of interests in contracts.

(f) The stock exchange should be notified of the appointment of an alternative director, if the company's shares are listed.

(g) Vacation of office. An alternate director may vacate office, and his powers cease:

(i) *by revocation*, that is, where the appointing director revokes his appointment;

(ii) *by death*, that is, if the appointing director dies or himself ceases to be a director, in which case revocation is automatic;

(iii) *on expiration of the term fixed* for the appointment;

(iv) *by his own act*, for example, retirement, resignation, etc.;

(*v*) *by disqualification*, that is, for any cause that would disqualify the appointer himself.

10. Remuneration.

(*a*) *Not a right*. A director has no implied right to remuneration; he is only entitled to remuneration where:

(*i*) it is provided for in the company's Articles; or

(*ii*) fixed by the company in general meeting, e.g. by a lump sum *ex gratia* payment, to be divided amongst all the directors.

(*b*) *Provisions of Articles*. When the director's remuneration is fixed by the Articles:

(*i*) it cannot be amended, except by special resolution;

(*ii*) a director can sue for it, even if there are no profits: *Re Lundy Granite Co. Ltd.; Lewis's Case* (1872).

(*iii*) he may prove for his remuneration, with other creditors, in a winding up;

(*iv*) his remuneration is deemed to cover his expenses, unless the Articles (or the company in general meeting) authorise an additional sum for expenses.

(*c*) *Wording of Articles*. The right to a proportionate part of a director's remuneration may depend upon the wording of the Articles.

(*i*) The Articles usually state that his remuneration shall be "at the rate of £........ per annum", which gives a resigning or disqualified director the right to receive a proportionate part of the yearly fee if he vacates office during the course of a year.

(*ii*) If, however, the Articles state that his remuneration shall be (say) "a yearly sum of £........" or "£........ per annum", there is some doubt whether the director is entitled to an apportionment of the yearly fee: *Inman* v. *Ackroyd Best Ltd.* (1901).

NOTE: The Apportionment Act 1870 provides that all salaries and other periodical payments of income shall be considered as accruing from day to day, and apportionable in respect of time accordingly. This is considered to be applicable to directors' remuneration; nevertheless, the wording the Articles ought to be explicit.

(*iii*) Table A (Article 76) expressly states that the remuneration of directors shall be deemed to accrue from day to day.

(*d*) *Tax-free remuneration*.

(*i*) The payment of tax-free remuneration to a director is now unlawful: s.189.

(*ii*) This applies equally to the payment of remuneration

varying with the amount of his income tax, or with the current rate of income tax.

(*iii*) Exception is made, however, in respect of any contract in force on 18th July 1945 which provided for tax-free remuneration to be paid to a director.

(*e*) *Disclosure in accounts.* Section 196 provides that emoluments (including expense allowances, pension contributions and benefits other than cash) must be shown in a note to the accounts prepared under s.1 of the Companies Act 1976.

NOTE: The Companies Act 1967, s.6, introduced additional requirements regarding the disclosure of directors' emoluments in a note to the accounts: (1) the emoluments of the chairman and of any director or directors who have received emoluments greater than those of the chairman; (2) the number of directors whose emoluments fall within various emolument brackets.

11. Compensation for loss of office: ss.191–193.

(*a*) It is illegal to pay a director compensation for loss of office—for example, on retirement or an amalgamation, with another company—unless:

(*i*) particulars, including the amount of compensation, are disclosed to the members;

(*ii*) approval is granted by the company in general meeting.

(*b*) If loss of office is due to transfer of the whole or part of the company's undertaking, any payment of compensation made illegally to a director is deemed to be held in trust for the transferee company.

NOTE: Section 196 provides that the *aggregate* amount of any compensation paid to directors or past directors for loss of office must be shown in a note to the accounts prepared under s.1 of the Companies Act 1976.

12. Loans to directors and connected persons. The Companies Act 1980, s.49, provides as follows, subject to various exceptions (*see* 13).

(*a*) A company must not make a loan to a director of the company or of its holding company, nor enter into any guarantee or provide any security in connection with a loan made by any person to such a director.

(*b*) A "relevant company" (*see* 14) must not:

(*i*) make a "quasi-loan" (*see* **14**) to a director of the company or of its holding company; or

(*ii*) make a loan or a quasi-loan to a person connected with such a director; or

(*iii*) enter into a guarantee or provide any security in connection with a loan or quasi-loan by any other person for such a director or a person so connected; or

(*iv*) enter into a credit transaction as creditor for such a director or a person so connected; or

(*v*) enter into any guarantee or provide any security in connection with a credit transaction made by any other person for such a director or a person so connected.

(*c*) A company must not arrange for the assignment to it or the assumption by it of any rights, obligations or liabilities under a transaction which, if entered into by the company, would contravene any of the above prohibitions.

(*d*) A company must not take part in any arrangement whereby another person enters into a transaction which, if it had been entered into by the company, would have been in contravention of any of the above prohibitions, and where that other person has obtained, or is about to obtain, any benefit from the company, or its holding company, or a subsidiary of the company or its holding company.

13. Exceptions. The following are the principal exceptions provided by s.50 of the 1980 Act (as amended).

(*a*) Where a relevant company is a member of a group of companies (a holding company and its subsidiaries) the prohibitions preventing a relevant company making a loan or a quasi-loan to a person connected with a director of the company or its holding company, or entering into a guarantee or providing any security in connection with a loan or quasi-loan made by any other person for such a director or a person so connected, shall not prohibit the relevant company from making a loan or quasi-loan to another member of that group or entering into a guarantee or providing any security in connection with a loan or quasi-loan made by any person to another member of the group, by reason only that a director of one member of the group is associated with another.

(*b*) A relevant company ("the creditor") is not prohibited from making a quasi-loan to one of its directors, or to a director of its holding company, if the terms of the loan require the director (or a person on his behalf) to reimburse the creditor within two months of the debt being incurred, and the aggregate amount of that quasi-loan and of the amount outstanding under each relevant quasi-loan does not exceed £1000.

(c) A company is not prohibited from making a loan to a director of the company or of its holding company if the aggregate of the relevant amount does not exceed £2500.

(d) A company is not prohibited from entering into any transaction for any person if the aggregate of the relevant amount does not exceed £5000, or any transaction which is in the ordinary course of business; and the value of the transaction is not greater, and the terms on which it is entered into are no more favourable, than it would be reasonable to expect the company to offer to any person unconnected with the company.

(e) Subject to various conditions, the following are also excepted from the prohibitions of s.49:

(i) a loan or quasi-loan by a company to its holding company; or

(ii) a company's entering into a guarantee or providing any security in connection with a loan or quasi-loan made by any person to its holding company;

(iii) a company's entering into a credit transaction as creditor for its holding company, or entering into a guarantee or providing any security in connection with any such credit transaction;

(iv) a company's doing anything to provide any of its directors with funds to meet expenditure incurred, or to be incurred, by him to enable him to perform his duties as an officer of the company;

(v) a loan or quasi-loan made by a money-lending company to any person, or a money-lending company's entering into a guarantee in connection with any other loan or quasi-loan.

NOTE: The exception in (e)(iv) applies only if prior approval of the company is given at a general meeting or, if not approved at or before the next following annual general meeting, the loan must be repaid within six months after the meeting. In any event, however, the exception in (e)(iv) does not apply if the aggregate of the relevant amounts exceeds £10,000.

14. Definitions (from the Companies Act 1980).

(a) "Relevant company" is defined in s.65(1), but might be more simply interpreted as meaning a public company or its subsidiary.

(b) "Quasi-loan", expansively defined in s.65(2), might be more briefly defined as payment by a creditor on behalf of the debtor—to a third party—where there is provision made for reimbursement.

(c) "Connected persons", fully defined in s.64, include a director's wife and child, a company or partner with which he is associated, and any person acting as trustee in any trust (other than in relation to an employees' share scheme or a pension scheme), the beneficiaries of which include the director himself or any of the connected persons already mentioned.

15. Penalties.

(*a*) Where a company enters into a transaction or arrangement which contravenes s.49 of the 1980 Act, it is *voidable* at the instance of the company, but subject to third party rights: Companies Act 1980, s.52.

(*b*) A director of a relevant company and a relevant company acting in contravention of s.49 provisions are guilty of an offence and liable to a fine and/or imprisonment. The same also applies to any person who procures a relevant company to enter into a transaction or arrangement knowing or having reasonable cause to believe that the company was thereby contravening s.49 of the 1980 Act: s.53.

16. Disclosure. Subject to certain exceptions, the group accounts of a holding company must contain specified particulars of any of the loan transactions or arrangements described above: Companies Act 1980, s.54.

17. Directors' interests in contracts with the company.

(*a*) At common law, a director of a company cannot himself contract with that company or have an interest in contracts between third parties and the company.

(*b*) Table A removes this prohibition to some extent by permitting a director:

(*i*) to be a director or other officer of another company with which it is contracting;

(*ii*) to have an interest in contracts with that company;

(*iii*) to retain remuneration or other benefits derived as a result, unless the company direct otherwise: Article 78.

(*c*) The Act imposes a statutory obligation under s.199 upon a director who is directly or indirectly interested in a contract, or proposed contract, to declare the nature of his interest, either:

(*i*) at a board meeting, when the contract is first considered or;

(*ii*) at the first board meeting held after he acquired an interest in the contract.

(*d*) A general notice to the directors to the effect that:

(*i*) he is a member of a specified company or firm and is to be regarded as interested in any contract which may, after the date of the notice, be made with that company or firm; or

(*ii*) he is to be regarded as interested in any contract which may, after the date of the notice, be made with a specified person who is connected with him;

shall be deemed to be sufficient declaration of interest in relation to any such contract, provided that no such notice shall be effective unless either it is given at a meeting of the directors, or the director takes reasonable steps to ensure that it is brought up and read at the next meeting of the directors after it is given: s.199, as amended by the Companies Act 1980.

(*e*) Where stock exchange regulations apply, a director is not permitted to vote on contracts in which he has an interest or, if he does vote, his vote shall not be counted.

(*f*) At general meetings, however, there is nothing to prevent a director from being included in the quorum and actually voting on matters affecting any contract in which he has a personal interest. In that case, he attends and votes merely as a member: *North-west Transportation Co.* v. *Beatty* (1887).

NOTE: The Companies Act 1967, s.16(1)(*c*), also requires disclosure in the director's report of certain contracts in which a director of the company has, or during the year had, an interest.

18. Contracts of employment of directors. Under the Companies Act 1980, s.47, subject to certain exceptions, any service agreement between a company and one of its directors which provides for continuance of the agreement beyond a period of five years and is terminable only in specific circumstances, or not at all, is *void* unless:

(*a*) the term of the contract is first approved by resolution of the company in general meeting; and

(*b*) a written memorandum setting out the proposed agreement and incorporating the term is available for inspection by members:

(*i*) at the registered office of the company for not less than the period of 15 days ending with the date of the meeting; and

(*ii*) at the meeting itself.

If, at the general meeting, no resolution is passed, the original agreement will be deemed to contain a term entitling the company to terminate it at any time by giving reasonable notice.

A company is required to keep copies of service contracts or written memoranda of such contracts of its directors: s.26 of the Companies Act 1967 (as amended). Members have a right to inspect such contracts or written memoranda.

19. Substantial property transactions involving directors etc. (Companies Act 1980, s.48, as amended).

(*a*) Subject to certain exceptions a company must not enter into any arrangement:

(*i*) in which a director of the company (or of its holding company), or a person connected with him, is to acquire non-cash assets of the requisite value from the company; or

(*ii*) in which the company is to acquire non-cash assets of the requisite value from such director, or from a person so connected; unless the arrangement is first approved by resolution of the company in general meeting.

(*b*) A *non-cash asset* is of requisite value if, at the time of the arrangement, its value is not less than £1000 but, subject to that, exceeds £50,000 or 10 per cent of the amount of the company's relevant assets.

(*c*) *Relevant assets* for this purpose is the value of the company's *net* assets, determined by reference to the accounts prepared and laid in respect of the last preceding accounting reference period, or, where no accounts have been prepared and laid before that time, the amount of its called-up share capital.

(*d*) Any arrangement made in contravention, and any transaction entered into in connection with such arrangement, is *voidable* at the instance of the company. The arrangement or transaction cannot, however, be avoided if:

(*i*) restitution cannot be made of the money or any other asset which is the subject-matter of the arrangement or transaction;

(*ii*) the rights of a third party would be affected by the avoidance; or

(*iii*) the arrangement is affirmed by the company within a reasonable period.

(*e*) *Disclosure:* subject to certain exceptions, notes to the group accounts prepared by a holding company must contain particulars of any of the transactions or arrangements described above: Companies Act 1980, s.54.

20. Register of Directors and Secretaries: s.200 (as amended).

(*a*) *Location.* Section 200 provides that every company must keep this register at its registered office.

(*b*) *Contents with respect to each director.* The following particulars must be included:

(*i*) present Christian name(s) and surname;

NOTE: The corporate name only is required in the case of a corporate director.

(*ii*) any former Christian name(s) and surname;

(*iii*) nationality;

(*iv*) usual residential address, or the address of the registered or principal office, in the case of a corporate director;

(*v*) business occupation (if any) and particulars of other directorships held by him or which have been held by him.

NOTE: However, it is not necessary for the register to contain on any day particulars of any directorship:

(*a*) which has not been held by a director at any time during the five years preceding that day;

(*b*) which is held by a director in any company which:

(*i*) is dormant or, in relation to the company keeping the register, is a relevant company; and

(*ii*) if he also held that directorship for any period during the five years immediately preceding that day, and was for the whole of that period either dormant or such a relevant company;

(*c*) which was held by a director for any period during the five years preceding that day in a company which for the whole of that period was either dormant or, in relation to the company keeping the register, a relevant company.

For these purposes a "dormant company" is one falling within s.12 of the 1981 Act (*see* **35**); and a "relevant company" is a wholly owned subsidiary of that other company or of another company of which that other is or was a wholly owned subsidiary.

(*vi*) date of birth;

NOTE: This is required only in the register of a company to which the age-limit set out in s.185 applies.

(*c*) *Contents with respect to the Secretary* (or, where applicable, of each joint Secretary). The following particulars are required:

(*i*) present Christian name(s) and surname;

NOTE: The corporate name only is required in the case of a corporate Secretary.

(*ii*) any former Christian name(s) and surname;

(*iii*) usual residential address, or the address of the registered or principal office in the case of a corporate Secretary.

NOTE: If there are *joint* Secretaries, particulars must be given for each of them, except where all the partners of a firm act as joint Secretaries, when the firm's name and the firm's principal office may be stated.

(*d*) *Registration of particulars.*

(*i*) Particulars of directors and Secretaries, similar to those set out in the register, must be filed with the Registrar within 14 days from the appointment of the first directors of the company.

(*ii*) The nature and date of any changes affecting the register, in respect of either directors or Secretaries, must be filed with the Registrar within 14 days of the change.

(*e*) *Inspection.* The register must be open for inspection for at least 2 hours per day during business hours:

(*i*) free of charge to members;

(*ii*) at a maximum charge of 5p to others;

The Court has power to compel an immediate inspection of the register.

21. Register of directors' interests.

(*a*) *Contents.* The Companies Act 1967, s.29, requires every company to keep a register for the purposes of s.27 of that Act and to record in it all information received from its directors under that section so that the entries against each name shall appear in chronological order.

(*b*) *Form.* The ruling on p. 250 will satisfy statutory requirements.

(*c*) *Location.* The register must be kept at the company's registered office or at any other office at which the company's register of members is kept.

Except where the register is kept at the registered office, the company must notify the Registrar of Companies where it is kept.

(*d*) *Purpose of the register.* The register is intended to reveal information concerning the interests of a person who is a director of a company in:

(*i*) shares in or debentures of the company; or

(*ii*) any other body corporate being the company's subsidiary or holding company; or

(*iii*) a subsidiary of the company's holding company,

and of any rights he, or his wife, or infant children, may be to subscribe for shares in or debentures of the company.

For this purpose it is the duty of directors to notify the company within *five days* of the acquisition of such securities by him, his wife or infant children, and the company must (if the securities are "listed") notify the stock exchange before the end of the following day: Companies Act 1976, ss.24 and 25.

Register of Directors' Interests

Director: C. I. Ess

Entry		Name of Company	Class of shares or debentures	Date of event	Date of Notifica- tion	No. or amount	Consideration	
No.	Date						Paid	Received

Grant of right to subscribe					Nature of event and remarks
Period during which exercisable	Consideration paid for grant	Consideration received for assignment	Subscription price	Name(s) in which registered	

(*e*) *Record of directors' interests.*

(*i*) The nature and extent of an interest recorded in the register of a director in any shares or debentures shall, if he requires, be recorded in the register.

(*ii*) The company shall not, by virtue of anything done for the purposes of Companies Act 1967, s.29, be affected with notice of, or put upon inquiry as to the rights of, any person in relation to any shares or debentures.

(*f*) *Inspection.*

(*i*) The register must be open for inspection for at least 2 hours per day during business hours,

(1) free of charge to members;

(2) at a charge of 5p (or such less sum as the company may prescribe) to others.

(*ii*) It must also be produced at the commencement of the annual general meeting of the company and remain open and accessible during the meeting to any person attending.

(*iii*) Anyone may require a copy of the register or any part of it on payment of 10p (or such less sum as the company may prescribe) for every 100 words or fractional part thereof, required to be copied; any copy so required must be sent within 10 days of the request.

(*iv*) In the case of refusal of an inspection of the register, or to supply a copy, the Court may, by order, compel compliance.

(*v*) If it appears to the Department of Trade and Industry that there are circumstances suggesting that contraventions have occurred in relation to (*inter alia*) disclosures of directors' interests (Companies Act 1967, s.27) they may appoint one or more inspectors to carry out any necessary investigations and report thereon.

(g) *Penalties for default.* The company and every officer in default shall be liable to default fines.

22. Particulars of directors in business letters, etc.: s.201 (as amended).

(a) A company to which this section applies shall not state, in any form, the name of any of its directors (otherwise in the text or as a signatory) on any business letter on which the company's name appears unless it states on the letter in legible characters the Christian name, or the initials thereof, and the surname of every director of the company who is an individual and the corporate name of every corporate director.

(b) The companies to which s.201 applies are as follows.

(i) Companies registered, and foreign companies which have established a place of business, in Great Britain, on or after 23rd November 1916.

(ii) Every company licensed under the Moneylenders Act 1927, whenever registered or whenever it established a place of business.

NOTE: The European Communities Act 1972, s.9, imposes an obligation on companies to show, on all business letters and order forms, the place of registration, the company's registration number, the address of its registered office and, if, in the case of a company having a share capital, there is a reference to share capital on its business letters or order forms, the reference must be to *paid-up* share capital.

23. Managing director.

(a) Appointment of a managing director. The directors of a company have no power to appoint one of their number as a managing director, unless they are permitted to do so by the company's Articles.

(b) Table A, Article 107, gives directors the power to appoint one or more of their body as managing director, to delegate any of their powers to him, and fix his remuneration.

(c) If the Articles make no provision for the appointment of a managing director, it can, of course, be made by the company in general meeting.

24. Special directors.

(a) *Purpose of appointing "special" directors.* In recent years, a number of companies have appointed quasi-directors bearing such titles as "special" director, "executive" director, "assistant" director and the like, usually for their senior executives. The purposes of such appointments are usually as follows:

(*i*) to provide a training ground for top management;

(*ii*) to improve the status of senior executives without, however, giving them the full stature of a director, principally to enable them to deal with customers and others on a "director" level.

(*b*) *Limited powers of "special" directors.* Companies making such appointments usually include in their Articles the power to appoint "special" directors "who will not become directors within the meaning of the expression 'director' as defined in s.455". As a rule, the Articles place severe restrictions upon the powers and rights of the "special" director.

(*i*) He is not to be a member of the board of directors or of any committee appointed by the board.

(*ii*) He is entitled to attend board or committee meetings only at the request of the board of directors.

(*iii*) The board has power to define and limit his powers, and to disqualify him.

(*iv*) His remuneration and duties are to be fixed and determined by the board.

(*c*) *Recording and filing particulars of "special" directors.* As "special" directors are not deemed to be "directors" within the meaning the Act, it is *not* usually considered necessary:

(*i*) to insert particulars concerning them in the Register of Directors and Secretaries; or

(*ii*) to give notice to the Registrar of their appointment of removal from office.

25. Shadow directors.

(*a*) The Companies Act 1980, s.63, creates a new class of directors: a "shadow director".

(*b*) A person so classified is "a person in accordance with whose directions or instructions the directors of a company are accustomed to act".

(*c*) If, however, the directors act on that person's directions or instructions only because his advice is given in a professional capacity, he will *not* be a director for the purpose of s.63(1). Nor will a holding company be a shadow director of any of its subsidiaries by reason only of this section.

(*d*) A shadow director who complies with the above requirements will be treated as a director of the company, and subject to provisions requiring disclosure of interests.

THE SECRETARY

26. Every company must have a Secretary: s.177. There may, however, be *joint* Secretaries.

27. Director as Secretary. Ordinarily, there is nothing to prevent a director acting also as Secretary, but *not* in the following cases:

(*a*) a sole director cannot also act as Secretary: s.177;

(*b*) a corporation, the sole director of which is a sole director of the company: s.178.

NOTE: Section 178 also prohibits a corporation from acting as sole director if its sole director is Secretary of the company.

28. Appointment.

(*a*) A Memorandum delivered for registration must be accompanied by a statement in prescribed form, signed by the subscribers to the Memorandum, giving particulars of the first secretary, and containing a consent signed by that person. On incorporation, the person named shall be deemed to have been appointed as first secretary of the company: Companies Act 1976, s.21.

(*b*) Subsequent appointments must be made in accordance with the Articles, which usually permit the directors to appoint the secretary and fix his remuneration.

29. The Secretary's status.

(*a*) He is a servant of the company.

(*b*) He is also an "officer" of the company, according to s.455 and, therefore, liable to penalties in that capacity.

(*c*) He is also, to some extent, an agent of the company, with power to bind the company:

(*i*) if acting within the scope of his duties as Secretary; and

(*ii*) expressly authorised by the directors (in respect of any act which the directors themselves have power to delegate) or by the company in general meeting.

30. The Secretary's capacity to act.

(*a*) Where the Act requires anything to be done or authorised by a director and the Secretary, the same person cannot act in dual capacity as both director and secretary: s.179.

(*b*) If the office of Secretary is vacant or if, for any other reason, there is no Secretary capable of acting, e.g. due to illness, his functions and responsibilities may be undertaken by:

    (*i*) an assistant or deputy Secretary; or

    (*ii*) any officer of the company, authorised generally or specially for the purpose by the directors, if there is no assistant or deputy secretary capable of acting: s.177(2).

31. The Secretary's signature.

(*a*) The Secretary's signature is an important feature on many documents, and on documents such as the Annual Return it is a statutory requirement.

(*b*) When signing any document on behalf of the company, he should take care to negative his own personal liability, by ensuring that he signs in a representative capacity; for example

"*For and on behalf of*...............................*Co. Ltd.*,

                            [*signed*].....................

                                     Secretary.

(*c*) He should also ensure that the company is correctly described by name, as a slight variation in the name, or even the omission of the word "Limited" from the name, may render him personally liable: *Penrose* v. *Martyr* (1858).

32. Qualifications.
The Companies Act 1980, s.79, at last gives statutory recognition to the post of company secretary, although its provisions apply only to *public* companies.

It is now the duty of the directors of a public company to ensure that the Secretary (or each joint Secretary) of the company is a person who appears to them to have the knowledge and experience to discharge the functions of Secretary of the company.

Such a person must be:

(*a*) one who on the appointed day held the office of Secretary (or assistant or deputy secretary) of the company; or

(*b*) one who for at least three years of the five years immediately preceding his appointment as Secretary held the office of Secretary of a company other than a private company; or

(*c*) a member of specified professional bodies, including Chartered Secretaries, Chartered Accountants, Certified Accountants, Cost and Management Accountants, Public and Financial Accountants; or (*d*) a barrister, advocate or solicitor called or admitted in the United Kingdom; or

(*e*) a person who appears to the directors to be capable of discharging those functions by reason of his holding, or having held, any other position, or his being a member of any other body.

33. Duties.

(*a*) It is difficult to specify precisely the duties of a company secretary for such vary with the size and nature of the company and the terms of the arrangement made with him.

(*b*) Many of his statutory obligations have been referred to in the text; however, the following may be proffered as a general summary of his obligations.

(*i*) He is present at all meetings of the company and of the directors, and is responsible for the taking of minutes thereof.

(*ii*) He issues, under the direction of the board, all necessary notices to members and others.

(*iii*) He conducts all correspondence with shareholders as regards calls, transfers, forfeiture and otherwise.

(*iv*) He is responsible for keeping the statutory books and administrative records of the company.

(*v*) He makes all necessary returns to the Registrar.

AUDITORS

The Companies Act 1976 repeals ss.159 and 160 of the Companies Act 1948 and, in ss.13 to 20, makes several changes concerning companies' auditors. The effects are summarised below.

34. Appointment of the first auditors.

(*a*) The first auditors may be appointed by the directors at any time before the first general meeting of the company, and auditors so appointed shall hold office until the conclusion of that meeting.

NOTE: The general meeting referred to is one at which the directors must lay before the company a copy of every document required to be comprised in the accounts of the company in respect of the appropriate accounting reference period: Companies Act 1976, s.1(6).

(*b*) If the directors fail to exercise their powers to appoint the first auditors, those powers may be exercised by the company in general meeting.

35. Subsequent appointments.

(*a*) Subsequently, at each general meeting (as defined above) the company shall appoint an auditor (or auditors) to hold office from the conclusion of that meeting until the conclusion of the next such general meeting of the company.

(*b*) Where at any general meeting satisfying the above requirements, no auditors are appointed or reappointed, the Secretary of State may appoint a person to fill the vacancy; and the company shall, within one week of the Secretary of State's powers becoming exercisable, give him notice of that fact.

(*c*) The directors, or the company in general meeting, may fill any casual vacancy in the office of auditor, but, while any such vacancy continues, the surviving or continuing auditor (or auditors), if any, may act.

36. Dormant companies.

(*a*) Section 12 of the Companies Act 1981 provides that where a company is one that is small for the purpose of the accounting exemptions provided by that Act, and has had no significant accounting transactions in the period concerned, it can relieve itself of the obligation to appoint auditors and deliver an auditors' report by passing a special resolution.

(*b*) A company is classified as small for the purposes of the accounting exemptions referred to above if it satisfies any two or more of the qualifying conditions, e.g.:

(*i*) the amount of its turnover must not exceed £1,400,000;

(*ii*) its balance sheet total must not exceed £700,000; and

(*iii*) the average number of persons employed by the company in the financial year in question (determined on a weekly basis) must not exceed fifty.

(*c*) A significant accounting transaction is one required by s.12 of the Companies Act 1976 to be entered in a company's accounting records though there is an exception for shares taken under an undertaking in the company's memorandum by a subscriber thereto, thus enabling a newly formed company to be considered dormant from its formation.

37. Resignation.

(*a*) An auditor of a company may resign his office by depositing a notice in writing to that effect at the registered office of the company, but the notice shall not be effective unless it contains either:

(*i*) a statement that there are no circumstances connected with his resignation which he considers should be brought to the notice of the members or creditors of the company; or

(*ii*) a statement of any such circumstances.

(*b*) Where a notice of resignation is deposited at the company's registered office, the company must, within 14 days, send a copy of the notice:

(*i*) to the Registrar of Companies; and

(*ii*) if the notice contained a statement, such as was referred to in (*a*)(*ii*) above, to every person entitled to be sent documents under s.158(1) of the Companies Act 1948.

(*c*) Provision is made in s.16 of the Companies Act 1976 to enable the company or any person claiming to be aggrieved by the statement to bring the matter to the notice of the court.

(*d*) Where an auditor's notice of resignation contains a statement of the kind defined above, provisions are made in the Companies Act 1976, s.17, which enable him:

(*i*) to require the directors to convene an extraordinary general meeting for the purpose of explaining the circumstances connected with his resignation; and

(*ii*) to request the company to circulate to the company's members a statement in writing of reasonable length before the general meeting at which his term of office would otherwise have expired, or before any general meeting at which it is proposed to fill the vacancy caused by his resignation, or convened on his requisition.

38. Removal of auditors.

(*a*) A company may, by ordinary resolution, remove an auditor before the expiration of his term of office, notwithstanding anything in any agreement between it and him.

(*b*) Where a resolution removing an auditor is passed at a general meeting of the company, the company must, within 14 days, give notice of that fact in prescribed form to the Registrar of Companies.

(*c*) *Special notice* shall be required for a resolution at a general meeting of a company to remove an auditor before the expiration of his term of office; and also in the following cases:

(*i*) to appoint as auditor a person other than a retiring auditor;

(*ii*) to fill a casual vacancy in the office of auditor; or

(*iii*) to reappoint as auditor a retiring auditor who was appointed by the directors to fill a casual vacancy.

(*d*) On receipt of the special notice of an intended resolution to *remove* an auditor, the company must forthwith send a copy of it to the auditor it is proposed to remove.

(e) He may then make representations in writing, of reasonable length, to the company. At the same time, he is entitled to request the company to notify members of his representations; or if his representations are not received in time by the company, that they be read out at the meeting.

(f) He is also entitled to receive notices of and to attend the general meeting at which his term of office would otherwise have expired, and at any general meeting at which it is proposed to fill the vacancy caused by his removal. At such meetings he is entitled to be heard on business which concerns him as former auditor of the company.

39. Qualifications.

(a) The bodies of accountants recognised by the Secretary of State whose members are qualified for appointment as auditors of a company shall be:

(i) The Institute of Chartered Accountants in England and Wales;

(ii) The Institute of Chartered Accountants of Scotland;

(iii) The Association of Certified Accountants;

(iv) The Institute of Chartered Accountants in Ireland, but the Secretary of State may amend this list: Companies Act 1976, s.13.

(b) The Secretary of State may refuse to accept qualifications obtained outside the United Kingdom if the country in which they were obtained does not offer reciprocal arrangements to persons qualified in the United Kingdom.

40. Disqualification. Apart from lacking qualification as member of a recognised accounting body, the following are disqualified from appointment as auditor of a company:

(a) an officer or servant of the company;

(b) a person who is a partner of, or in the employment of, an officer or servant of the company;

(c) a body corporate;

(d) a person who, because of the previous provisions, is already disqualified from appointment as auditor of that company's holding company, subsidiary or fellow-subsidiary.

No person shall act as auditor of a company at a time when he knows he is disqualified for appointment to that office, and if he knows that he has become disqualified he must then vacate office and give notice in writing that he has vacated it, giving the reason for so doing.

41. Remuneration.

(*a*) In the case of an auditor appointed by the directors or by the Secretary of State his remuneration may be fixed by the directors or by the Secretary of State, as the case may be.

(*b*) In other cases it will be fixed by the company in general meeting, or in manner determined by the company in general meeting

NOTE: For this purpose, "remuneration" includes any sums paid by the company in respect of the auditor's expenses.

42. Auditor's rights. The rights of the auditors may be summarised as follows:

(*a*) to have free access to books, accounts and vouchers at all times;

(*b*) to require from officers of the company any information and explanations they think necessary in the performance of their duties;

(*c*) to receive the same notices as members are entitled to of all general meetings of the company;

(*d*) to attend and be heard at general meetings of the company on any business with which they are concerned.

43. Auditors' duties.

(*a*) To examine the company's books and accounts.

(*b*) To make a report to the members on the accounts examined by them and on every balance sheet, every profit and loss account and all group accounts laid before the company in general meeting during their tenure of office.

(*c*) To report on particulars of assets and liabilities, profits and dividends included in any prospectus issued by the company.

44. The auditors' report.

(*a*) The auditors must report to the members on the accounts examined by them, and on every balance sheet, every profit and loss account and all group accounts laid before the company in general meeting during their tenure of office: Companies Act 1967, s.14(1).

(*b*) The report must state with any necessary qualifications whether in their opinion a true and fair view is given:

    (*i*) in the case of the balance sheet, of the state of the company's affairs as at the end of its financial year;

(*ii*) in the case of the profit and loss account (if it is not framed as a consolidated profit and loss account), of the company's profit or loss for its financial year;

(*iii*) in the case of group accounts submitted by a holding company, of the state of affairs and profit or loss of the company and its subsidiaries dealt with thereby, so far as concerns members of the company: Companies Act 1967, s.14(3).

(*c*) In preparing their report the auditors must carry out such investigations as will enable them to form an opinion as to whether:

(*i*) proper accounting records have been kept by the company and proper returns adequate for their audit have been received from branches not visited by them; and

(*ii*) the company's balance sheet and (unless it is framed as a consolidated profit and loss account) profit and loss account are in agreement with the accounting records and returns.

If the auditors are of the opinion that either of these requirements has not been satisfied or if they fail to obtain the information and explanations which they consider necessary for the purpose of the audit, they must state any such conclusion in their report: Companies Act 1967, s.14(4) and (6).

(*d*) The report must given particulars of directors' emoluments or loans if these are not adequately or correctly disclosed in the accounts: Companies Act 1967, s.6; Companies Act 1980, s.59.

(*e*) By s.23A of the Companies Act 1967 it is the duty of the auditors in preparing their report to consider whether the information given in the directors' report relating to the financial year in question is consistent with those accounts. If there is any inconsistency in this respect, the auditors must state such in their report: Companies Act 1981, s.15.

(*f*) In preparing their report the auditors must carry out the investigations specified in s.14 of the Companies Act 1967; they may require information from any subsidiary company and its auditors: Companies Act 1976, s.18; and by s.19 of the 1976 Act it is a criminal offence for any officer of a company knowingly or recklessly to supply false or misleading information to auditors.

(*g*) The report drawn up by the auditors must be attached to the accounts when sent to the members: s.156, and by s.14(2) of the Companies Act 1967 it must be read before the company in general meeting and shall be open to inspection by any member.

(*h*) By s.11 of the Companies Act 1981 when full accounts (which includes for these purposes modified accounts in the case of exempted companies) are published, the auditors' report relating thereto must be published with them; and where abridged accounts are published the company may not publish the auditors' report, but must state, in this respect, whether the report was unqualified.

DIRECTORS' REPORT

45. The directors' report.

(*a*) Section 157 of the Companies Act 1948 requires the directors to append to every balance sheet laid before the company in general meeting a report with respect to the company's affairs. The section as amended by the Companies Act 1981 details what is to appear in the report and ss.15–24 of the Companies Act 1967 as amended by the Companies Act 1981 specify a number of others matters which must be included.

(*b*) The disclosure requirements for the directors' report may be summarised as follows:

(*i*) A fair review of the development of the business of the company and its subsidiaries during the financial year and of their position at the end of it: s.157 as amended by s.13(1) of the 1981 Act;

(*ii*) Proposed dividend: s.157;

(*iii*) Proposed transfers to reserves: s.157;

(*iv*) Names of directors at any time in the period concerned: s.16(1) of the 1967 Act;

(*v*) Principal activities of the company and of its subsidiaries during the period and any significant changes therein: s.16(1) of the 1967 Act;

(*vi*) Significant changes in fixed assets of the company, or of any subsidiaries, during the period: s.16(1)(*a*) of the 1967 Act;

(*vii*) An indication of the difference between the book and market values of land and buildings of the company, or any of its subsidiaries, if significant: s.16(1)(*a*) of the 1967 Act;

(*viii*) In relation to the company and its subsidiaries:

(1) particulars of any important events which have occurred since the end of the financial year;

(2) an indication of likely future developments in the business; and

(3) an indication of any activities in the field of research and development: s.16(1)(*f*) of the 1967 Act, as amended by s.13(3) of the 1981 Act;

(*ix*) Interests in shares or debentures of group companies (negative statement where applicable) as recorded in the register of directors' interests at:

(1) the beginning of the period (or later date of appointment), and

(2) the end of the period.

to be given in respect of each person who was a director of the company at the end of the financial year: s.16(4A) of the 1967 Act, as amended by s.13(4) of the 1981 Act.

NOTE: This information may be given, instead, in the notes to the accounts.

(*x*) Total of United Kingdom political and charitable contributions of the company (or, if any made by subsidiaries, of the group), unless together such do not exceed £200. It must state also the amount and name of the political party or person paid in respect of political contributions exceeding £200. Wholly owned subsidiaries of companies incorporated in Great Britain are exempt: s.19 of the 1967 Act.

(*xi*) Where the company's average number of employees is over 250, it must state the company's policy as to:

(1) employment of disabled persons;

(2) continued employment and training of persons who become disabled while in the company's employment, and

(3) otherwise for the training, career development and promotion of disabled persons: S.I. 1980 No. 1160.

(*xii*) Detailed particulars of the acquisition and disposal by a company of its own shares: s.16A of the 1967 Act, as amended by s.14 of the 1981 Act.

46. Stock exchange requirements. Companies subject to stock exchange regulations are required to include in the report of their directors various matters additional to those specified by the Acts. In particular:

(*a*) A statement by the directors of the reasons for any significant departure from standard accounting practices.

(*b*) An explanation in the event of trading results shown by the accounts for the period under review differing materially from any published forecast made by the company.

(*c*) If the company or, as the case may be, the group trades outside the United Kingdom a statement showing a geographical analysis of its trading operations.

(*d*) The name of each country in which each subsidiary operates.

(*e*) If the company or, as the case may be, the group has interests in associated companies, a list giving for each:

(*i*) its name and country of operation;

(*ii*) particulars of its issued share and loan capital and the total amount of its reserves;

(*iii*) the percentage of each class of share and loan capital attributable to the company's interest (direct and/or indirect).

(*f*) A statement as at the end of the financial year detailing bank loans and overdrafts and other borrowings of the company or group.

(*g*) A statement relating to the financial year involved, of the amount of interest capitalised by the company or the group during the year, with an indication of the amount and treatment of any related tax relief.

(*h*) A statement as at the end of the financial year detailing the interests of each director in the share capital of the company and its subsidiaries appearing in the register of directors' interests.

(*i*) A statement detailing entries in the register of interests in shares.

(*j*) A statement as to whether or not the company is a close company for taxation purposes.

(*k*) Particulars of any arrangement whereunder any director has waived or agreed to waive any remuneration.

(*l*) Particulars of any arrangement under which a shareholder has waived or agreed to waive any dividends.

INSIDER TRADING ·

47. Prohibition on stock exchange deals by insiders: Companies Act 1980, s.68.

(*a*) *Individuals affected.* The following "insiders" are prohibited under s.68 of the 1980 Act from dealing on a recognised stock exchange in listed securities of a company:

(*i*) a person who is, or at any time in the preceding six months has been, knowingly connected with that company, and has, or would reasonably be expected to have, unpublished price-sensitive information relating to that company's securities;

(*ii*) a person who is contemplating, or has contemplated making, a takeover offer for a company, in a particular capacity, knowing that he is in possession of unpublished price-sensitive information concerning that company's securities;

(*iii*) a person who has knowingly obtained, either directly or indirectly, information from an "insider" in either of the above categories concerning price-sensitive securities of a company.

(*b*) *Exceptions.* The above provisions do not apply to the following.

(*i*) A person in any of the above categories who possesses price-sensitive information concerning securities is not prohibited from dealing with them if his object in so doing is not to make a profit or avoid a loss (whether for himself or for another person) by the use of that information.

(*ii*) A person acting in the capacity of liquidator, receiver, or trustee in bankruptcy is not prohibited under s.68 from entering into a transaction where he exercises his function in good faith.

(*iii*) A person engaged as a jobber is not prohibited from using information obtained in the course of his business, so long as he uses it in good faith in the course of that business.

NOTE: A "jobber" is defined as an individual, partnership or company dealing in securities on a recognised stock exchange and recognised by the Council of the Stock Exchange as such.

(*iv*) A trustee, a personal representative (or a person who acts on behalf of a corporate trustee or personal representative) is also excepted from the prohibitions of s.68 if he either deals in securities or counsels or procures another person to deal in them. He is, in such circumstances, presumed to have acted otherwise than with a view to making a profit or avoiding a loss by using any unpublished price-sensitive information, if he acted on the advice of a person who appeared to him to be an appropriate person from whom to seek such advice, and who did not appear to him to be prohibited from dealing in listed securities.

(*v*) An individual will not be prohibited as an "insider" by reason only of his having information relating to any particular transaction from dealing on a recognised stock exchange in any securities, or from doing any other thing in relation to securities, which he is prohibited from dealing in by s.68, if he does that thing in order to facilitate the completion, or carrying out of, that transaction.

48. Prohibition on the abuse of information obtained in official capacity: Companies Act 1980, s.69.

(*a*) *Individuals affected.* The prohibitions laid down in s.69 apply to any information which is held by:

(*i*) a Crown servant (or former Crown servant) by virtue of his position (or former position as a Crown servant); or

(*ii*) any individual who knowingly obtained such information, directly or indirectly, from a Crown servant (or from a former Crown servant), knowing, or having reasonable cause to believe, that the latter held the information by virtue of his position.

(*b*) *Prohibitions*. An individual in either of the above categories is prohibited from:

(*i*) dealing on a recognised stock exchange in any relevant securities;

(*ii*) counselling or procuring any other person to deal in any such securities, knowing, or having reasonable cause to believe, that that other person would deal in them on a recognised stock exchange; and

(*iii*) communicating to any other person the information held by or obtained by him, if he knows, or has reasonable cause to believe, that that person or some other person will make use of the information for the purpose of dealing, or of counselling or procuring any other person to deal, on a recognised stock exchange in such securities.

(*c*) *Exceptions*. The exceptions listed above in 1(*b*) also apply to s.69 prohibitions.

49. Off-market deals.

(*a*) *Prohibitions*. The prohibitions of ss.68 and 69 are applicable also to "off-market deals".

(*b*) *Definitions*.

(*i*) *Off-market deals*. These are defined in s.70 as dealings otherwise than on a recognised stock exchange in the advertised securities of any company through an off-market dealer, or as an off-market dealer who is making a market in those securities, or as an officer, employee or agent of such a dealer acting in the course of the dealer's business. The market in which such deals take place might be described as an "over-the-counter market".

NOTE: The prohibitions of ss.68 and 69 relating to counselling, procuring and communicating information are also applicable in relation to off-market deals.

(*ii*) *Off-market dealer* means a person who holds a licence under s.3 of the Prevention of Fraud (Investments) Act 1958; or is a member of a recognised stock exchange or recognised association of dealers in securities within the meaning of that Act; or is an exempted dealer within the meaning of that Act.

(*iii*) *Advertised securities*, in relation to a particular occurrence, means listed securities, or securities in respect of which, not more than six months before that occurrence, information indicating the prices at which persons have dealt, or were willing to deal, in those securities has been published for the purpose of facilitating deals in those securities.

(c) *Exceptions.* The exceptions listed above in **47**(b) also apply to s.70 prohibitions.

50. International bonds: Companies Act 1980, s.71 (as amended).

(a) *Definition.* An international bond issue (or Eurobond issue) means an issue of debentures of a company all of which are offered, or to be offered, by an off-market dealer to persons (whether principals or agents) whose business includes the buying or selling of debentures.

If, however, the debentures are denominated in sterling, the issue will not be classified as an international bond issue unless not less than 50 per cent (nominal value) of the debentures are offered to persons who are neither citizens of the United Kingdom and Colonies nor companies incorporated or otherwise formed under the law of any part of the United Kingdom.

(b) *Protection for managers* of international bond issues. The activities of managers of international bond issues, and any related persons, who would otherwise fall within the provisions of s.68 and also s.70 (in relation to off-market deals) will *not* be prohibited under either of those sections from doing anything in relation to any debenture, or any right to subscribe for, call for, or make delivery of any debenture, if:

(i) that thing is done by an issue manager, or officer, employee or agent of an issue manager for that issue, in good faith in connection with an international bond issue not later than three months after the issue date or (in a case where the issue is not proceeded with), before the decision is taken not to proceed with the issue; or

(ii) he is an issue manager for an international bond issue who is making a market in that debenture or right, or is an officer, employee or agent of such an issue manager, and that thing is done by him in good faith.

NOTE: The above exceptions will only apply if in either case, the unpublished price-sensitive information (that would otherwise preclude those persons from dealing under s.38 provisions) is information held by an individual by virtue of being (or having been) an issue manager or an officer, employee or agent of an issue manager, and is information which it would be reasonable to expect him to have obtained in that capacity.

51. Contravention of ss.68 and 69.

(a) *Penalty*. The penalty for contravening ss.68 or 69 is laid down in s.72(1) as follows:

(*i*) on conviction on indictment to imprisonment for a term not exceeding two years or a fine, or both; and

(*ii*) on summary conviction, to imprisonment for a term not exceeding six months, or a fine not exceeding the statutory maximum, or both.

(b) *Proceedings* for an offence under this section in England and Wales can be instituted only by the Secretary of State or by, or with the consent of, the Director of Public Prosecutions.

(c) *Legal effect*. No transaction will be void or voidable by reason only of its contravening ss.68 or 69.

PROGRESS TEST 14

1. (a) The Companies Act 1948 prohibits the appointment of directors who attain the age of 70. Can this requirement be excluded or modified?

(b) You are asked by a newly-appointed director what action he has to take regarding acquiring qualification shares in the company. Advise him. *ICSA* (**3, 4**)

2. (a) How may a director be removed from office?

(b) In what circumstances may he be disqualified from office? *ICSA* (**5–7**)

3. Comment on the appointment of an alternate director, indicating circumstances in which you consider this desirable. (**9**)

4. Explain fully how and by whom a change in the constitution of a board of directors may be effected and who should be notified of such a change. (**5–9**)

5. Draft a form for circulation to directors to ensure that they are aware of and fully comply with the requirements of s.196 of the Companies Act 1948, relating to disclosure of directors' emoluments. (**10**)

6. What approval is required for the payment of compensation for loss of office to a director? *ICSA* (**11**)

7. (a) The directors (who are also the shareholders) of a private company are proposing that the company lends them money (to avoid drawing profits as salaries and paying tax). Ignoring the tax consequences, explain whether this may be done.

(b) The directors (all of whom hold executive office) wish to know if there are any restrictions regarding their remuneration. Advise them. *ICSA* (**10, 12**)

8. Advise the directors of your company regarding the disclosure of their interests in any contracts entered into by the company. Consider also whether they can vote on any such contracts. *ICSA* (**17**)

9. Are directors allowed to be interested in contracts with the company? *ICSA* (**17**)

10. Set out in the form of a letter to the directors the requirements regarding disclosure of their interests in shares in the company. *ICSA* (**21**)

11. The directors of your company ask you what is meant by special (or associate) directors. Write (*a*) a brief memorandum explaining the significance of such appointments, and (*b*) set out in numbered paragraphs the points to be covered in the Articles of Association providing for such appointments. *ICSA* (**24**)

12. Summarise the matters to be attended to upon the appointment of a new director. *ICSA* (**3, 4, 10, 13**)

13. A director has just been appointed to the board of a private company of which you are secretary. Write to him requesting from him the matters he is liable to disclose in order for you to file the notice of appointment and to comply with other statutory requirements. *ICSA* (**3, 6, 17, 19, 21**)

14. Who may be appointed auditors of a company? How is an auditor removed? *ICSA* (**35, 35, 36**)

15. Some members of the company of which you are secretary have given notice that at the forthcoming annual general meeting they intend to nominate for election as auditor a person other than the retiring auditor. What are your duties on receiving this intimation, and what further duties might follow? (**34**)

16. Apart from account books and vouchers, what documents and records are likely to be required by auditors, and how can the secretary of a company facilitate the auditor's work? (**38, 39, 40**)

17. In relation to auditors state (*a*) how they are appointed, (*b*) who may be appointed, (*c*) the action required when an auditor becomes aware of his disqualification. *ICSA* (**31–36**)

18. List the contents of the directors' report. (**45, 46**)

19. How has the Companies Act 1980 sought to curb the abuse of insider trading? (**47–51**)

CHAPTER XV

Borrowing Powers; Trust Deeds; Receiverships

METHODS OF BORROWING

1. Borrowing as an alternative to further share issue. When a company requires further capital to develop its business, it must decide whether to issue further shares or to borrow. If it has the necessary borrowing power, it may be considered advantageous to make use of it, but the question then arises: what form of borrowing is best suited for the purpose, having regard to amount required, the period for which it is to be borrowed, and what security can be offered?

2. Methods of borrowing.

(*a*) *A bank loan or overdraft.* These methods would not normally meet the company's long-term loan requirements, as banks are usually averse to the making of long-term loans for the purpose of capital developments. Moreover, the bank would almost certainly require some form of security.

(*b*) *An issue of debentures* would probably meet requirements more adequately where a large loan is required for an extended period—where, for example, it is required for extensive capital development.

3. Shares or debentures? When deciding between shares and debentures, the following factors ought to be considered.

(*a*) *Redemption.* If the company would prefer to have the opportunity to clear off the debt within a given period, debentures would obviously meet this requirement, as redeemability is an important feature of that type of security.

Against this, it might be argued that the advantage of redeemability can be gained by the issue of redeemable shares, but the rather stringent conditions laid down in the Act for their issue and redemption frequently rules them out.

(*b*) *Interest.* Another way of making debentures more attractive than shares is to offer interest at a fixed rate and payable (usually half-yearly) irrespective of the company's trading results.

Preference shares might be considered as an alternative, but the fixed dividend on such shares is dependent upon the company's trading results and may be passed over or carried forward.

(*c*) *Security.* If the company is in a position to offer adequate security to prospective debenture-holders, that would be yet another way of making debentures more attractive than shares.

On the other hand, the directors might regard the creation of a charge upon the company's assets as a disadvantage in that it is likely to be restrictive as regards the assets so charged. If, however, the security is in the form of a "floating" charge, this objection can be put aside.

(*d*) *Economy.* Because the above advantages can be offered along with debentures, they can usually be issued at a lower rate of interest—that is, as compared with the rate of dividend that it would be necessary to offer to prospective preference shareholders.

(*e*) *Membership.* As debenture holders are merely "loan creditors" of the company, the raising of funds by way of debentures does not extend the membership and therefore by the same token there is no further spread of voting power.

Against this, it must be accepted that the preference shares of many companies carry no voting power. Furthermore, in recent years an increasing number of companies have appeared to favour the issue of non-voting ordinary shares.

(*f*) *Convertibility.* A debenture is available which might prove attractive to the investor who is undecided between debentures and shares. This is the convertible debenture, referred to later in 6(*h*) below.

(*g*) *Taxation.* Debenture interest is chargeable against profits, whereas dividend on shares is regarded as a distribution of profits—a very important consideration as regards taxation.

(*h*) *Capital duty.* If the company has already issued the whole of its authorised capital, the issue of debentures, as an alternative to an issue of shares, would save the company the trouble and expense of increasing its authorised capital and paying capital duty on the increased amount. It is not suggested that this would be a weighty consideration; nevertheless, it would entail a saving of £10,000 capital duty where the increased authorised capital amounted to £1,000,000.

DEBENTURES

4. Definition. A debenture is a document acknowledging a debt, but the term is also loosely applied to the debt itself. It is difficult to define in precise terms, because debentures as a group may have some or all of the following features, according to the type.

(*a*) *Form.* Debentures are almost invariably under seal, although this is not a statutory requirement.

(*b*) *Redeemability.* All debentures are redeemable, the company undertaking to repay the loan within a specified period, or upon the happening of various specified contingencies.

(*c*) *Security.* Most debentures are secured on the property or undertaking of the company, by way of a fixed or "floating" charge. Evidence of the charge is usually set out in the form of a trust deed.

(*d*) *Interest.* In most cases, the company undertakes payment of interest at a fixed rate (usually half-yearly) irrespective of trading results.

5. Borrowing *ultra vires* the company.

(*a*) *Company's powers.* Before issuing debentures or adopting any other method of borrowing, it is necessary to ensure that the company has power and, if so, within what limits. In this connection, the following points are relevant.

(*i*) A trading company has an implied power to borrow: *General Auction Estate Co.* v. *Smith* (1891).

(*ii*) The implied power of a trading company may be limited, or even excluded, by its Memorandum or Articles.

(*ii*) A non-trading company has no implied borrowing power, but that may be conferred by its Memorandum.

(*iv*) Power to give security. A company with express or implied power to borrow is also entitled to mortgage or charge its assets as security, unless restricted by its Memorandum or Articles: *Re Patent File Co., ex parte Birmingham Co.* (1870).

(*b*) *The effects of* ultra vires *borrowing.* The effects of borrowing beyond the company's express or implied powers are as follows.

(*i*) The borrowing is *void*, and does not create any debt, either at law or in equity, on the part of the company: *Sinclair* v. *Brougham* (1914).

(*ii*) Security, if any, given for the loan is *void*.

(*iii*) Lender's remedies. The lender cannot sue the company for return of money borrowed *ultra vires* because, as already stated, a debt was not legally created; however, the lender may have certain remedies:

(1) to obtain an injunction preventing the company from spending the money;

(2) to apply to the Court for a tracing order and, if he can identify any money or assets purchased with it in the hands of the company, recover such money or property as can be traced;

(3) to be subrogated to the rights of creditors of the company who have been paid with money borrowed from him;

(4) to take action against the directors of the company for breach of warranty of authority, that is, in exceeding the company's powers: *Firbank's Exors.* v. *Humphreys* (1886).

NOTE: Following the European Communities Act 1972 there is the possibility that in such circumstances the lender concerned may be able to bring himself within s.9(1) of that Act and the protection afforded thereby.

6. Types of debenture.

(*a*) *Mortgage debentures.* The name applied in a general way to all debentures which are secured on the property or undertaking of the company, i.e. in the form of:

(*i*) a "floating" charge;

(*ii*) a fixed (or specific) charge; or

(*iii*) both floating and fixed charges.

(*b*) *Simple (or naked) debentures.* A comparatively rare form of debenture, issued without security. On the winding up of the company, the holders of these debentures would rank with the unsecured creditors.

(*c*) *Redeemable debentures.* These are issued subject to the condition that the company shall redeem them on or before a fixed date, or within a specified period.

The company usually reserves the right to redeem at an earlier date, in which case it may be able to buy up some or all of its debentures on the open market before the redemption date.

(*d*) *Irredeemable (or perpetual) debentures*: s.89. These are issued without fixing any specific date or period for redemption. The fact that they are described as "irredeemable" or "perpetual" simply means that the debenture holders can demand repayment only on the happening of one of a number of specified contingencies, such as default in payment of interest, or winding up of the company.

NOTE: It is, in fact, illegal to issue debentures which are never to be redeemed, but s.89 sanctions the issue of irredeemable or perpetual debentures such as are described above.

(e) *Registered debentures*. Certificates are issued to the holders of these debentures and their names and addresses recorded in the Register of Debenture Holders.

Interest is paid to the registered holder, or to his order, in the same manner as applies to the payment of dividend on shares.

Transfer and transmission procedure is basically the same as that used for shares, e.g. as regards form of transfer and registration.

(f) *Bearer debentures*.

(i) *Transfer* is by simple delivery. The document is a negotiable instrument and can, therefore, be handed over without the formality of a transfer instrument or payment of transfer duty. Furthermore, the transferee acquires a good title, so long as he acted in good faith and gave value for the debentures.

(ii) *Interest* is usually payable against the presentation of coupons attached to the debenture.

(iii) *Stamp duty*. As already indicated, no stamp duty is payable at the time of transfer, but it must be paid in a lump sum when the debentures are first issued.

(g) *Income debentures*. The holders of these securities usually have the right to a fixed rate of interest, but only out of the current year's profits. If no profits are earned, no interest may be payable, or it may be reduced in a poor financial year.

Debentures of this type are not popular with investors, and are comparatively rare nowadays.

(h) *Convertible debentures*. These give the holder the option to convert his debentures into ordinary or preference shares, so long as he exercises his option within the period stated in the conditions of issue.

(i) *Debenture stock*. This differs from debentures as stock differs from shares; that is—in theory at least—debenture stock is divisible and transferable in fractional amounts, whereas debentures are indivisible and can be transferred only in complete units. For the sake of convenience, the conditions of issue usually provide that the stock must be transferred in multiples of fixed amount.

Debenture stock differs from stock created out of shares in that it *can* be issued originally as debenture stock.

7. Floating charge. Earlier in this chapter, reference was made to floating and fixed (or specific) charges in connection with mortgage debentures. The main characteristics of a floating charge are as follows:

(*a*) It gives a charge on all the assets of the company for the time being; that is, on the whole of the company's undertaking as a going concern.

(*b*) It does not become fixed on any specific assets, unless or until an event occurs upon the happening of which the charge is said to "crystallise", for example:

(*i*) on the company's default in payment of interest on the debentures concerned; or any other "event" specified in the conditions of issue;

(*ii*) on liquidation of the company.

(*c*) The company can deal with the property charged in the ordinary course of business, and for that reason the floating charge is a popular form of security.

8. Fixed (or specific) charge.

(*a*) This creates a charge on one or more specific assets of the company which are clearly identifiable, such as (say) leasehold or freehold property.

(*b*) The company is unable to deal freely with the assets charged; it must not, for example, create any prior charge on the assets affected, nor dispose of any of them without the agreement of the debenture holders.

PROCEDURE ON ISSUE OF DEBENTURES

9. Issue procedure. This is similar in many respects to that for the issue of shares. Where important differences occur, attention has been drawn to them in the following itemised procedure.

(*a*) *Preparation of a Prospectus.* On the assumption that debentures are being offered to the public, a Prospectus must be prepared, bearing in mind that the requirements of the Fourth Schedule to the Act apply equally to an issue of debentures. It is, of course, possible that both shares *and* debentures are being included in the same prospectus.

(*b*) *Arrangements for underwriting the issue.* There is, of course, no restriction on the amount or rate payable, as s.53 does not apply to debentures.

(*c*) *Board meeting.* Convene a board meeting for the purpose of authorising the issue of the Prospectus.

(d) *Issue of the Prospectus.* This will probably be done through advertising agents and by the distribution of Prospectus forms through the company's bankers, brokers, etc., and to the stock exchange.

(e) *Application and allotment.* Procedure is similar to that for an issue of shares, except that it will be unnecessary to make a return of allotments to the Registrar.

(f) *Registration of charges.* Where applicable, i.e. if a charge is created for the purpose of securing the debentures, particulars of the charge must be filed with the Registrar within 21 days after the date of its creation, i.e. the date on which the charge is executed: *see* **10** *below.*

(g) *Register entries.* The company's Register of Charges must then be written up, giving particulars of any specific and/or floating charge, in accordance with s.104.

(h) *Register of Debenture Holders.* On the assumption that the debentures issued are registered debentures, the Register of Debenture Holders is now written up.

NOTE: The Register of Debenture Holders is not one of the statutory books but a company is often required to have one to comply with the conditions of issue of their debentures, in which case it must conform to the requirements of the Act: ss.86 and 87. These are referred to in **13** below.

(i) *Certificate of registration.* When the Registrar issues a certificate of registration of the charge (referred to in (f) above), a copy of the certificate must then be endorsed on every debenture or debenture stock certificate before issue.

NOTE: The Registrar's certificate of registration of a charge is conclusive evidence of compliance with the Act as to registration formalities: s.98.

(j) *Copies of instruments creating charges* are required to be kept at the company's registered office: s.104. If applicable, therefore, a copy of one debenture in a series must be kept, also a copy of any trust deed creating a charge.

10. The Register of Charges. The Act requires every company to keep a Register of Charges and sets out the following provisions as to its contents, location, inspection, etc.

(a) *Contents.* It must contain the following particulars concerning every specific and floating charge created by the company:

    (i) amount of the charge;

(*ii*) short description of the property charged;

(*iii*) names of the persons secured—except in the case of bearer securities.

(*b*) *Location*. The register must be kept at the company's registered office, together with a copy of every instrument creating a registerable charge; but a copy of *one* debenture in a series will be adequate: s.104.

NOTE: The Act does *not*, in this case, provide for any alternative location.

(*c*) *Inspection*: s.105.

(*i*) The register and any copies of instruments creating registerable charges must be open for inspection of creditors and members, free of charge, for at least two hours per day during business hours.

(*ii*) Any other person may inspect the register on payment of a fee not exceeding 5p.

(*iii*) The Court has power to compel immediate inspection of the register and documents.

NOTE: There is no provision requiring the company to provide copies of the register or of any document creating a charge.

(*d*) *Effects of non-compliance*, i.e. as to keeping a register of charges or failing to make an entry:

(*i*) the security itself is *not* prejudiced;

(*ii*) every officer of the company knowingly or wilfully authorising the omission is liable to a fine: s.104.

11. Registrar's Register of Charges: s.98.

(*a*) *Contents*. The Act requires the Registrar to keep a Register of Charges of each company, with particulars of the charges.

(*b*) *Inspection*. The register is available for inspection by the public, on payment of a search fee. Thus persons dealing with the company can ascertain for themselves to what extent it has mortgaged its property: s.98(3).

(*c*) *Certificate of registration*. As already stated when describing the procedure on issue of debentures, the Registrar is required to issue a certificate of registration when all the requirements of the Act as to registration have been complied with. The certificate is conclusive to that effect: s.98(2).

12. Registration of Charges: s.95.

(*a*) Particulars of charges created by companies registered in

England must be filed with the Registrar of Companies within 21 days after the creation of the charge.

(b) The charges to be registered are as follows:

(i) a charge to secure debentures;

(ii) a charge on uncalled share capital;

(iii) a charge by an instrument which, if made by an individual, would require registration as a bill of sale;

(iv) a charge on land, or on any interest therein;

(v) a charge on the company's book debts;

(vi) a floating charge on the undertaking or property of the company;

(vii) a charge on calls made but not paid;

(viii) a charge on a ship or on any share in a ship;

(ix) a charge on goodwill, on a patent, or trademark.

(c) Failure to register within 21 days of creation has the following effects.

(i) The charge is void against the liquidator and any creditor; that is, it ceases to be preferential.

(ii) The obligation to repay is not prejudiced.

(iii) The money lent and secured by the charge becomes immediately repayable.

(iv) The company and every officer in default becomes liable to a default fine.

(d) If default is shown to be accidental or inadvertent, the time for registration may be extended by the Registrar.

13. Register of Debenture Holders. As already indicated in **9**(h) above this is *not* one of the statutory books. If however, a company keeps a Register of Debenture Holders in compliance with the conditions of issue of its debentures, the register must conform to the following provisions.

(a) *Location.* The register must be kept at the company's registered office, or at any office where it is written up, within the company's domicile.

(b) *Notice of location.* Notice must be given to the Registrar of the place where the register is kept, and of any change, unless it has always been kept at the company's registered office: s.86.

(c) *Inspection.* The register must be open for inspection for at least two hours per day:

(i) to debenture holders and shareholders without fee;

(ii) to other persons on payment of a fee not exceeding 5p.

(*d*) *Copies*. Any person may require a copy of the register or any part of it, on payment of 10p per 100 words.

(*e*) *Closing the register*. The company may close the register for a period or periods not exceeding 30 days on the whole in any year, in accordance with its Articles or as provided in the conditions of issue of its debentures.

(*f*) *Inspection refused*. If inspection or a copy of the register is refused;

(*i*) the Court may compel the company to afford immediate inspection and direct that the copies required be sent;

(*ii*) the company and every officer in default are liable to default fines.

14. Reissue of debentures.

(*a*) Section 90 permits the reissue of debentures which have been redeemed, or the issue of other debentures in their place, unless:

(*i*) the Articles provide to the contrary, expressly or by implication; or

(*ii*) any contract entered into by the company contains express or implied provisions to the contrary; or

(*iii*) the company has done some act, by resolution or otherwise, manifesting or implying intention to cancel the debentures.

(*b*) Debentures reissued by the company will rank *pari passu*, i.e. as to rights and priorities, with the debentures which they replace.

(*c*) For the purpose of stamp duty, reissued debentures must be treated as new debentures: s.90(4).

15. Memorandum of Satisfaction: s.100.

(*a*) A company may produce evidence to the Registrar of Companies, in the form of a Memorandum of Satisfaction under common seal of the company and accompanied by a statutory declaration:

(*i*) that the debt secured by a charge previously registered with him has been paid or satisfied, in whole or in part; or

(*ii*) that part of the property or undertaking charge has been released from the charge, or has been disposed of.

(*b*) The Registrar may then enter the Memorandum of Satisfaction in his Register of Charges, and, if required, provide the company with a copy of the Memorandum.

(*c*) Appropriate entries must also be made in the company's Register of charges, financial books and (if applicable) Register of Debenture Holders.

(*d*) A resolution approving the signing and sealing of the Memorandum should be passed by the board and recorded in the minute book. The resolution may take the following form:

RESOLVED: That £200,000 9% debenture stock issued on .... 19... be and is hereby redeemed and cancelled, and that the Chairman and Secretary be and are hereby authorised to sign and seal a Memorandum of Satisfaction for deposit with the Registrar of Companies.

16. Sinking fund (or debenture redemption fund).

(*a*) *Purpose.* A sinking fund may be created by a company for the purpose of redeeming its debentures.

(*b*) *Annual investment.* The most satisfactory method is to provide the fund by making an annual investment outside the business in, say, gilt-edged securities.

(*c*) *The amount invested* is based upon tables which show the amount which, with compound interest for a given number of years, will produce the sum required on the date of redemption.

17. Alternative methods used for redeeming debentures are as follows.

(*a*) *A service fund.* This is sometimes created by setting aside fixed annual sums to cover both debenture interest and the sum required for redemption of the debentures.

(*b*) *Purchase on the open market.* If the conditions of issue of the debentures permit, the company may purchase them on the stock exchange before the date for redemption. Money accumulated in the sinking fund may be used for this purpose.

(*c*) *Tender by debenture holders.* Debenture holders may be permitted to tender their debentures, stating the price at which they are prepared to sell them back to the company for cancellation.

(*d*) *Annual drawings.* The company may have power under the conditions of issue to redeem annually a stipulated number of debentures by drawings, i.e. the debentures are "drawn" from a container in which the number of all unredeemed debentures have been deposited.

TRUST DEEDS

18. Trust deeds.

(*a*) *Nature.* Debenture and debenture stock are often secured by a trust or covering deed conveying property of the company to trustees in favour of the debenture holders, charging other property and containing a number of ancillary provisions regulating the respective rights of the company and the debenture holders.

(*b*) *Advantages.* The existence of a trust or covering deed improves and strengthens the security. It constitutes trustees charged with the duty of looking after the rights and interests of the debenture holders. The debenture holders can by these trustees enter and sell the property comprised in the security; the trustees will have a legal mortgage over the company's land, so that persons who subsequently lend money to the company cannot gain priority over the debenture holders secured through the trust deed.

(*c*) *Contents.* The trust deed will usually provide for the following:

(*i*) the appointment of the trustee;

(*ii*) the amount of the issue, the rate of interest and date of payment, terms of redemption, conversion rights, if any etc.;

(*iii*) the creation of a charge over some or all of the company's assets as security;

NOTE: This will usually consist of a legal mortgage of the freehold and leasehold property of the company, and a general charge by way of floating security on the rest of the assets and undertaking. Such gives the trustees a fixed and not merely a floating charge so that the freeholds and leaseholds cannot be sold or dealt with without the trustees' consent. This as stated strengthens the security of the debenture holders.

(*iv*) the various events on the happening of which the security is to become enforceable;

(*v*) the powers and duties of the trustees in particular with regard to the enforcement of the security;

(*vi*) the imposition on the company of additional obligations, regarding the submission of information and similar matters;

(*vii*) the holding of meetings of the debenture holders.

RECEIVERSHIPS

19. Remedies of debenture holders.

(*a*) The remedies of a debenture holder vary according to whether he is unsecured or secured.

(*b*) If the debenture holder is unsecured he has the same remedies as any other creditor, and may enforce payment of principal or interest by an action for debt or through taking steps to have the company wound up.

(c) Where, however, the debenture holder is secured he has in addition to the remedies available to an unsecured debenture holder the following methods of enforcing his security:

(i) if the debenture is issued under the common seal of the company he has under s.101(1) of the Law of Property Act 1925 a power to sell the property or to appoint a receiver of its income in specified circumstances of default;

(ii) utilisation of any express power given by the debenture to be exercised on the occurrence of any one of specified happenings or defaults of the company;

(iii) application to the court for an order for:

(1) sale;

(2) delivery of possession;

(3) foreclosure;

(4) appointment of a receiver of the property subject to the charge.

NOTE: The court will only order a sale or appoint a receiver when the principal or interest is in arrears, when the company has gone into liquidation and when the security is in jeopardy.

20. Appointment of a receiver.

(a) The office of receiver may only be held by a human person: s.366 disqualifies a corporation. Further, s.367 disqualifies an undischarged bankrupt and s.188 (as amended) and s.9 of the Insolvency Act 1976 (as amended) exclude those subject to disqualification orders made under those provisions (see XIV, 6). Section 368 provides that where a company is in compulsory liquidation the Official Receiver may be appointed.

(b) A receiver appointed by the court is an officer of the court and his remuneration is determined by the court. A receiver appointed out of court under powers given by the debenture would be an agent of the debenture holders, but the terms of the debenture will generally provide that he is to be an agent of the company and thus establish that it is the company rather than the debenture holders which is liable for his actions. In either case s.369(2) provides the receiver with a right of indemnity against the assets of the company.

(c) Every invoice, order or business letter of the company must state that a receiver has been appointed: s.370; and notice of his appointment must be given to the Registrar within seven days by the person who made or applied for it: s.102.

(*d*) The appointment of a receiver will bring about the crystallisation of all floating charges. Further, where appointed by the court, all servants of the company are automatically dismissed, though the receiver may re-employ them. Where the receiver is appointed out of court and the receiver is the agent of the company, contracts of employment are not determined: *Re Mack Trucks (Britain) Ltd.* (1967). During the continuation of the receivership the powers of the directors are suspended, though the directors may exercise them in so far as the receiver does not wish to do so and provided the receiver is not prejudiced thereby: *Newhart Developments Ltd.* v. *Commercial Co-operative Bank Ltd.* (1978).

21. Statutory duties of the receiver.

(*a*) Where a receiver is receiver of the company's undertaking, i.e. its entire business and not merely of some specific assets, he may be appointed receiver and manager or have a manager appointed to assist him.

(*b*) In the circumstances set out above the receiver must send to the company notice of his appointment forthwith and the company must within (usually) fourteen days make out and submit to the receiver a statement as to the affairs of the company: s.372. This statement must:

(*i*) show the date of the receivers appointment, particulars of the company's assets and liabilities, and particulars as to the creditors and securities held by them;

(*ii*) be verified by affidavit (or statutory declaration where the receiver was appointed out of court) of a director and the secretary, and past directors, employees and officers of the company, and persons who have taken part in the formation of the company may, in certain cases, be required by the receiver to submit and verify the statement: s.373.

(*c*) Within two months of receipt of the statement the receiver sends to the Registrar (and to the court if appointed by the court) a copy of the statement of affairs and of his comments on it. He also sends to the Registrar (and to the court if applicable), to the company and to the debenture holders a copy of a summary of the statement and his comments: s.372(1)(*c*).

(*d*) The receiver must also within two months after the end of each year, and within two months after he ceases to act as receiver, send to the Registrar, to the trustees for debenture holders, if any, to the company and the debenture holders an abstract of his receipts and payments during the relevant period: s.372(2).

(e) Where s.372(2) is not applicable, a receiver or manager appointed by debenture holders must deliver to the Registrar an abstract of his receipts and payments at six-monthly intervals, and within one month after he ceases to act as receiver.

(f) On ceasing to act the receiver must give notice of that fact to the Registrar and, formally advise the company and surrender possession of any property not realised.

PROGRESS TEST 15

1. Write explanatory notes to distinguish between:
(a) certification of a transfer and registration thereof;
(b) retirement of a director by rotation and vacation of office;
(c) a call and an instalment;
(d) redeemable and convertible debenture stock.
ICSA (IV, **3**; VIII, **1, 6**; XIV, **5, 6**; XV, **6**)

2. What do you understand by the term "5 per cent Debenture Stock, 1963/67"? What is a trust deed and what provision would you expect such a document to contain with respect to the aforementioned stock? (**4, 6**)

3. Your company is proposing to take an interest in another company by way of taking up Convertible Debenture Stock. Outline the main provisons you would expect to find in the Trust Deed. ICSA (**4, 6**)

4. What are the respective advantages of debentures secured by fixed and floating charges? ICSA (**6, 7, 8**)

5. In what ways does the register of charges kept by the Registrar of Companies with respect to every company differ from the register of charges required to be kept at the registered office of every limited company? Give (a) two examples of charges which must be registered with the Registrar, and (b) one example of a charge which needs to be recorded only in a company's own register. (**10–12**)

6. Explain what is meant by registration of charges secured on the property of a company. ICSA (**12**)

7. A company has issued £500,000 of debenture stock in units of £1. The debenture trust deed requires that, each year, 500 lots of 100 units each must be redeemed by drawing. Outline, in numbered paragraphs, the procedure to be followed. ICSA (**17**)

8. (a) What information has to be recorded by a company in respect of any debentures which it has issued?
(b) What are the usual methods by which debentures are

redeemed? *ICSA*   (**9, 10, 12, 13, 16, 17**)

9. Discuss the ways in which debenture stock may be redeemed. What is a Memorandum of Satisfaction? *ICSA*   (**15–17**)

10. Your directors are proposing the repayment of debentures and a new issue at a lower rate of interest. How would such a scheme be carried out?   (XII, **4**)

11. What is a debenture trust deed? What are the advantages of utilising a debenture trust deed?   (**18**)

12. What are the effects of the appointment of a receiver?   (**20**)

Examination Technique

1. Preliminaries.

(*a*) *Preparation.* Ample preparation, followed by thorough revision to consolidate the knowledge already gained, is necessary for any examination. Without it, a list of examination hints is virtually useless. Nevertheless, even a well-prepared candidate can fail through faulty presentation of his work, waste of valuable time, and irrelevancy; it is for such a candidate that these hints have been compiled.

(*b*) *In the examination room.* Even before he comes to grips with the actual questions on the examination paper, the candidate can improve upon, or mar, his chances; therefore, at this stage, the following points ought to be borne in mind.

(*i*) *Read carefully* the instructions on the outside cover of the answer book.

(*ii*) *Fill in the information required* on the outside cover, e.g. date, subject, candidate's letter and number.

(*iii*) *Follow carefully the other instructions* as and when they become applicable, e.g. it is customary to require the candidate finally to arrange his answers in numerical order.

(*iv*) *Write answers legibly* on both sides of the paper provided, but commence each answer on a fresh sheet. An instruction to this effect is usually given on the outside cover.

(*v*) *Number the answers.* Be careful to number the answers so as to indicate the questions to which they refer, and, where applicable, continue the numbering on to any additional sheet or sheets.

(*vi*) *Use the paper provided.* Usually the examining body provides headed paper, with spaces left for subject, and candidate's identification letter and number. This paper only must be used, and the spaces properly completed.

(*c*) *Planning the approach.* Having followed and/or memorised the procedural instructions, the candidate may now turn to the examination paper itself. *This is the crucial stage of the examination*, and the following suggestions for a planned approach are not to be regarded as wasteful of time; just the reverse, in fact, as an answer

285

which has been planned (and is, therefore, logically arranged) saves time in the writing of it and, moreover, avoids much repetition. Another important advantage is that the finished answer will be less haphazard, easier to mark; therefore, the examiner is less likely to miss the points you have attempted to make, and may even be sufficiently appreciative to award bonus marks for a well-planned answer.

(*i*) *Read carefully through the examination paper*. This enables the candidate to get a general impression of the nature and apparent difficulty (or relative simplicity) of the questions, from which he can plan his approach.

(*ii*) *Read the instructions*. Return to the beginning of the paper to read (or re-read) the instructions, for example, number of questions to be attempted overall and (where applicable) from each section of the paper; compulsory questions, if any; number of marks allotted to each question, where some questions carry higher marks than others, and any other special instructions.

(*iii*) *Allot the available time* according to the number of questions to be answered, taking into account those cases where some questions earn higher marks than others. An allowance of, say, five or ten minutes ought to be made for the final reading through of the answers.

(*iv*) *Choose the first question* to be attempted. Obviously, it is quite unnecessary to answer the questions in the same order as they appear in the paper, but the candidate must decide at this point whether to deal first with a compulsory question (where applicable), one of the questions earning higher marks, or one of the simpler (or shorter) questions earning lower marks. So long as the compulsory questions are not overlooked, the choice is not vitally important, although it is usually advisable to deal first with a question that the candiate feels is well within his ability to handle. A good start engenders confidence and may well boost his morale.

(*v*) *Plan the answer* to the first question. Having read the question again in order to understand what is required, it will probably be found that it consists of two, three or more distinct parts. Underline the key word of each part and then make a note of the various key words on a separate rough working sheet. Alongside, or underneath, each key word jot down your ideas at random, leaving space for any afterthoughts. Re-arrange the various points you have made and commit them to your examination script in a logical sequence. In this way the candidate will ensure that each part of the question is dealt with; moreover, he is less likely to omit important points which the examiner is looking for in the answer.

Plan answers to the remaining questions in the same way.

(d) *Rough notes on working paper.* If the candidate uses a separate sheet (or sheets) for his rough notes, it should be securely attached to his examination script, but he must be careful to cancel the sheet or mark it clearly as "rough notes". Failure to do this might cause some confusion for the examiner and prove disastrous for the candidate.

2. Answering the questions. The foregoing hints might well be applied to practically any written examination, but it is now necessary to deal more specifically with examinations in Company Secretarial Practice. The questions in this subject may be classified roughly into three types, and each type merits individual treatment.

(a) *Procedures.* Questions requiring an outline of a company's procedure, e.g. alteration of a company's objects, are set quite regularly. To answer this type of question, the following points ought to be borne in mind.

(i) The procedure must be logically arranged, and each stage in the procedure should be numbered, headed and (where applicable) sub-headed.

(ii) If the question refers to a company whose shares are "listed", relevant stock exchange requirements ought to be introduced at the appropriate points.

(iii) Entries in the appropriate statutory books and the filing of documents with the Registrar must also be inserted where necessary in the procedure.

(iv) As procedural questions often require somewhat lengthy answers, there is no need to deal in detail with each item of the procedure; usually a brief outline is all that is necessary.

NOTE: Students preparing for an examination in Company Secretarial Practice are rarely able to rely upon their *practical* knowledge of procedures; therefore, they would be well advised to memorise a number of "cut and dried" procedures of the kind that occur most frequently in examination papers.

(b) *Documents, statutory and other books.* These are also a popular source of examination questions in which the candidate is required to state the purpose, contents, legal effects etc. of various documents (e.g. share certificates, transfer instruments, statutory declarations, probates, etc.) or the contents of and statutory provisions affecting such books as the Register of Members, Register of

Directors' Shareholdings, Register of Charges, etc. The main considerations when answering such questions are as follows.

(*i*) These are principally factual questions and call for factual answers. Avoid long preambles (which merely annoy the examiner) and simply state the facts—preferably, wherever possible, by enumeration.

(*ii*) When setting out the purpose and legal effects of documents or books used by the company, take the opportunity, where relevant, to support your statements by citing an appropriate case.

(*iii*) Questions of this type demand concise but, nevertheless, *precise* answers, as most of them are concerned with statutory requirements—principally of the Companies Act 1948. It is not usually essential to refer to the section of the Act concerned; if however, the candidate can do so, he may earn for himself one or two bonus marks.

(*iv*) When citing cases, accuracy is, of course, essential, but the candidate need not refrain from citing a case merely because he is not entirely certain of the full names of the parties to it, or of the date, e.g. *Ruben* v. *Great Fingall Consolidated* (1906) might reasonably be cited as "*Ruben* v. *Great Fingall*" or *Eley* v. *Positive Government Security Life Assurance Co.* (1876) as "*Eley's Case*". On the other hand, it is obviously inadvisable to take a chance by citing a case which is entirely irrelevant to the matter in hand.

(*c*) *Secretary's duties and problems.*

(*i*) Many of the questions on these lines are *not* "textbook" questions; that is, ideally they call for practical experience and an ability to *apply* knowledge of company law to the Secretary's everyday problems; if the candidate has little or no practical experience of company secretarial work, he must use his imagination to replace the practical experience. In many cases, there may be *no* precise answer to the problem; if, however, the candidate presents a well-reasoned, imaginative answer, he will, no doubt, merit high marks, even though his solution to the problem is not the one which the examiner originally had in mind.

(*ii*) Questions which require the candidate to deal with shareholders' enquiries or complaints are fairly common. If called upon to write to a complaining or inquiring shareholder, it is important to bear in mind that he is one of the proprietors of the business and must, therefore, be treated civilly and tactfully.

(*iii*) Reports and memoranda are often called for, and candidates must take great care in the drafting of these documents. If the candidate is required to draft a report, he ought to regard this as a two-part question, i.e. the *form* of the report, for which the examiner has, no doubt, allotted a certain number of marks, and the *subject* of the report.

Index

291

Details of some other Macdonald & Evans
books on related subjects can be found on
the following pages.

For a list of titles and prices write for the
complimentary Macdonald & Evans Business catalogue,
available from: Department BP1, Macdonald &
Evans Ltd., Estover, Plymouth PL6 7PZ

Auditing

LESLIE R. HOWARD

Auditing may be defined as the examination of certain statements covering the transactions over a period and the financial position of an organisation on a certain date in order that the auditor may issue a report on them.

However, as with all accountancy-related subjects, raised standards in the world of business have demanded an even greater depth of knowledge on the part of the practitioner. This, allied to the increasing complexity of auditing procedures, has necessitated a complete revision of the text for the seventh edition of this successful M&E HANDBOOK. All recent changes in auditing techniques and legislation are covered in this edition, which closely follows the latest recommendations of the professional bodies. The text incorporates the sections of the Companies Acts (including the Companies Act 1980) which affect the auditor. Although rewritten for students up to and including final examination standard, it will also be useful to intermediate students and those with no previous knowledge of auditing procedure as an aid both to understanding and memorising the subject. Recommended by the Association of International Accountants and the London Chamber of Commerce and Industry.

Leslie Howard is Dean of the Faculty of Business Studies at Lingnan College, Hong Kong.

Business Administration

L. HALL

This HANDBOOK has been specifically written for students preparing for examinations in business management, and in particular those set by the ACA, ICMA, ICSA and certain BEC higher level courses. It is also recommended reading for the Association of Accounting Technicians Level III examination in Business organisation.

The author gives a detailed analysis of the general principles of management, including the most up-to-date techniques, and the organisation and control of office procedure.

Business and Financial Management

B.K.R. WATTS

The author has drawn on considerable lecturing and consultancy experience to write this HANDBOOK, which will give a sound introduction to the subject to those students studying for financial and accounting examinations, and for non-financial managers who need to understand the terminology of accountancy. As such it will be useful for students preparing for the Diploma in Management Studies as well as for ICA, ACCA and ICMA examinations, or for any other professional examinations. Furthermore, the experience of previous editions has shown that it is a valuable text for study and supplementary reading on training courses for middle and senior managers. "This book is a most competent and concise summary on a wide range of financial matters." *Director* Recommended by the Institute of

Commercial Management, the Association of Certified Accountants and the British Society of Commerce.

Mr Watts is Principal Lecturer of the Faculty of Management at Slough College of Higher Education.

Capital Transfer Tax

R.C. IND

This HANDBOOK contains a concise but clear survey of the most important aspects of this tax, and is aimed primarily at students of accountancy and law. It includes a section on transfer tax mitigation which will furnish the practitioner with useful ideas and the student with a helpful summary of the taxing provisions. The latest edition has been prepared to take account of developments since the previous edition was published. "The book is warmly recommended to students and practitioners alike." *The Accountants' Magazine* Recommended by the Institute of Cost and Management Accountants.

Cases in Company Law

M.C. OLIVER

This CASEBOOK, now in its third edition, can be used independently or as a companion volume to the author's HANDBOOK on Company Law. Since the significance of a case lies mainly in its content rather than in the ultimate verdict, the author has chosen to include a small but important selection of cases, all of which are presented chronologically and as comprehensively as possible. No authorial comment is made, thus enabling the reader to draw his own conclusions. "A commendable little book, . . . doubtless it will be found useful by many." *The Law Teacher* Recommended by the Institute of Cost and Management Accountants.

Mary Oliver was formerly Dean of the Faculty of Law, and Lecturer in Company Law at the City of London Polytechnic.

Cases in Income Tax Law

HENRY TOCH

This CASEBOOK is relevant to all students and practitioners of income tax law. May be used independently or in conjuction with the HANDBOOK *Income Tax 1983/84* Recommended by the Society of Company and Commercial Accountants.

Corporation Tax

B.S. TOPPLE

This HANDBOOK assumes no prior knowledge of taxation on the reader's part. It provides a basic introduction to the principles of company taxation, with chapters covering capital allowances and losses, the treatment of income tax and close companies. The author gives typical examples of firms' accounts in the text to illustrate each point. ". . . difficult to recommend a better book for a basic introduction to the subject. *Accountancy* Recommended by the Association of International Accountants and the Institute of Cost and Management Accountants.

Company Accounts
J.O. MAGEE

During recent years company accounting has become more complex in its operations, and the legal requirements of the subject are ever more demanding. The need therefore for a clear yet detailed introduction to the subject is self-evident. This HANDBOOK aims to show the basic principles underlying the main aspects of accountancy in relation to limited companies.

For this third edition the text has been thoroughly revised to cover the requirements of legislation such as the Companies Act 1981 and the latest SSAP issued by the leading accounting bodies, and includes a completely new chapter dealing with inflation accounting. Contents include limited company accounts, profit and reserves, sinking funds, redemption of debentures, redeemable preference shares, accounting requirements of the Companies Act 1981, purchase of a business, company reconstructions, reduction of capital for internal reconstructions, amalgamations and absorptions, sources and applications of funds, consolidated balance sheets, consolidated profit and loss accounts, valuation of shares, inflation accounting. Recommended by the Institute of Administrative Accountants.

Company Law
M.C. OLIVER

Since this well-established HANDBOOK was first published in 1966, there has been an almost uninterrupted flow of company law legislation. The maze of company law which exists, formulated and amended by the five Companies Acts, can seem daunting to the student whose examination syllabus requires a knowledge of the subject. To this end the author has sought to present the key facts, in their entirety, in a way which renders the subject interesting and easily assimilable. As a teacher herself, she is well placed to understand the difficulties experienced by many students and this comparatively simple presentation of an immensely technical subject will undoubtedly help to eliminate these problems. For this ninth edition, the provisions of the Companies Act 1981 have been taken into account, and a Table of Statutes added.

"To pack into a pocket-sized book . . . the wealth of detail required, at least for examination purposes, of aspiring company secretaries, accountants and students of business management is no mean achievement in itself; add to this the bonus of progress tests at the end of each chapter, a selection of test papers and the author's comforting advice on learning and examination technique, and the reasons for the book's continuing popularity are clear." *The Solicitors' Journal* Recommended by numerous professional bodies, including the Institute of Bankers, the Institute of Commercial Management, the Institute of

Cost and Management Accountants and the Association of Cost and Executive Accountants.

Mary Oliver was formerly Dean of the Faculty of Law and lecturer in company law at the City of London Polytechnic.

Company Secretarial Practice

L. HALL, *revised by* G.M. THOM

This HANDBOOK has been specifically written to meet the requirements of students preparing for the final examinations of the Institute of Chartered Secretaries and Administrators. It also covers the corresponding syllabus of Polytechnic Diplomas by which students may earn exemption from certain of the Institute's examinations. In addition, students preparing for the Higher Stage Company Secretarial Practice examination of the London Chamber of Commerce and Industry will find it useful supplementary reading.

This revision takes full account of the latest company legislation and much of the material formerly contained in the appendixes is now included in the main body of the text.

L. Hall was formerly Senior Lecturer at the City of London Polytechnic, whilst George Thom is Senior Lecturer in Law at the Department of Business Studies, Bristol Polytechnic.

Income Tax 1983/84

HENRY TOCH

This successful HANDBOOK, now in its thirteenth edition, is primarily intended for students of the various professional bodies whose courses demand an understanding of the basic principles of income tax law. These principles are set out in a clear, concise and practical way, and it is also hoped that this logical presentation of the key facts will prove of value to the lay reader. The authority for each principle is clearly stated and since the application of the law involves a knowledge of accountancy, the theory is well-supported with practical examples. The material used is based on the author's extensive practical experience as a tax inspector, consultant, examiner and teacher, and this new edition incorporates a thorough revision of the existing text in addition to new material dealing with the 1983 Finance Act. The book should be particularly useful for students of the Institute of Chartered Accountants, the Institute of Taxation, the Institute of Cost and Management Accountants, the Building Societies Institute, the Institute of Chartered Secretaries and Administrators, the Law Society, the Chartered Institute of Public Finance and Accountancy, the Association of Certified Accountants and BEC Higher National Certificate. Recommended by the Society of Company and Commercial Accountants.

Intermediate Accounts

L.W.J. OWLER

This HANDBOOK offers a lucid and compact coverage of the subject, progressing from first principles by clear and logical steps to the standard required for intermediate examinations. Each new topic is followed by a typical examination question and a fully worked-out answer. The book will be of use to students taking the professional examinations of the ICA, ICSA, AIB and LCCI and for those on BEC courses. ". . . it is a book which can be recommended to all students, and College Librarians . . . ." *Education & Training*

Meetings
L. HALL

This HANDBOOK can be treated either as an independent set of study notes on the Law and Practice of Meetings, or as a companion to the author's *Company Secretarial Practice* (q.v.), and will be invaluable to students seeking to master the details of meetings practice. Recommended by the Institute of Chartered Secretaries and Administrators.

Office Administration
J.C. DENYER, *revised by* A.L. MUGRIDGE

Office administration is a subject fast becoming increasingly complex, and the need for the student to keep abreast of the latest developments cannot be too strongly emphasised.

The fourth edition of this HANDBOOK is intended for all students sitting examinations of which office management and secretarial practice form an integral part, including relevant BEC examinations. Much of the material included in the third edition has required fundamental revision, whether due to the effects of recent legislation, or the reappraisal of long-established office systems occasioned by word-processing and microtechnology.

This edition, therefore, covers the recent changes in industrial relations legislation and PAYE procedure, as well as the effects of computerised technology and office procedure.

Topics covered include organisation and personnel, office equipment and records and general services. The book is on the recommended reading list of the Society of Company and Commercial Accountants and the Association of Accounting Technicians.

Mr Denyer's original book has been revised by A.L. Mugridge, formerly Principal Lecturer in the Business Studies Department of Bristol Polytechnic.

Partnership Accounts
J.O. MAGEE

This HANDBOOK covers the entire field of partnership accounting. The method employed is to explain in simple language the various matters which are peculiar to the accountancy problems relating to partnerships and then, by graded examples, to illustrate the type of problems involved. "This excellent M&E *Handbook* will be of great assistance to examination students." *Education & Training*

Public Administration
MICHAEL P. BARBER, *revised by* ROGER STACEY

Public administration is a field currently beset by widespread problems. This HANDBOOK not only identifies and analyses these, but also provides a study of the theory and structure of the system, its practical aspects and the contemporary "management" approach to the subject. As such it will be useful for all students of public administration, whether studying for the examinations of the Local Government Examinations Board, the Diploma in Public Administration from the University of London or for relevant BEC courses. It does not aim to replace completely existing textbooks but provides a succinct yet thorough coverage of all the topics which may arise in any of the above examinations.

This third edition, whilst retaining the same format and aims as its predecessor, has been updated in the light of recent legislation. This includes an analysis of the new investigative select committee system of Parliament, and the administrative arrangements of the European community. This latter topic exemplifies the problems of public as opposed to private administrative systems. Finally, in keeping with the changing requirements of examining bodies, the emphasis has been laid on the effect of wider political forces in society. Recommended by the Institute of Purchasing and Supply.

Secretarial and Administrative Practice

L. HALL

Specifically written for students preparing for relevant professional examinations such as those of the ICSA, this HANDBOOK provides a concise and comprehensive course of study. An updated glossary of stock exchange terms and a new section on statistics have been included. ". . . the continuing success of the handbook seems well assured." *Times Educational Supplement*

Working Capital

LESLIE R. HOWARD

No other aspect of the financial management of a business can be more influential than the handling of working capital. The author describes the various methods to be employed in its efficient management, and the book should therefore be of value to management accountants and students.